Parallelization of Automotive Control Software

TECHNISCHE UNIVERSITÄT
**ILMENAU**

FAKULTÄT FÜR INFORMATIK UND AUTOMATISIERUNG
FACHGEBIET TELEMATIK / RECHNERNETZE

# Dissertation
zur Erlangung des akademischen Grades
Doktoringenieur (Dr.-Ing.)

# Parallelization of
# Automotive Control Software

|  |  |
|---|---|
| vorgelegt von: | Dipl.-Inf. Sebastian Kehr |
| geboren am: | 22. September 1985 in Eisenach |
| Datum der Einreichung: | 8. April 2016 |
| Datum der Verteidigung: | 2. November 2016 |
| Betreuender Gutachter: | Prof. Dr.-Ing. Günter Schäfer |
| Gutachter: | Prof. Dr.-Ing. Winfried E. Kühnhauser |
| Externer betreuender Gutachter: | Dr.-Phil. Eduardo Quiñones |

**Bibliografische Information der Deutschen Nationalbibliothek**
Die Deutsche Nationalbibliothek verzeichnet diese Publikation in der
Deutschen Nationalbibliografie; detaillierte bibliografische Daten sind im Internet
über http://dnb.d-nb.de abrufbar.
1. Aufl. - Göttingen: Cuvillier, 2016
   Zugl.: (TU) Ilmenau, Univ., Diss., 2016

© CUVILLIER VERLAG, Göttingen 2016
   Nonnenstieg 8, 37075 Göttingen
   Telefon: 0551-54724-0
   Telefax: 0551-54724-21
   www.cuvillier.de

   ISBN 978-3-7369-9431-7
   eISBN 978-3-7369-8431-8

# Abstract

The embedded multicore processor is seen as the hardware platform that satisfies the steadily increasing performance requirements of automotive control software. It provides a higher absolute performance and consumes less energy than an equal amount of single-core processors. As a result, low sensor/actuator latencies and low resource consumption per *electronic control unit (ECU)* are enabled.

An application is developed according to the *AUTomotive Open System ARchitecture (AUTOSAR)* standard. *Runnables*, i.e. elementary code pieces, within software-components implement the controller's functional behaviour. The *unit of scheduling (UoS)* is the task. Executing the runnables in the correct order and frequency realizes the control function. Runnables are mapped to tasks to achieve this. However, existing control software must be re-used for the multicore ECU, because the code is well tested and much effort was spent on its optimization.

Consequently, this Ph.D. thesis focuses on the migration of AUTOSAR legacy software to multicore ECUs. For this, the thesis addresses two main challenges: first, a large amount of data dependencies limits the parallelism. Second, the original *data-flow* must be reproduced in the parallel program to guarantee the same functional behaviour without exhaustive validation and testing efforts. Common approaches rearrange the runnables in new tasks to increase the level of parallelism, but this requires a costly re-validation of the functional correctness. The associated expenditure is high and therefore undesirable.

The approach in this Ph.D. thesis uses the original application's configuration for the single-core processor to derive side constraints for the parallelization. Precedence and latency constraints are extracted and the original mapping of runnables to tasks remain unchanged. This is a reasonable approach to keep the functional properties of the application, because the configuration describes a well-tested and validated system configuration.

On *runnable-level*, the allocation algorithm *RunPar* distributes runnables and not tasks. Furthermore, the introduced concept of a *Supertask* maximizes the level of parallelism. A Supertask groups runnables of consecutively scheduled AUTOSAR tasks into a unique scheduling entity and is then scheduled with RunPar. Both methods keep the sequential execution of tasks, which maintains the original data-flow. Hence, the validation effort after the migration to the multicore ECU is drastically reduced. For the evaluation, a real diesel engine management system is used to investigate the performance and efficiency with a real application as an example. Both methods achieve a high performance and efficiency on two cores. The use of Supertasks further improves the performance. This suggests runnable-level parallelism is ideal for few cores and activated tasks. Nevertheless, a low efficiency is observed on larger processors. This motivated deeper analysis of the impact of inter-task communication.

Consequently, on *task-level timed implicit communication (TIC)* decouples inter-task communication to allow parallel execution of producer and consumer, while the same data-flow is achieved on all multicore ECUs. TIC is implemented in the AUTOSAR *run-time environment (RTE)* and, thus, no modifications of source code are required. The method provides a high efficiency for numerous cores and activated tasks. As a side effect, TIC introduces an artificial delay due to buffering of data. A comparison with runnable-level parallelism suggested the use with task-level parallelism as complementary strategy.

A coordination strategy, based on an *evolutionary algorithm (EA)*, is proposed to combine both methods and take individual shortcomings or advantages into account. The traversal of data from sensor to actuator is explicitly modelled. This enables consideration of the latency imposed by parallelization techniques. Task periods and the processor's clock rate are adjusted to guarantee the system's original worst-case sensor/actuator latency. The thesis establishes the *parallel schedule quality (PSQ)* metric for quantifying the success of the parallelization. This enables the EA to select the best parallel schedule from a set of feasible solutions. The EA selects the schedule with the highest PSQ. As a result, the coordination guarantees the sensor/actuator latency of the reference system and minimizes the energy consumption.

# Zusammenfassung

Der eingebettete Mehrkernprozessor wird als die Hardware-Plattform angesehen, welche den stetig steigenden Rechenanforderungen von Steuerungs-Software an Steuergeräte in Automobilen gerecht wird. Dieser verfügt über eine höhere Rechenleistung und verbraucht dabei weniger Energie als die gleiche Anzahl von Einkernprozessoren. In der Folge ermöglichen diese Plattformen sowohl eine geringe Latenz zwischen Sensor und Aktuator als auch einen geringeren Energieverbrauch je Steuergerät.

Steuerungs-Software wird entsprechend dem *AUTomotive Open System ARchitecture (AUTOSAR)*-Standard entwickelt. Sogenannte *Runnables*, elementare Code-Abschnitte bzw. verteilbare Aufgaben, bilden strukturiert angeordnet in Software-Komponenten das funktionale Verhalten des Reglers ab. Die Steuerungsaufgabe wird durch die Ausführung von Runnables in korrekter Reihenfolge und Häufigkeit realisiert. Hierfür werden die Runnables den Tasks der Anwendung zugeordnet. Bei der Migration auf Mehrkernprozessoren soll existierende Steuerungs-Software wiederverwendet werden. Der Grund hierfür ist die ausgiebige Erfahrung mit existierendem Quellcode. Dieser wurde ausgiebig getestet und die Software-Architektur wurde über viele Jahre hinweg, durch tiefgreifende Optimierung, verbessert.

Gegenstand dieser Dissertation ist die Migration existierender AUTOSAR-Steuerungs-Software auf Mehrkernprozessorsteuergeräte. Dafür befasst sich die Arbeit mit zwei wichtigen Herausforderungen. Erstens wird die Parallelität durch eine große Anzahl an Datenabhängigkeiten begrenzt. Zweitens muss der ursprüngliche Datenfluss des Einkernprozessors nachgebildet werden, um anschließend dasselbe funktionale Verhalten ohne aufwändige Validierung oder Tests zu erreichen. Existierende Ansätze arrangieren Runnables in neuen Tasks, um die Parallelität zu erhöhen. Das allerdings erfordert die erneute Validierung der parallelisierten Software. Der damit verbundenen Arbeitsaufwand sowie die Kosten sind hoch und daher unerwünscht.

Der Ansatz dieser Dissertation verwendet die ursprüngliche Konfiguration der Anwendung für den Einkernprozessor, um daraus Randbedingungen für die Parallelisierung abzuleiten. Es werden Vorrang- und Latenzbeschränkungen extrahiert. Außerdem bleibt die ursprüngliche Zuordnung von Runnables zu Tasks erhalten. Dies ist ein sinnvoller Ansatz, um die funktionalen Eigenschaften der Anwendung zu erhalten. Da diese Konfiguration bereits sorgfältig getestet und validiert ist.

Auf *Runnable-Ebene* verteilt der Allokationsalgorithmus *RunPar* Runnables statt Tasks. Darüber hinaus wird die Parallelität auf dieser Granularitätsstufe durch das Konzept der *Supertask* maximiert. Eine Supertask gruppiert Runnables von nacheinander ausgeführten AUTOSAR Tasks in eine Scheduling-Einheit, deren Runnables anschließend mittels RunPar verteilt werden. Beide Methoden behalten die sequenzielle Ausführungsreihenfolg der Tasks bei, wodurch der ursprüngliche Datenfluss erhalten bleibt. Daher ist der Validierungsaufwand nach der Migration erheblich reduziert.

Die Evaluierung wurde mit einer echten Dieselmotorsteuerung als repräsentatives Beispiel durchgeführt. Beide Methoden erreichen eine hohe Performanz und Effizienz mit zwei Rechenkernen, wobei Supertasks zu einer signifikanten Verbesserung führen. Dies legt nahe, dass die Parallelisierung auf Runnable-Ebene ideal für eine kleine Anzahl an Rechenkernen und aktivierten Tasks ist. Jedoch zeigt sich für größere Prozessoren eine geringe Effizienz. Dies motiviert eine tiefgehende Analyse des Einflusses von Inter-Task-Kommunikation.

Folglich wird *Timed Implicit Communication* (TIC) als Parallelisierungsmethode auf *Task-Ebene* eingeführt. TIC entkoppelt die Kommunikation zwischen Tasks, um die parallele Ausführung von produzierender und konsumierender Task zu ermöglichen. Hierbei wird derselbe Datenfluss auf allen Mehrkernprozessorsteuergeräten erreicht. TIC ist in die AUTOSAR *Run-time Environment* integriert, weshalb Modifikationen von Quellcode vermieden werden. Die Evaluierung zeigt eine bessere Performanz und eine höhere Effizienz als die Parallelisierung auf Runnable-Ebene, wenn eine große Anzahl Tasks aktiv ist und viele Rechenkerne zur Verfügung stehen. Der Vergleich legt nahe, dass es sich bei Runnable- und Task-Ebenen-Parallelisierung um einander ergänzend einzusetzende Strategien handelt.

Schließlich wird eine koordinierende Strategie vorgeschlagen, die basierend auf einem *evolutionären Algorithmus (EA)*, beide Parallelisierungsebenen kombiniert. Hierbei werden die individuellen Vor- und Nachteile der Methoden berücksichtigt. Der Verarbeitungspfad von Sensor zu Aktuator wird explizit modelliert. Dies ermöglicht die Berücksichtigung der Latenz, die durch die Parallelisierung entsteht. Task-Perioden und Prozessortakt werden anschließend so angepasst, dass Leerlaufzeiten minimiert und kritische Antwortzeiten eingehalten werden. Die Metrik Parallel Schedule Quality (PSQ) wird eingeführt, um den Erfolg der Parallelisierung zu quantifizieren. Damit wird es dem EA möglich den besten parallelen Ausführungsplan aus einer Liste zulässiger Lösungen auszuwählen. Der EA wählt den Ausführungsplan mit dem höchsten PSQ-Wert. Insgesamt wird dieselbe Antwortzeit wie im Referenzsystem erreicht. Gleichzeitig wird der Energieverbrauch des Steuergerätes minimiert.

Für meine Familie.

# Danksagung

Ich danke allen, die zum Gelingen dieser Arbeit beigetragen haben.

Vor allem gilt mein Dank meinem Doktorvater Prof. Dr.-Ing. Günter Schäfer, welcher mir in meiner Zeit als externer Doktorand, ungeachtet der Entfernung, jederzeit mit Rat und Tat zur Seite stand sowie immer seine kritische und konstruktive Meinung geäußert hat. Außerdem danke ich Dr.-Phil. Eduardo Quiñones, der durch die gute Zusammenarbeit, im zugrundeliegenden Forschungsprojekt, schließlich zu einem weiteren Betreuer dieser Arbeit und zu einem geschätzten Freund wurde. Des Weiteren danke ich dem Gutachter Prof. Dr.-Ing. Winfried E. Kühnhauser für seine Bereitschaft diese Arbeit zu lesen sowie für seine wertvollen und konstruktiven Anmerkungen.

Besonderer Dank gebührt meinem Chef, Dr. Bert Böddeker, der mich während meiner Zeit als Doktorand bei DENSO immer unterstützt hat und mir in Hochlastzeiten den Rücken frei gehalten hat. Er hat mir im umfangreichen AUTOSAR-Standard Orientierung gegeben, Ideen diskutiert, Kontakte hergestellt und mir in einem Großunternehmen ein Arbeitsumfeld ermöglicht, in dem diese Arbeit entstehen konnte.

Ich danke auch meinen Studenten, Jorge "Schorsch" Becerril Sandoval und Ahmad Hassan (späterer Kollege), für ihren wichtigen Beitrag zur Evaluierung. Ohne diese notwendige "Handarbeit" hätten die Ergebnisse so nicht zu Stande kommen können. Ich danke auch Miloš Panić für die gute Zusammenarbeit, wodurch initiale Ergebnisse dieser Arbeit erst entstanden sind. Auch danke ich Dr.-Ing. Michael Roßberg und Franz Girlich vom Fachgebiet Telematik/Rechnernetze dafür, dass sie mir für die umfangreichen Untersuchungen zum Ende der Arbeit Rechencluster zur Verfügung gestellt haben. Außerdem danke ich den Korrekturlesern Emanuel Berndl, Felix Kaiser und Vera Höfflin.

Ich danke auch meinen japanischen Vorgesetzten Naoki Matsumoto-san, Ichiro Yamauchi-san und Masahiro Goto-san für Ihre breite Unterstützung in allen Stadien dieser Arbeit und die Möglichkeit internationale wissenschaftlichen Konferenzen besuchen zu dürfen. Ebenfalls möchte ich die mir gewährten Freiheiten mit großer Anerkennung hervorheben. Darüber hinaus bin ich sehr dankbar dafür, die japanische Lebens- und Arbeitskultur kennengelernt zu haben.

Außerdem danke ich meinem Kollegen Dr.-Ing. Robert Schmidt, der seine Erfahrungen als externer Doktorand mit mir geteilt hat. Er hatte stets ein offenes Ohr für ein kurzes Gespräch und einen guten Rat. Danken möchte ich außerdem Dr. Dominik Langen für die Visualisierung der prototypischen Implementierung, die anregenden Diskussionen sowie für die gute Zusammenarbeit bei der Weiterführung der Arbeit. Für patentrechtliche Unterstützung danke ich Wolfgang Stalder, Moritz Ernicke und Enrico Bannies.

Ohne die Unterstützung meiner Familie wäre diese Arbeit undenkbar gewesen. Ich danke meinem Vater Reinhard, meiner Mutter Karin, Walter, Oma Frieda, Opa Walter, meinen Schwestern Cindy und Conny sowie meiner zauberhaften Freundin Vera. Ihr habt mich ein Leben lang unterstützt und an mich geglaubt. Ohne dieses Vertrauen und die Zuversicht hätte diese Arbeit nicht entstehen können.

Ich danke auch meinen Freunden, Micha, Jennifer, Thomas, Uly, Markus, Claudi, Franz, Julia und Philipp, die mich von Zeit zu Zeit auf andere Gedanken gebracht haben und mir somit den nötigen Ausgleich gegeben haben. Sei es auf einer Moped-Tour, bei einem Grillabend, bei einer sportlichen Aktivität oder bei einem Musikfestival.

Vielen Dank! Arigatou gozaimashita!

# Acknowledgements

I am grateful to everyone who contributed to the success of this work.

Above all, my thanks go to my supervisor Prof. Dr.-Ing. Günter Schäfer who, in my time as an external doctoral student, always supported me with help and advice regardless of distance. He always expressed his critical and constructive opinion. I also thank Dr.-Phil. Eduardo Quiñones who, through the good cooperation in the underlying research project, finally became a second supervisor of this work and a valued friend. I would also like to thank Prof. Dr.-Ing. Winfried E. Kühnhauser for his willingness to read this work as well as for his valuable and constructive remarks.

Special thanks go to my boss Dr. Bert Böddeker, who has always supported me during my time as a doctoral student at DENSO and has kept my back in high-load times. He gave me an orientation in the extensive AUTOSAR standard, discussed ideas, established contacts, and enabled me in a large company to create a work environment in which this work could be created.

I thank my students, Jorge "Schorsch" Becerril Sandoval and Ahmad Hassan (later colleague), for their important contribution to the evaluation. Without this necessary "manual work" the results could not have been achieved. I also thank Miloš Panić for the good cooperation, whereby initial results of this work were the outcome. I thank Dr.-Ing. Michael Roßberg and Franz Girlich, from the Telematics/Computer Networks Group, for providing access to compute cluster resources for comprehensive calculations towards the end of the work. I also thank the proofreaders Emanuel Berndl, Felix Kaiser and Vera Höfflin.

I would also like to thank my Japanese superiors Naoki Matsumoto-san, Ichiro Yamauchi-san and Masahiro Goto-san for their broad support at all stages of this work and the opportunity to visit international scientific conferences. I would also like to emphasize, with great credit the privileges, granted to me. In addition, I am very grateful for having met the Japanese life and work culture.

Furthermore, I would like to thank my colleague Dr.-Ing. Robert Schmidt, who shared his experiences as an external doctoral student with me. He always had a sympathetic ear for a short conversation. I also want to thank Dr. Dominik Langen for the visualization of the prototypical implementation and the stimulating discussions as well as for the good cooperation in the continuation of the work. I would like to thank Wolfgang Stalder, Moritz Ernicke and Enrico Bannies for support regarding patent legislation.

Without the support of my family, this work would have been unthinkable. I would like to thank my father Reinhard, my mother Karin, Walter, Grandma Frieda, Grandpa Walter, my sisters Cindy and Conny as well as my wonderful girlfriend Vera. You have supported me for a lifetime and believed in me. Without this trust and confidence, this work would not have been possible.

I also thank my friends, Micha, Jennifer, Thomas, Uly, Markus, Claudi, Franz, Julia and Philipp, who have brought me from time to time to other thoughts and thus gave me the necessary balance. Whether on a moped tour, a barbecue evening, a sporting activity or a music festival.

Thank you so much! Arigatou gozaimashita!

# Contents

# 1 | Introduction

> "Software gets slower faster
> than hardware gets faster."
>
> Niklaus Wirth, 1995

The performance requirements for an automotive embedded system have increased steadily in recent years and this also raised the number of *electronic control units (ECUs)* per car. Today, they contain a complex in-vehicle network of 70 or more ECUs [Für10], which realize thousands of control functions altogether. Each of these ECUs consumes electrical energy and this leads to a higher overall energy consumption of the car. Nevertheless, the demand for more functionality continues and this means more control functions must be integrated. This requires more computational power in the form of ECUs and it increases the overall electrical power consumption of the car. As a result, minimizing the resource consumption per car and per ECU is an important design objectives for automotive embedded system design [Mös10].

On the contrary, numerous control functions in a car must guarantee upper bounds on the response time to realize the desired functionality. This marks an essential difference between general purpose computing and automotive control software. For this reason, minimizing the latency of critical sensor/actuator paths is a typical optimization objective for automotive embedded systems [Nat+07]. An example for a critical sensor/actuator latency is the maximum time between pushing the gas pedal and the point in time when the driver recognizes the acceleration. The more control functions the *engine management system (EMS)* ECU has to compute (active cylinder management, exhaust gas recirculation, pre- and post-injection, etc.) the longer is the response time.

Increasing the processor's clock rate in the ECU was a first countermeasure to satisfy the increasing performance requirement. However, this solution leads to a higher electrical power consumption and heat dissipation, whereas the additional gained compute power is low. Moreover, this technique faces physical limits with the result that it is impractical to further increase the clock rate. The automotive industry is therefore searching for alternative hardware platforms that satisfy the performance and efficiency requirements.

Fortunately, embedded multicore processors, like the Infineon AURIX [Inf] or the Freescale Qorivva [Fre15], have become widely available for the automotive industry. These processors were designed for safety critical applications in the first place, but they also provide a surplus of computational power, in comparison to a single-core processor. This makes it possible to efficiently exploit *thread-level parallelism* of automotive control software.

Consequently, the ECU can either execute a more complex algorithm or execute the same application on multiple cores with a reduced clock rate, such that deadlines are still kept, to save electrical energy. Thus, multicore ECUs are seen as the hardware platform for current and future automotive control software in cars.

However, introducing multicore ECUs is a great challenge [MB09] for the automotive industry. Until now, software is developed and optimized for the execution on a single-core ECU. This software is well tested and much effort was spent on the optimization and maintenance. As a result, most existing (legacy) control software is supposed to be re-used, because the code is known to be reliable and the development process can be shortened. Consequently, the migration of automotive legacy software to multicore ECUs must be supported. This is a fundamental step for the adaptation of multicore ECUs in the automotive domain and for taking full advantage of these platforms. Consequently, this Ph.D. thesis focuses on the migration of automotive legacy control software to multicore ECUs.

Automotive control software is developed according to the *AUTomotive Open System ARchitecture (AUTOSAR)* standard [AUT14a]. The standard established an industry-wide understanding, a uniform development methodology, and a uniform terminology for automotive control software. A hierarchical *software-component (SW-C)* model describes the application according to the concept of a *virtual function bus (VFB)*. In this concept, *runnables*, i.e. elementary code pieces; a schedulable job, within SW-Cs implement the functional behaviour of the component. Each SW-C realizes a part of the overall control and runnables frequently communicate with each other. Executing the runnables in the correct order and frequency realizes the control function.

However, multicore ECUs have significantly different properties than general purpose multicore processors and automotive control software strongly differs from inherently parallel *high performance computing (HPC)* programs. This makes the parallelization a non-trivial task that demands for a specific approach, as the next section describes in more detail.

## 1.1 Problem Statement and Approach

The central requirements for embedded systems design are *predictability* and *robustness* [Hen08]. The consequences for automotive software parallelization are twofold:

a) *Predictability* — The execution order of runnables must be deterministic to form a predictable data-flow, i.e. an order in which runnables process data, from sensors to actuators.

b) *Robustness* — An upper bound on the sensor/actuator latency must be guaranteed.

The cores of a multicore processor perform calculations independent of each other, but they share resources such as the bus, memory, or other peripherals. That means the parallel execution on multiple cores requires a coordination of accesses to these shared resources to avoid unforeseen computational interleaving. This is necessary to avoid *data races*, i.e. concurrent access to the same shared memory location from at least two cores. Otherwise, inconsistent data might be the result or the data-flow between a sensor and an actuator might break. Another important factor is the duration of this computation, which should be as small as possible in automotive control software. Consequently, *the challenge in this Ph.D. thesis* is to schedule tasks to cores in a way that the data-flow between sensor and actuator produces a valid result with a low latency.

To achieve this, constraints must specify the correct functional behaviour to create the same sensor/actuator data-flow like in the former sequential execution. Unfortunately, the information about the legacy application is limited. However, this original application's configuration for the single-core ECU describes a correct functioning system and it can be used to derive parallelization constraints. Hence, the parallelization approach in this thesis relies on the original application's configuration for the single-core ECU. This approach leads to further challenges that are described in the following.

Automotive control software typically contains a high number of data dependencies. Many runnables frequently exchange data with each other. Every runnable is a consumer and a producer of interim results in a data-flow from a sensor to an actuator. This results in a dense *task dependence graph (TDG)*. Sensor data flows into this TDG in different runnables, traverses it on multiple paths, and the results leave it in different runnables. Thereby, paths overlay each other and a clear distinction between relevant and less relevant data-flows is hard.

Runnables consume and produce data with a fixed period and they have to be executed in the correct order to realize a data-flow from the sensor(s) to the actuator(s). This results in a large amount of *precedence constraints* that must be respected during parallelization and this frequently forces serialization of producer and consumer runnable. This imposes the question:

⋄ *How can parallel execution of communicating runnables be enabled, but sensor/actuator data-flows be guaranteed with a worst-case latency?*

Furthermore, the AUTOSAR standard itself imposes limitations on the parallelization. A runnable is seen as smallest schedulable entity that requires an allocation to a core and a mapping to a task. The runnable is allocated indirectly by assigning the SW-C, containing the runnable, to a core. Hence, if two independent runnables are mapped to the same core, no parallel execution is possible. A parallelization approach beyond the state of the art potentially requires extensions of the existing standard. The challenge here is to minimize these changes and remain compliant to the standard as far as possible.

⋄ *Which extensions for the AUTOSAR standard are required to guarantee efficient and deterministic parallel execution on a multicore ECU?*

This Ph.D. thesis attempts to answer these research questions. The contributions are described in the following section.

## 1.2   Contributions of this Thesis

This thesis was developed in the context of the research projects parMERASA [par11; Ung+16] and EMC[2] [EMC14]. The research activities in the projects were conducted in close collaboration with project partners and thus results have been published jointly. During the parMERASA project, a processor architecture was developed to address the challenge of overestimations in the *worst-case execution time (WCET)* by pessimism. The design of the processor architecture follows the demands of automotive software. The WCET estimations are thus less pessimistic than usual. Nevertheless, the approach in this thesis is applicable to any automotive control software.

Initially, a set of functional and non-functional objectives for automotive software parallelization has been defined based on the challenges described previously. A qualitative comparison and discussion of existing approaches has been conducted. As a result, the following main deficiencies have been identified in state-of-the-art approaches:

▷ Reconfiguring approaches define an efficient new application configuration for which a re-validation of the functional correctness is required. Moreover, their applicability is limited to systems with specific scheduling policies. Contrarily, preserving approaches maintain the same data-flow and fulfil most of the requirements, but they are not compatible with AUTOSAR.

▷ The AUTOSAR standard does not provide a method for predictable interprocessor communication between parallel executed tasks. The proposed interprocessor communication mechanisms either access shared memory locations in an unpredictable order or data dependencies force frequent serialization of the task scheduling. Strong *deterministic multithreading (DMT)* and *time-triggered architectures (TTAs)* ensure determinism. However, the former one misses a link between the internal artificial clock and real time. The latter one has strict time budgets that cannot be exceeded or the data-flow can break.

▷ A relaxation of inter-task data dependencies for improving parallel performance by reading less up-to-date input data is possible. However, state-of-the-art approaches do not define rules for transforming inter-task communication in such a manner that the sensor/actuator data-flow is predictable and reproducible. Moreover, the end-to-end latency constraints are maintained.

These deficiencies motivate for a parallelization approach that achieves determinism and robustness by considering the original application's configuration. Therefore, precedence constraints are derived between runnables of the same release period, using the original control flow, and between tasks with different release periods, using the original task priority. Latency constraints are derived, for relevant end-to-end chains, by taking precedence constraints and the original task period into account. These constraints build the foundation for further parallelization steps. The following sections describe the contributions of this Ph.D. over the state of the art.

**Runnable-level Parallelization**—The static partitioned scheduler RunPar [Pan+14] is proposed for the separate parallelization of tasks, which schedules runnables and not tasks. RunPar is a result of collaborative work in the parMERASA project. The author of this thesis mainly contributed in formulating the problem, analysing the case study, and conducting experiments. RunPar uses a bin-packing heuristic and a priority rule to assign the longest chain of dependent runnables first. The heuristic guarantees predictability, robustness, and data consistency of the parallel program by construction. The runtime overhead is low and a re-validation is unnecessary. The implementation can be done efficiently and only minimal modifications at operating system level are required. A complex diesel EMS is used to extensively evaluate RunPar. The results show that RunPar efficiently reduces a task's WCET on two cores, but the improvement on higher core counts is minor. The reason for this is that RunPar executes tasks in sequential order and this limits the achievable parallelism.

Consequently, this thesis proposes a new AUTOSAR structure named *Supertask*, which further exploits runnable-level parallelism of AUTOSAR tasks and still maintains the original data-flow of the application. Runnables from (originally) consecutive scheduled tasks are grouped into one Supertask, which then becomes a unique scheduling entity with a period equal to the least common multiple of tasks composing it. Runnables of the Supertask are then scheduled with RunPar, whereas inter-task data dependencies are respected. This allows for maintaining the original data-flow and increasing the parallelism in the legacy application. The scalability of Supertasks is evaluated and compared against separate parallelization with RunPar. The results report a significant improvement over RunPar, but more than two cores cannot be used efficiently with runnable-level parallelization.

These results also show that the original target of the parallelization is achieved only in parts. Consequently, distributing complete tasks is investigated as an alternative strategy.

**Task-level Parallelization**—The high number of precedence constraints between tasks causes frequent serialization, when RunPar is used and prevents an efficient usage of computational resources. The target of task-level parallelization is a relaxation of constraints that were respected by RunPar, so that communicating tasks can execute in a parallel way and still communicate in a predictable manner.

Therefore, this thesis proposes the novel communication mechanism *timed implicit communication (TIC)* [Keh+15], which overcomes the shortcomings of AUTOSAR implicit communication (an unpredictable data-flow). TIC [Keh+15] allows dependent tasks to execute in a parallel way, while maintaining the application's data-flow independent of the task schedule. Therefore, the communication between producer and consumer is decoupled by shifting the reception of data by one producer period (and bound to the task period). The producer task stores data in a buffer and attaches a publication timestamp, which is the end of the current producer period. Afterwards, the consumer task reads from the previous producer instance (compared to the single-core ECU execution) by selecting a value with the appropriate timestamp from the buffer. Thereby, the functional behaviour is independent from the point in time at which a task instance is scheduled within its period.

The communication between tasks is transformed in a predictable manner, which guarantees an identical data-flow for all target platforms. Thus, predictability and reproducibility are guaranteed. The approach is compliant to AUTOSAR and is implemented at AUTOSAR *run-time environment (RTE)* level and does not require modification of source code. The runnable-to-task mapping remains unchanged, which guarantees a correct data-flow within a task. The evaluation of TIC showed a speed-up of a 2.7 times faster execution on four cores and a 4.5 times faster execution on eight cores execution, when the utilization is at its maximum. However, the end-to-end latency is increased due to delayed transmission. Despite the benefits of TIC, it requires careful choice in applying this mechanism.

For this reason and for a better classification, runnable-level parallelization (with Supertasks and separate parallelization with RunPar) is compared to task-level parallelization (with TIC). The results show that Supertasks provide a higher speed-up under low processor utilization and TIC provides better performance under high processor utilization. Interestingly, these observations suggest the use of Supertasks and TIC as complementary strategies for increasing the overall system performance. Therefore, a method for deriving a hyperperiod schedule must be aware of the end-to-end latency and it must apply TIC and RunPar selectively. The coordination of RunPar and TIC is thus investigated.

**Coordination of Runnable- and Task-level Parallelization**—Introducing TIC allows parallel execution, but it also introduces an additional delay between a sensor and an actuator. Combining runnable- and task-level parallelization can compensate the negative impact on the latency and exploit the performance of the multicore ECU at the same time.

Coordinating runnable- and task-level parallelization means to optimize contradictory targets. However, each approach has individual advantages that can be used to compensate the shortcomings in the other. To achieve this, an evolutionary algorithm for solving the *resource-constrained project scheduling problem* is adapted to generate a set of possible hyperperiod schedules. The *parallel schedule quality (PSQ)* is established as a metric for quantifying the quality of a schedule. This allows for selecting the schedule with the highest overall benefit from parallelization and finding a satisfactory solution in reasonable time.

The computed schedule is predictable, robust, efficient, cost-effective, and can be implemented in AUTOSAR straightforward. The *first-in-last-out (FILO)* latency is identical to the reference platform and reducing the processor's clock rate to a minimum utilizes idle intervals. All task periods are scaled with the same value for this.

RunPar and TIC significantly reduce the clock rate, whereas TIC achieves a much lower value (58% less than RunPar). Thus, solely using RunPar provides an overall better performance, if less than half of the inter-task communication uses TIC. The trend reverses when more inter-task communication is replaced and thus the best solution is found in this region. However, combining runnable- and task-level parallelism outperforms the individual approaches and provides the best overall performance.

**Proof of Concept**—The proposed approach is applied to a real diesel EMS to investigate the performance and efficiency with a real application as an example. In the first instance the mechanisms are applied and evaluated in simulation studies. Promising techniques are selected for implementation on an Infineon AURIX platform. The studies on the real platform are conducted to analyse the performance of simulative studies and deployment on a real platform. Finally, a migration process for an industrial environment is derived from these experiences. One section describes a step by step process. This eases the migration of legacy software to a multicore ECU.

## 1.3 Thesis Outline

Chapter 2 provides the background to this thesis and introduces fundamental terms. Automotive control software is explained and a short overview about the AUTOSAR software architecture standard is given. Fundamental work steps of software parallelization are explained. The processor architecture, which is used for the evaluation of the approach, is explained as well as its simulation environment. An overview about timing analysis techniques for the estimation of WCETs is given.

Chapter 3 begins with a definition of functional and non-functional objectives, taking the properties of legacy automotive embedded control software and the AUTOSAR methodology into account. Afterwards, state-of-the-art approaches for each parallelization step are explained and discussed in the context of the previously defined objectives. This specifically includes methods for automotive or embedded systems and more general methods. A discussion in the context of the objective is conducted. The chapter concludes with a summary of deficiencies.

Chapter 4 introduces the partitioned scheduling approach RunPar for runnable-level parallelization and introduces the optimization with Supertasks. The implementation in AUTOSAR and the handling of interrupts are described. The approaches are evaluated and compared against each other in an evaluations section.

Chapter 5 introduces a mechanism for predictable task-level communication called TIC that allows for parallel execution of tasks. Moreover, the migration with TIC and the implementation in AUTOSAR are described. The evaluation of the approach investigates the performance, buffer, and latency overhead. The findings motivate the combination of TIC with RunPar.

Consequently, chapter 6 describes the combination of the approaches from chapters 4 and 5 in a coordinated manner. Rules for the classification of communication are defined and a self-adaptive evolutionary algorithm, for combining the approaches, is described. The evaluation first compares the individual approaches against each other and investigates the performance of the combined approach afterwards.

The chapters 4 to 6 contain a qualitative analysis of each approach. A list of research questions is derived to motivate for experimental investigations. The results are discussed in the context of these questions and main findings from experiments are summarized in each chapter separately.

Finally, chapter 7 summarizes the main findings of the three main chapters 4 to 6 in this thesis and draws conclusions on the results. Moreover, ideas for improvements and future work are given.

Appendix A describes the applicability of the approach in an industrial mass production environment. Moreover, the chapter lists the tools required to implement the parallelization approach and it describes the migration process step by step to ease reproducing. Finally, the applicability of the approach is shown with an implementation on the Infineon AURIX processor.

# 2 | Background

"There is nothing more
practical than a good theory"

Kurt Lewin, 1952

This chapter introduces the fundamentals for this thesis. Section 2.1 explains automotive control software basically. Domain specific wording, which is used throughout the following chapters, is introduced. Section 2.2 gives an overview about software parallelization. This includes fundamentals about subtask decomposition and dependency analysis. Section 2.3 describes the extraction of relevant parallelization constraints from automotive control software and it introduces necessary notations. Section 2.4 describes the considered processor architecture and employed tools. The last section in this chapter provides a summary of the main points.

## 2.1  Automotive Control Software

Automotive software is described according to the *AUTomotive Open System ARchitecture (AUTOSAR)* standard [AUT14a]. The consortium behind the standard is a worldwide development partnership of car manufacturers, suppliers, and companies from the electronics, semiconductor, and software industry. AUTOSAR standardises the software architecture, services, and a methodology comprising configuration and description methods. The software architecture covers a superset of properties from existing software and common development practices. AUTOSAR shaped a uniform understanding of control software across the whole automotive industry and harmonises the development process. The terminology is used throughout this thesis.

Automotive control software is integrated in an embedded real-time system; the *electronic control unit (ECU)*. In the scope of this thesis, this device executes one application with real-time properties. The model of automotive control software is derived from a classical task model presented in the fundamental work of Liu and Layland [LL73] as well as the formulation of Forget and Pagetti et al. [For+10; Pag+11].

**Definition 2.1 (Real-time application):** *A real-time application consists of a set of n tasks:*

$$\mathcal{A} = \{\tau_i \mid 1 \leq i \leq n, i \in \mathbb{N}\}. \tag{2.1}$$

*The real-time attributes* $(\pi_i, T_i, C_i, O_i, D_i)$ *characterise each task* $\tau_i \in \mathcal{A}$.

▷ $\pi_i$ *is the priority.*

▷ $\tau_i$ *is instantiated periodically with period* $T_i$.

▷ $\tau_i^p$ *denotes the p-th iteration of task* $\tau_i$.

▷ $C_i$ *is the worst-case execution time (WCET) of* $\tau_i$ *expressed in time units.*

▷ $O_i$ *is the release time of the first instance of* $\tau_i$, *i.e. the offset with respect to the start time of the system.*

▷ $D_i \leq T_i$ *is the relative deadline of* $\tau_i$; *they are implicitly defined, i.e.* $D_i = T_i$.

▷ *The release time of* $\tau_i^p$ *is* $o_i^p = O_i + pT_i$.

▷ *The absolute deadline of* $\tau_i^p$ *is* $d_i^p = o_i^p + D_i$.

Automotive control applications are real-time applications in the sense of definition 2.1. Later in this chapter, in section 2.3.2.2, the formulation is extended to describe and derive latency constraints. Chapters 4 to 6 consider different aspects of automotive control applications and adapt this definition for the specific needs.

Automotive control software has strict real-time constraints and the order in which output is produced matters. This mainly distinguishes the parallelization of such software from others, for example from the area of high performance computing. For this reason, precedence constraints are extracted to define a partial order for the execution of runnables, and latency constraints are extracted to specify the acceptable response time of the application.

## 2.1.1 AUTomotive Open System ARchitecture (AUTOSAR)

The software architecture of automotive control software is divided in three parts as shown in figure 2.1. A hierarchical component-based model describes the control application on the top layer. In this model, elementary code pieces (*runnables*) within the components implement the functional behaviour. Each component realizes a subtask of the overall control and communicates frequently with other components.

The structure of such an application is a block diagram, as they are characteristic for control engineering and similar to the representation in a model-based development environment like MATLAB. Executing the runnables of the blocks in the appropriate order guarantees the data-flow through the blocks. Therefore, runnables with the same

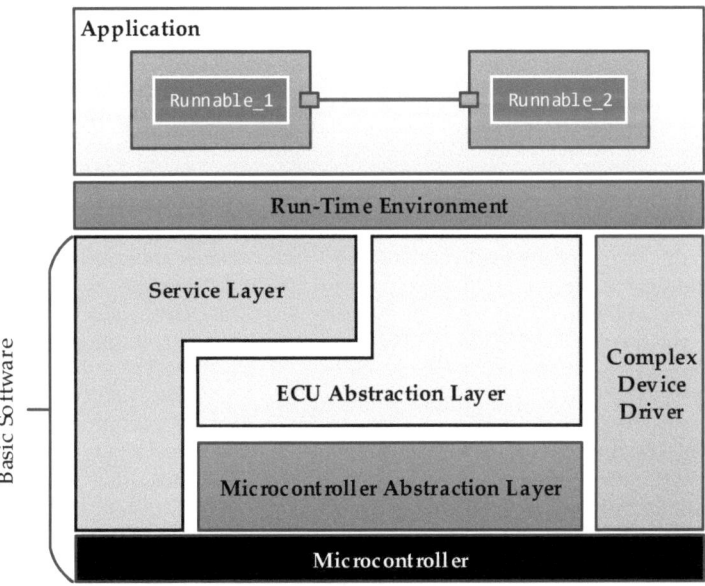

Figure 2.1: The AUTORSAR Software Architecture.

release time (periodic or sporadic) are grouped into AUTOSAR task structures and scheduled by the AUTOSAR OS, which is part of the *basic software (BSW)*. In contrast to the application layer, the BSW has a layered architecture and many hardware-specific components. Thus, the *run-time environment (RTE)* serves as separation between them. This makes the control application independent from the hardware architecture below.

The *AUTOSAR operating system (AR-OS)* [AUT14a] supports *periodic* and *sporadic* task execution. Deadlines are defined implicitly, which means a task instance must finish its execution before the release of the next task instance. Typically, a fixed priority-preemptive scheduling with *rate monotonic (RM)* priority assignment [LSD89] is used.

### 2.1.1.1 Virtual Function Bus

The *virtual function bus (VFB)* is a model for describing an AUTOSAR control application. A particular characteristic is the independence from the ECU's hardware architecture. The model has a component-based structure, describes the functional separation, and the communication between components. This allows for easier re-use of components.

The structural element is the *software-component (SW-C)*, which can be nested. No limitation about the number hierarchy levels is made. Within a SW-C runnables implement the functional behaviour. Within the component, they can exclusively exchange data through *inter-runnable-variable (IRV)*, which cannot be accessed from runnables in another SW-C. This concept is similar to the encapsulation of private data in a class instance of an object oriented programming language.

Interaction across component boundaries is possible through *ports*. Within the SW-C a runnable is associated to the port whose data are either read or written. Outside of a SW-C ports are associated with each other with an *assembly-connector*. One port can have multiple connections with other ports and multiple runnables can read from or write to the same port. That means the port serves as an interface and a runnable does not have a direct connection to another runnable, although they communicate with each other practically.

A *port-interface* further specifies a port. Multiple kinds of port-interfaces can be specified, because this is the only point for inter-component interaction. Most relevant for this thesis are sender-receiver communication, for transmitting a datum, and client-server communication, for invoking operations.

The developer can define the communication via IRVs, within a SW-C, or through a sender-receiver port, between SW-C, either as *explicit* or as *implicit*. By default, communication is explicit, i.e. a precedence constraint is imposed from producer runnable to consumer runnable, defining a strict order of execution. The consumer reads the most recent value of the producer. Implicit communication means that a datum is distributed to all consumer runnables after the producer runnable has finished its execution. On the consumer side, the datum is buffered and calculations are performed on a copy meanwhile. As a result, concurrent execution of runnables is possible, because the datum is buffered, but delivered with a delay. This is a form of *asynchronous communication*. Storing data in a queue is another possibility, but their use is rare and is therefore not considered in this thesis.

In client-server communication, the provider of the operation is denoted as *server* that offers an operation to one or more *clients*. That means the client-runnable triggers the execution of a server-runnable through a well-defined interface. The server-runnable typically maintains an internal state and parallel execution is therefore not possible.

Apart from those communication mechanisms, four other kinds of ports can be specified:

1) a *parameter* interface provides a constant value or calibration data,

2) a *non-volatile data* interface provides access to non-volatile memory,

3) a *trigger* interface immediately starts the execution of a runnable,

4) and a *mode-switch* interface notifies a SW-C about the state from the mode manager to adjust the component's behaviour.

### 2.1.1.2  Run-Time Environment

The AUTOSAR RTE serves as a separation between the layered architecture design of the BSW and the component-based design of the application. It makes the application independent from a specific ECU and is the realization of the port-interfaces in the VFB model of an application. This includes the application's access to the BSW modules, the connections to the AUTOSAR OS, and communication services. A SW-C can only access the BSW modules on the same ECU, but it can communicate with SW-Cs on another ECU through the RTE. The RTE therefore hides the concrete implementation of the communication behind a standardised *application programming interface (API)*.

The RTE guarantees data consistency for IRVs and sender-receiver communication. Additionally, it is possible to use *per-instance memory (PIM)* for direct memory accesses, but the RTE does not guarantee consistency in this case and thus PIM is not recommended and consequently not considered in this thesis.

The RTE is in addition responsible for scheduling SW-Cs from the application and from the BSW. Therefore, runnables with the same release period are typically grouped into the same task. Although, this is not stipulated by the standard, but it represents a reasonable and logic combination. The task bodies and schedule tables are automatically generated from the RTE configuration. The OS starts the tasks and the runnables within the task are executed one after another. Guards may check if all runnables must be executed. The RTE and the BSW scheduler are generated for each ECU to ensure efficiency of the implementation.

### 2.1.1.3  Basic Software

The *microcontroller abstraction* makes the layers above independent from the underlying processor architecture. This layer has direct access to the microcontroller hardware, contains the hardware-specific drivers, and provides a standardized set of interface functions to the ECU *abstraction* layer above. ECU abstraction provides interfaces to the hardware drivers of the microcontroller abstraction, contains external drivers, and it provides an API for accessing peripherals and devices regardless of their physical location. The communication service for example is part of this layer. A *complex device driver* allows direct access from the RTE to the microcontroller hardware. This interface is used to integrate proprietary functions, implement time-critical or complex sensor/actuator operations, or encapsulate legacy functions in the architecture. The *service* layer provides basic services to the application and BSW modules. It contains amongst others the AUTOSAR OS, which is based on the specification *Offene Systeme und deren Schnittstellen für die Elektronik in Kraftfahrzeugen (OSEK)* [OSE05].

## 2.1.2    Migration to AUTOSAR

AUTOSAR is now introduced in the *electrical/electronic (E/E)* architecture development processes of car manufacturers. The standard enables shorter design cycles and easier re-use of legacy software [DT11]. Nevertheless, a large fraction of legacy control software is not compliant to AUTOSAR standard. The migration is necessary to ensure interoperability and re-use in the future.

Migrating legacy control software to AUTOSAR is twofold. It can be distinguished in defining the communication, on application layer with the VFB (SW-Cs, ports, runnables, etc.), and configuring the BSW, i.e. OS tasks, runnable-to-task mapping, etc. The description and configuration are defined according to the AUTOSAR meta-model and stored in a standardised XML-file format. The application's source code is refactored. Concretely, the communication is replaced by RTE API calls and the original *operating system (OS)*, drivers, etc. are replaced by the BSW.

The migration to AUTOSAR becomes more relevant in the context of parallelization, because the SW-C structure of the application has a direct impact on the achievable degree of parallelism. The reason for this is runnables are distributed to cores indirectly by assigning a SW-C to a core. As a result, if a component contains two independent runnables no parallel execution is possible. The migration must therefore create a fine-grained VFB model, in which a SW-C contains only one runnable to allow for a maximal degree of parallelism in later steps.

Only few publications about the migration of legacy software to AUTOSAR are available, because this activity often concerns proprietary or confidential contents. Reports about the migration in the context of parallelization are rare. However, existing literature concerns two kinds of legacy software. The software can either be available as a model in a proprietary model-based environment like MATLAB/Simulink or it can be plain source code.

### 2.1.2.1    Migration of Model-based Legacy Software

A development environment for model-based automotive software often allows for direct export of an AUTOSAR XML description and source code. For example, the commercial tool Embedded Coder [The15a] for MATLAB and Simulink supports these features [The15b].

Manufacturers that maintain an own proprietary model can transform their model with the ATLAS *Transformation Language (ATL)* [Jou+06]. The language specifies the transformation from an arbitrary source model to and target model with a mixture of declarative and imperative constructs. The work by Selim et al. [Sel+12] describes the migration of the *General Motors (GM)* meta-model to the AUTOSAR meta-model via model transformation with ATL. Horizontal transformation manipulates models at the same abstraction level, but possibly expressed in different formalisms. An example is the transformation of a MATLAB state machine into an UML state machine. Vertical transformation manipulates different abstraction levels. An example is generating a deployment model from a software and hardware architecture model.

The migration steps cover the application layer only and the configuration of the BSW is done in a separate step. The generated SW-C structure is equivalent to the model from which it is generated. Thus, the hierarchy can have multiple levels with independent runnables within the same SW-C. Model transformation techniques do not consider software parallelization. The transformation from a (proprietary) meta-model to the AUTOSAR meta-model is straightforward, because the source model contains explicit information about the control function, data dependencies, etc. and the transformation can be done without loss of information.

### 2.1.2.2 Migration from Plain Source Code

The migration from plain source code is complex and the expenditure is high. An in-depth analysis of data dependencies is needed. Common techniques are explained later in section 2.2.2. The result from this analysis must be interpreted to create an application model, the BSW must be configured, and the source code must be refactored to use the RTE API.

A helpful tool for creating a VFB model is the AUTOSAR Tool Platform (Artop) [Knü+10]. Artop is a textual description language, which can be used royalty free by all AUTOSAR members. The tool is based on Eclipse and provides base functionality for creating design and configuration tools for AUTOSAR. Several subprojects provide a textual modelling environment (ARText), for describing SW-Cs, timing, variant handling, etc., or a test environment (ARUnit), for implementing test cases.

Kum et al. [Kum+08] describe the migration of a legacy software including the AUTOSAR BSW. The methods separate the application's source code into parts: the control application, ECU devices, communication, other services, and peripherals. These parts are mapped to the equivalent part in AUTOSAR afterwards. For example, peripherals are mapped to the microcontroller abstraction in the BSW.

The control application is first divided into SW-Cs and second broken down into runnables. A data-flow between two runnables is interpreted as sender-receiver communication and a function call is interpreted as client-server communication. This interpretation is advantageous, because the RTE guarantees data consistency in both cases. However, the actual implementation of the process is not described.

Contrarily, the case study by Scheidemann et al. [SKS10a; SKS10b] is an example for the usage of ARText. Like the approach of Kum et al., a static data and control flow analysis is conducted first. The information about function calls, read and write access to global variables, and data types of variables and parameters are used to map the communication to AUTOSAR communication paradigms in ARText.

The RTE (runnable-to-task mapping, client-server communication, and events) and communication stack are configured in a separate ECU development phase. The OS is replaced by an AUTOSAR compliant one and the parameters are determined from the former OS configuration. Contrarily, Scheidemann et al. already consider the multicore ECU and thus a mapping is generated (this is discussed in more detail in chapter 3) first. The BSW is configured in a semi-automatic way afterwards, because it depends on the mapping.

### 2.1.3 Case Study: Diesel Engine Control

The performance and the efficiency of the approach in this thesis need to be evaluated. Using a real application is advantageous, because this allows for drawing conclusions in a real deployment. To that end, a diesel *engine management system (EMS)* is used as example, because the application contains a large amount of highly connected runnables.

The examined EMS comprises roughly 1200 runnables that implement the behaviour of numerous SW-Cs. They exchange data via sender-receiver and IRV communication. The SW-C's internal states are updated at different rates, e.g. sensor values are polled with a greater or equal frequency than they are processed. Therefore, runnables with the same released period are mapped to the same task.

Figure 2.2 provides a simplified description of the task set in the diesel EMS. The nodes in this directed graph represent tasks and the edges represent communication between them.

The task $\tau_1$ executes after an interrupt from the camshaft sensor (*crank-angle task*). Tasks $\tau_2$ to $\tau_{12}$ execute with the period denoted by the label close to the node, task $\tau_5$ has a period of one millisecond for example.

A solid edge represents explicit communication between two tasks, which is imposed by the runnables mapped to this task. As a result, communication between takes place with different frequencies. The dashed edges represent implicit communication. In this example, only the communication with the sporadic crank-angle task $\tau_1$ is implicit.

The EMS also contains client-server communication. This requires a mechanism for maintaining memory coherency, when a server-runnable updates the internal state of the SW-C it belongs to. This is out of the scope of this thesis. To still conduct a performance evaluation, calls are enclosed in *ticket-locks* [ORS14]. They block other runnables until the execution of the server-runnable has finished. These locks can

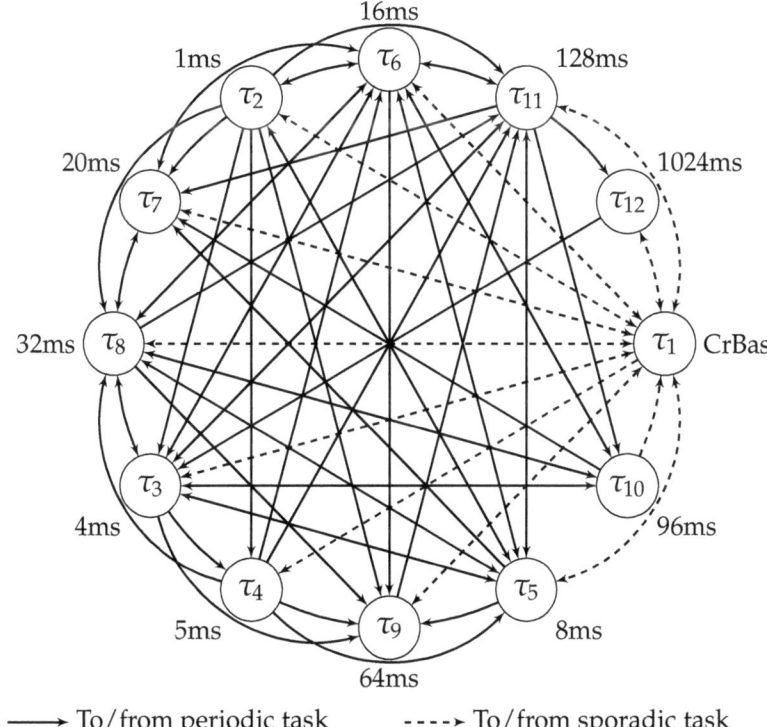

Figure 2.2: Communication in a diesel EMS.

be integrated within the RTE and are transparent to the client and the server. Thus, no changes of the application are required. Data consistency and data coherency are guaranteed.

## 2.2 Software Parallelization

The central topic of this thesis is the parallelization of control software. This section gives a brief overview about this large topic. According to Sinnen [Sin07a] software parallelization can be divided in the following three broad categories.

a) *Subtask decomposition* — This category contains methods that divide a program into subtasks. Generally, subtasks are not independent and precedence constraints are derived to define a partial order for the execution thereof.

b) *Dependency analysis* — The methods of this category identify data dependencies between subtasks, for example high level language statements, of a program. The analysis for data dependencies constitutes the foundation for the definition of precedence constraints between subtasks. Thus, this step is necessary to define the partial order for the execution of subtasks.

c) *Scheduling* — This category refers to methods that define the temporal (the *schedule*) and spatial assignment (the *mapping*) of tasks to processors. The scheduling of tasks requires an existing mapping.

In practice, these steps cannot be separated as described above. A *reconfiguration step* typically supplements the subtask decomposition, in which subtasks are grouped to form a longer (in execution time) *unit of scheduling (UoS)*. This must reduce the overall synchronization time and thus increase fraction of parallel execution. Moreover, Culler and Singh [CSG99] denote this step as *orchestration* and Foster [Fos95] denotes this step as *agglomeration*.

The problem of scheduling a program for parallel execution is discussed in the next chapter as it is subject to the state of the art and the problem analysis in this thesis. Contrarily, the subtask decomposition and dependency analysis are fundamental to this thesis and therefore described in more detail in the following.

## 2.2.1 Subtask Decomposition Fundamentals

The decomposition of software can be accomplished in several ways. The book of Grama [Gra03] describes the following commonly used techniques.

a) *Recursive decomposition* — The program is recursively decomposed into subtasks, whereas a tree is created. This method is well suited for programs that implement a divide-and-conquer strategy.

b) *Data decomposition* — data, on which computations are performed, are identified and they are partitioned across tasks. The partitioning induces a problem decomposition and can be done in various ways. An exemplary usage of this technique is the parallel matrix multiplication.

c) *Exploratory decomposition* — These techniques go along with the execution of the program, for example when computations are used to search within a state space. Computation possibilities are represented in a tree-like structure and computed by independent tasks. This is similar to the recursive decomposition.

d) *Speculative decomposition* — Speculative approaches schedule tasks regardless of data dependencies and they perform a roll-back, if the dependency manifests at runtime. The performance of these techniques depends on the amount of data dependencies in the program and they are typically used when independent tasks cannot be identified a-priori.

e) *Hybrid decomposition* — In practice, programs can often be decomposed with different techniques. Methods that combine several decomposition techniques are thus denoted as hybrid decomposition techniques.

The decomposition can be implemented in various ways. An obvious and convenient way is the integration in a parallelizing compiler [Wol96; PW86; Aug+11; GGL12], because the source code is analysed for data dependencies in any case.

The automatic parallelization can thus be implemented as an optimization step afterwards. The above mentioned parallelizing compilers focus on extracting parallelism from loops in the first place. Recent speculative techniques [Ram+10; Joh+12] avoid or eliminate data dependencies between tasks by transformation of the program.

## 2.2.2 Dependence Analysis Fundamentals

Source code analysis is, according to David Binkley [Bin07], the process of extracting information about a program from its source code using automatic tools. It is one of the first steps in program compilation, optimization, or transformation. The result of this process is commonly represented in the form of a graph. Central to parallelization is the *dependence graph*, as August et al. describe in [Aug+11]. The process of deriving the dependence graph is thus denoted as dependency analysis and refers to compiler analyses for *disproving* various kinds of data dependencies that may exist between different imperative program units.

A wide range of analysis techniques were proposed in the past decades. The most relevant analysis techniques are:

▷ Reaching definition and liveness analysis [ASU86]

▷ Flow-sensitive analysis [Muc97]

▷ Context-sensitive analysis [CH00]

▷ Pointer analysis [Hin01]

▷ Array dependency analysis [KA02]

▷ Field-sensitive analysis [PKH07]

However, exactly determining data dependencies between all statements in a program is undecidable [MHL] in general and there is a trade-off between the scalability of the analysis and its accuracy. That means a fast analysis reports more data dependencies than a slow one [PK03].

Analysing data dependencies first requires representing the program in the form of a *control flow graph (CFG)* [Aug+11]. The nodes of this directed graph represent program statements and edges represent the control flow relation by sequential composition and branch statements.

**Definition 2.2 (Data Dependence Graph (DDG)):** *The data dependence graph (DDG) is a graph $G = (V, E)$, in which $V$ is a set of nodes and $E$ is a set of edges in the graph. Each $v \in V$ represents one statement in the program; one node for each statement. The edges of the graph represent data dependencies between statement A and statement B, if a valid path in the CFG from A to B exists.*

A distinction is made between the following kinds of data dependencies:

a) *Flow dependence* — A writes the same memory location that is read by B afterwards, i.e. *read-after-write (RAW)*.

b) *Anti-dependence* — A reads from the same memory location that is written by B afterwards, i.e. *write-after-read (WAR)*.

c) *Output dependence* — A and B write to the same memory location, i.e. *write-after-write (WAW)*.

The DDG is a general concept and can be used for any kind of optimization. The abstraction level can be adapted for the optimization, for example to low-level assembly instructions, individual statements in a compiler intermediate representation (like the LLVM [LA04]), or high-level language program statements or functions.

Another helpful form of representation is the *control dependence graph (CDG)*. The node B is said to be control dependent on a node A if:

a) There is an execution path p in the CFG from A to B.

b) B post-dominates every node C in p, which means every path from C to an exit node in the CFG has to necessarily pass through B.

c) B does not post-dominate A.

In addition to the DDG and the CFG, alternative forms of presentation have emerged for software parallelization. The most relevant graph representations are explained in the following.

The *program dependence graph (PDG)* is proposed by Ferrante et al. [FOW87], as a single compiler intermediate program representation. It represents the DDG and the CFG in one graph. The PDG contains two kinds of edges: *control dependence edges* and *data dependence edges*. The combination of both kinds of data dependencies allows for more efficient operation of program optimizations.

The *hierarchical task graph (HTG)* is proposed by Girkar and Polychronopoulos [GP94] as an intermediate program representation. The graph is used for program optimization and extraction of functional parallelism [GP92]. The HTG is a layered graph of acyclic control flow graphs and it is overlaid with data- and control-dependence graphs. It contains simple (basic statement) and hierarchical (loop or function body) nodes, which represent the hierarchy of program statements and edges represent the data dependencies between tasks at the corresponding hierarchy level. Thus, parallelism can be exploited at each level of the HTG.

The work by Cordes et al. [CMM10] extends the HTG with communication in- and out-nodes to allow for automatic parallelization process for real-time applications. Moreover, node weights (measurement-based execution time) and edge weights (communication cost) supplement the graph. This makes it possible to extract parallelism for each node in isolation.

The compiler OSCAR [KOI01; Ish+05] uses a *macro-flow graph (MFG)*, which is similar to the DDG. The program is decomposed in three kinds of blocks (they are also denoted as *macro tasks (MTs)*):

a) *Basic blocks* — They represent a single statement of the program and are thus the most fine-grained blocks. That means further decomposition of these blocks is impossible.

b) *Subroutine blocks* — These are coarse-grained blocks that can contain other blocks. Further decomposition into basic, repetition, or subroutine blocks is possible.

c) *Repetition blocks* — They represent loop statements and contain the loop body. Additionally, they can contain basic blocks, repetition blocks or subroutine blocks. That means further decomposition is possible here. OSCAR automatically parallelizes loops, whereas independent blocks represent iterations.

The main difference between the MFG and the DDG is the fixed granularity of blocks in the MFG. The DDG is a more general concept and the MFG can thus be seen as specialization.

Bernstein [Ber66] denotes the set of memory locations that are read by a program portion $i$ as *ReadSet(i)* and the set of memory locations that are written by a program portion $j$ as *WriteSet(j)*. Two portions of a program $i$ and $j$ can execute in parallel if the following three conditions hold true:

$$
\begin{aligned}
&1.)\ \text{ReadSet}(i) \cap \text{WriteSet}(j) = \varnothing \\
&2.)\ \text{WriteSet}(i) \cap \text{ReadSet}(j) = \varnothing \\
&3.)\ \text{WriteSet}(i) \cap \text{WriteSet}(j) = \varnothing
\end{aligned}
\tag{2.2}
$$

Later Randy Allen et al. [ACK87] formulated this in a more general way, when they stated that two processes, which access a shared memory location, must be serialized if at least one those processes modifies the memory location. The CFG defines the order in which the serialization takes places. Thus, finding a partial order for the execution of a program requires a dependency analysis, an appropriate graph representation, and the use Bernstein's/Allen's rule.

## 2.3 Parallelization Constraints in Automotive Software

The extraction of parallelization constraints, as described in section 2.2, from automotive control software, as described in section 2.1, is a mandatory preparation step during the parallelization process. In addition, latency constraints are needed to specify the input/output behaviour of the control application.

Precedence constraints express an order. For example, consider the direction of communication from one runnable $r_1$ to another runnable $r_2$ ($r_1 \rightarrow r_2$) or consider the execution order of one task $\tau_1$ and another task $\tau_2$ ($\tau_1 \rightarrow \tau_2$). A graph that describes precedence constraints needs to be free of cycles to be causal. Latency constraints must span over multiple task instances, so that the latency of a chain from a sensor to an actuator is verifiable.

### 2.3.1 Extraction of Precedence Constraints

The structure of an automotive application does not necessarily represent a decomposition into parallel or independent components. But, each component realizes a subtask, implemented by runnables, of the overall control and it communicates frequently with other components. Figure 2.3a illustrates this with a simple application model. A runnable $r_1$ in the SW-C $A$ sends a datum to a runnable $r_2$ in the SW-C $B$ through a sender-receiver port. The two runnables cannot execute in parallel, although they belong to independent SW-Cs.

The VFB model does not explicitly describe, if it is correct to execute $r_1$ before $r_2$ or not. It is possible to consider further information of the model though. If both runnables execute with the same period, it is probably safe to assume that $r_1$ must execute before $r_2$. If the runnables execute with different periods, it is probably safe to assume a higher priority for the runnable with the smaller period. The reason for this is rate monotonic priority assignments are usual in automotive software and the runnables with the higher priority executes first in this case. However, it is impossible to determine the correctness of this decision based on the information available in the VFB model.

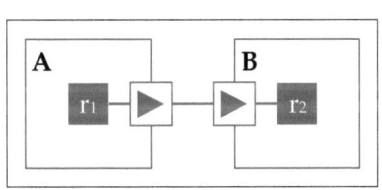

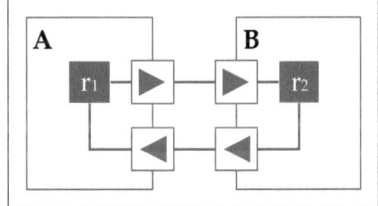

(a) Unidirectional communication.    (b) Bidirectional communication.

Figure 2.3: Example for application model with unidirectional communication (left) and bidirectional communication (right).

The situation is more difficult, if two runnables communicate in a bidirectional way as shown in figure 2.3b. It is impossible to derive a partial order for runnables that execute with the same period. One of the runnables works on a less up-to-date datum, from the last execution of the producer. Such situations are common, because bidirectional communication is frequent and the internal state of an ECU is continuously calculated. That means decomposing an automotive control application must follow the data-flow of the implemented control function and not solely the component structure.

Fortunately, the configuration of the BSW for the original single-core implementation is well-tested and validated. This configuration is known to produce a valid data-flow and lead to correct functional behaviour. Hence, it is reasonable to use the configuration for extracting parallelization constraints. Thereby, the functional properties and the task set of the application remain unchanged.

This approach has smaller migration cost, because re-arranging the runnables in new tasks increases the level of parallelism. However, this approach requires a re-validation of the functional correctness. That means extensive tests must be conducted whose cost is high and this is undesirable. Deriving parallelization constraints from the original application's configuration is therefore a reasonable alternative.

Julien Forget et al. [For+10] make a distinction between two types of precedence constraints for multiperiodic systems:

a) *Simple precedence constraints* — They define the execution order between tasks of the same release period.

b) *Extended precedence constraints* — They define the execution order between tasks with different release periods. This covers only the relation between periodic tasks, because an unforeseen event (like and interrupt or alarm) usually triggers a sporadic task. Thus, they are associated with a higher priority than periodic tasks.

Simple precedence constraints for a real-time application according to definition 2.1 are directly derived from the PDG and formally defined as follows.

**Definition 2.3 (Simple Precedence Constraint):** *Let $\mathcal{T}$ be a set of tasks and let $\tau_i$ and $\tau_j$ be two task in $\mathcal{T}$. The simple precedence constraints are represented by the relation $\rightarrow$, which is a subset of $\mathcal{T} \times \mathcal{T} : \tau_i \rightarrow \tau_j$ such that $\tau_i$ must execute before $\tau_j$.*

Simple precedence constraints are commonly represented as *directed acyclic graph (DAG)* [Bar+12] $G = (V, E)$, where $V = \mathcal{T}$ and with an edge $(\tau_i, \tau_j) \in E$ for every $\tau_i \rightarrow \tau_j$.

Tasks in automotive software produce data for each other, and there are many possible deterministic communication schemes between two tasks. Determining the correct order can be difficult. Forget et al. propose the usage of RM [LSD89] or *deadline monotonic (DM)* [Aud+91] task priority assignment to derive inter-task data dependencies between tasks with different release periods. These dependencies are denoted as extended precedence constraints and defined as follows.

**Definition 2.4 (Extended Precedence Constraint):** *For any $k \in \mathbb{N}$, let $\mathcal{I}_k = [0, k]$ and let $\mathrm{lcm}(a, b)$ be the least common multiple of $a$ and $b$. Let $\tau_i^n \rightarrow \tau_j^{n'}$ denote a precedence from the instance $n$ of $\tau_i$ to the instance $n'$ of $\tau_j$. Let $p_{i,j} = \mathrm{lcm}(T_i, T_j)$. The tasks $\tau_i$ and $\tau_j$ are periodically instantiated with $T_i$ and $T_j$, respectively. The extended precedence constraints are:*

$$M_{i,j} = \{(n, n') \mid \tau_i^n \rightarrow \tau_j^{n'}, (n, n') \in \mathcal{I}_{\frac{p_{i,j}}{T_i}} \times \mathcal{I}_{\frac{p_{i,j}}{T_j}}\} \tag{2.3}$$

The precedence relation between two tasks repeats every time when both tasks are released simultaneously. Thus, extended precedence constraints are described as a repetitive pattern. A precedence constraint between two tasks $\tau_i$ and $\tau_j$ corresponds to a set of constraints between the instances of the tasks.

**Definition 2.5 (Periodic Extended Precedence):** *The periodic extended precedence $M'_{i,j}$ are imposed by the extended precedence constraints $M_{i,j}$ such that:*

$$M'_{i,j} = \left\{(n, n') \;\middle|\; \begin{array}{l} \exists k \in \mathbb{N}, (m, m') \in M_{i,j}, \\ (n, n') = (m, m') + (k\frac{p_{i,j}}{T_i}, k\frac{p_{i,j}}{T_j}) \end{array}\right\} \tag{2.4}$$

A simple precedence $\tau_i \rightarrow \tau_j$ is actually a particular case of periodic extended precedence constraints where $M_{i,j} = \{(0, 0)\}$. In other words, the extended precedence constraints express a subset of all possible communication patterns between instances of $\tau_i$ and $\tau_j$.

Figure 2.4 illustrates this with an example for

$$M_{1,4} = \{(0,0)\} : \quad \tau_1 \xrightarrow{\{(0,0)\}} \tau_4 \tag{2.5}$$

, with $T_1 = 1$ ms and $T_4 = 4$ ms, respectively. This represents the precedence constraints $\tau_1^0 \to \tau_4^0$, $\tau_1^4 \to \tau_4^1$, etc.

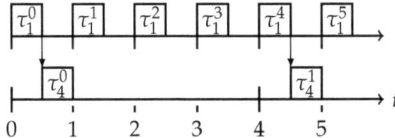

Figure 2.4: Example for periodic extended precedence.

Forget et al. use this model to schedule dependent task sets without synchronization mechanisms deterministically. Therefore, the release time and the deadline of each task are adjusted. In automotive software, the execution order of runnables is constraint by simple and extended precedence constraints. They result from the communication among runnables with the same or different release period, respectively. As a result, simple precedence constraints only exist within tasks, while extended precedence constraints only exist among tasks.

### 2.3.2 End-to-end Paths and Latency Semantics

The configuration of the legacy application defines a well-tested and validated *data-flow*. It specifies the order in which runnables process data. Each sensor value traverses several runnables in different task instances until an output value is produced. Hence, it specifies an upper bound on the sensor/actuator end-to-end latency for this data-flow.

Minimizing the latency of a critical sensor/actuator paths [Nat+07] is a typical optimization objective for embedded systems. An example for a critical sensor/actuator latency is the maximum time between the push on a gas pedal and the resulting final injection in a diesel engine, see section 2.1.3. The optimization must guarantee the satisfaction of reaction requirements even under worst-case conditions. The parallelization must guarantee, apart from the precedence constraints, the same upper bound on the end-to-end latency of critical paths as the original single-core implementation does. This marks an essential difference between classical and automotive software parallelization.

### 2.3.2.1    Different Semantics of End-to-end Latency

The compositional framework of Feiertag et al. [Fei+08] describes end-to-end path and end-to-end latency metrics that are relevant to automotive control software and commonly used in practice.

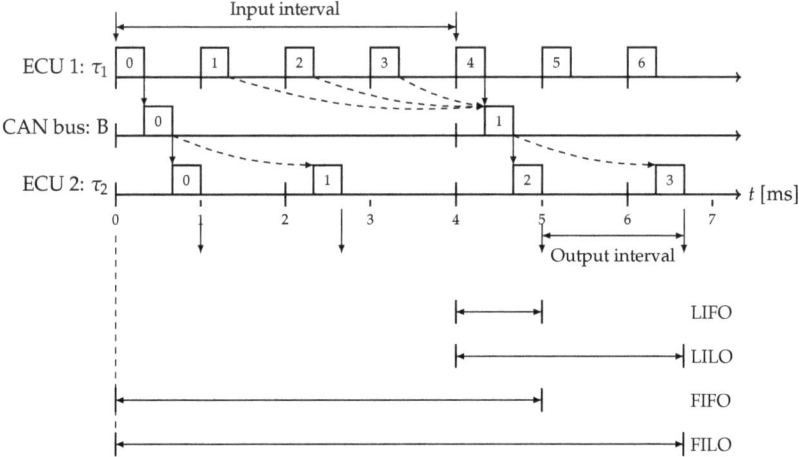

Figure 2.5: *First-in-last-out (FILO)* end-to-end latency semantic.

Figure 2.5 illustrates the semantics for an exemplary distributed system with two tasks $\tau_1$ and $\tau_2$ with a period of 1 ms and 2 ms, respectively. The tasks run on different ECUs. That means they exchange data through a field bus. In this figure, B represents communication on a *controller area network (CAN)* bus with a period of 4 ms between ECU 1 and ECU 2. The communication between tasks is defined as *overwriteable*, i.e. a new datum overwrites the existing one, and *sticky*, i.e. a datum remains in the buffer until it is overwritten.

There exists a large amount of possible data-flow paths between a sensor/actuator pair, because input values are overwritten several times before they are consumed and input values are processed several times before they are updated. In this example, an input datum is periodically read from a sensor by a runnable in $\tau_1$ and further processed by this task. The result is transmitted from ECU 1 through the CAN bus (B) to ECU 2; where $\tau_2$ processes the datum and eventually produces an output on an actuator.

The communication through register buffers results is different paths, because input values are overwritten several times. For example, $\tau_1$ overwrites its output at $t = \{1, 2, 3, 4\}$ before the result is sent to the CAN bus B at $t = 4^1/3$). $\tau_2$ processes the same input value from the CAN bus two times; at $t = \{4^2/3$ and $t = 6^1/3\}$. Generally, the following paths and latency values are seen as most relevant:

  a) *Last-in-first-out (LIFO)*: the latency between the last non-overwritten input and the first output.

  b) *Last-in-last-out (LILO)*: the latency between the last non-overwritten input and the last output.

It is important to capture the system's reaction delay after a value change in situations where input data arrive asynchronously (for example by sensor interrupts). Then, an additional sampling delay is considered before the actual processing, before the LIFO or LILO latency. In single-rate systems without jitter the delay is equal to the period of the first task in the path [GG08]. In multiperiodic systems over- or under-sampling introduce extra internal delay. As a consequence, overwritten values from the past are considered. These latency values are denoted as:

  c) *First-in-first-out (FIFO)*: the latency between the first non-overwritten input and the first output.

  d) First-in-last-out (FILO): the latency between the first non-overwritten input and the last output.

To that end, the primary focus in this thesis is on the FILO latency, because it represents an upper bound on the reaction time of the controller. It is the worst possible latency that can appear in the control software.

### 2.3.2.2 Model for End-to-end Paths

Rajeev et al. [Raj+10] refined the framework of Feiertag et al. and they provided a formal model. The model is generally defined for a distributed system of ECUs. It considers processing of data in a task and through a field bus with analysable timing characteristics, e.g. an CAN [Int15; THW94], as data transmission channel. Hence, applying the framework to multicore ECUs is possible, if the processor's bus is considered as data transmission channel.

A distributed embedded system that runs a real-time application, according to definition 2.1, needs to additionally consider message transfers between ECUs. Therefore, Rajeev et al. introduce the set of schedulable objects $\varepsilon_i \in \mathcal{O}$ as superordinate set. Each object in $\mathcal{O}$ is either a task $\tau_i$ from the task set $\mathcal{T}$ or a message $m_i$ from the message set $\mathcal{M}$. The transmission of a message does not finish instantaneously. It takes a minimal positive time to transmit one message from one ECU to another. As a result, a best-case execution time $(C_i^b)$ is considered as a lower bound and the worst-case execution time $(C_i^w)$ is considered as an upper bound for an object.

Analogous to definition 2.1, a distributed real-time application can be defined as follows.

**Definition 2.6 (Distributed real-time application):** *A distributed real-time application consists of n schedulable objects*

$$\mathcal{O} = \{\varepsilon_i \mid 1 \le i \le n, i \in \mathbb{N}\}. \tag{2.6}$$

*, whereas each object is either a task $\tau_i \in \mathcal{T}$ or a message $m_i \in \mathcal{M}$. The real-time attributes $(\pi_i, T_i, [C_i^b, C_i^w], O_i, D_i)$ characterise each task $\tau_i \in \mathcal{O}$.*

> ▷ $\pi_i$ *is the priority.*

> ▷ $\varepsilon_i$ *is instantiated periodically with period $T_i$.*

> ▷ $\varepsilon_i^p$ *denotes the p-th instance (activation/occurrence) of object $\varepsilon_i$.*

> ▷ $\hat{c}_i^p \in [C_i^b, C_i^w]$ *is the execution or transmission time of $\varepsilon_i^p$ expressed in time units.*

> ▷ $O_i$ *is the release time of the first instance of the object, i.e. the offset with respect to the start time of the system.*

> ▷ $D_i \le T_i$ *is the relative deadline, which is implicitly defined for tasks, i.e. $D_i = T_i$.*

> ▷ *The release time of $\varepsilon_i^p$ is $o_i^p = O_i + pT_i$.*

> ▷ *The absolute deadline of $\varepsilon_i^p$ is $d_i^p = o_i^p + D_i$.*

The distributed application is executed on a set of resources $\mathcal{R}$ comprised of ECUs in $\mathcal{E}$ and CAN buses in $\mathcal{B}$. The allocation of a task (or a message) to an ECU (or bus) is given by the function

$$\text{alloc} : (\mathcal{T} \to \mathcal{E}) \cup (\mathcal{M} \to \mathcal{B}). \tag{2.7}$$

The set $\mathcal{L} \subseteq \mathcal{O} \times \mathcal{O}$ describes the data dependency links between tasks and messages, where a link $(\varepsilon_i, \varepsilon_j) \in \mathcal{L}$ is seen as a register buffer between the objects $\varepsilon_i$ and $\varepsilon_j$. For example, a task sending data to another task through a shared memory location, a task sending a message on the CAN bus and so forth.

A single execution of a distributed real-time system according to definition 2.6 is denoted as a *run* $\sigma$. Each run produces a different execution sequence of *timed events*, i.e. the execution order of schedulable objects from $\mathcal{O}$. An element in the sequence of timed events is a 2-tuple of event (ev$_i$) and timestamp (ts$_i$):

$$(\text{ev}_1, \text{ts}_1), \dots, (\text{ev}_n, \text{ts}_n). \tag{2.8}$$

The instance $\varepsilon_i^p$ produces a start event and a finish event, which corresponds to the object activation or termination, respectively. The sequence $\text{ts}_1, \dots, \text{ts}_n$ forms an increasing order.

Closer observation of events allows for deriving data-flow paths within the application. A closer look at the timestamps gives the timing properties of the derived data-flow path. Both are explained in the following.

If the objects that correspond to timed events have a data dependency link, a *chain*:

$$\zeta = \varepsilon_{i_1}^{n_1} \dots \varepsilon_{i_\ell}^{n_\ell} \tag{2.9}$$

, with length $\ell \in \mathbb{N}, \ell > 1$, of objects can be derived. A chain begins with the source object $\varepsilon_{i_1}^{n_1}$ and terminates with the sink object $\varepsilon_{i_\ell}^{n_\ell}$. Formally, a sequence of timed events $\text{ev}_1, \cdots, \text{ev}_\ell$ forms a chain $\zeta$ of length $\ell$, if for all objects $\varepsilon_{i_1}^{n_1} \dots \varepsilon_{i_\ell}^{n_\ell}$ holds

$$\forall j \in \{1, \dots, \ell - 1\} : (\varepsilon_{i_j}, \varepsilon_{i_{j+1}}) \in \mathscr{L}. \tag{2.10}$$

Please note, this definition does not require that events of a chain appear immediately one after the other. In particular, several chains can overlap each other.

The timing properties of the extracted chain $\zeta$ are represented by a *timed path (TP)* $\kappa$. For a single system run $\sigma$, with $k_j \in \mathbb{N}$ denoting the activation time and $e_j \in [C_j^b, C_j^w]$ denoting the execution or transmission time, the sequence

$$\kappa = (k_1, e_1), \dots, (k_j, e_j), \dots, (k_\ell, e_\ell) \quad j = 1, \cdots, \ell \quad k_1 = \varepsilon_{i_1}^{n_1} \quad k_\ell = \varepsilon_{i_k}^{n_k} \tag{2.11}$$

is called a TP if the first start event of the $k_{j+1}$-th activation of $\varepsilon_{i_{j+1}}^{n_{j+1}}$ occurs after the finish event of $k_j$-th activation of $\varepsilon_{i_j}^{n_j}$, i.e. $\text{ft}_{i_j}^{n_j} < \text{st}_{i_{j+1}}^{n_{j+1}}$. The set of all timed paths for run $\sigma$ is denoted as $\text{TP}_\sigma$.

The latency of a timed path $\kappa$ is computed as

$$\text{latency}(\kappa) = \text{ft}_{i_\ell}^{n_\ell} - \text{st}_{i_0}^{n_0} \tag{2.12}$$

As explained before, register buffers can be overwritten by the producer. The TP $\tilde{\kappa}$ *overwrites* the TP $\kappa$ (overwrites($\tilde{\kappa}, \kappa$)) if:

a) $\tilde{\kappa}$ begins after $\kappa$:

$$\widetilde{\text{st}}_{i_0}^{n_0} > \text{st}_{i_0}^{n_0}$$

b) The output of the $k_j$-th activation of $\varepsilon_{i_j}^{n_j}$ is overwritten by the output of the $\tilde{k}_j$-th activation of $\varepsilon_{i_j}^{n_j}$ before it could be read by the $k_{j+1}$-th activation of $\varepsilon_{i_{j+1}}^{n_{j+1}}$:

$$\forall j \in \{2, \dots, l - 1\} : \tilde{k}_j \geq k_j$$

c) The paths finish simultaneously:

$$\widetilde{ft}_{i_\ell}^{n_\ell} = ft_{i_\ell}^{n_\ell}$$

A *life path* is a TP that is not overwritten. The set of all live paths corresponding to a run $\sigma$ is defined as:

$$TP_\sigma^{\text{live}} = \{\kappa \in TP_\sigma \mid \forall \tilde{\kappa} \in TP_\sigma : \neg\, \text{overwrites}(\tilde{\kappa}, \kappa)\}. \tag{2.13}$$

Based on this definition, the LILO paths for a run $\sigma$ are represented by the set

$$TP_\sigma^{\text{LILO}} = \{\kappa \in TP_\sigma^{\text{live}} \mid \forall \tilde{\kappa} \in TP_\sigma^{\text{live}} : \neg(\widetilde{st}_{i_0}^{n_0} = st_{i_0}^{n_0} \wedge \widetilde{ft}_{i_\ell}^{n_\ell} > ft_{i_\ell}^{n_\ell})\}. \tag{2.14}$$

Consequently, the LILO end-to-end latency for $\zeta$ is

$$LILO_\zeta = \max\{\text{latency}(\kappa) \mid \kappa \in \bigcup_r TP_\sigma^{\text{LILO}}\}. \tag{2.15}$$

The FILO paths $TP_\sigma^{\text{FILO}}$ and end-to-end latency $FILO_\zeta$ are derived analogously. For this reason, a sampling delay is considering the before $LILO_\zeta$.

## 2.4 Considered Processor Architecture and Analysis Tools

Applying the approach in this thesis to a real use case requires tools and knowledge about the processor architecture. This section explains:

1) the dependency analysis tool,

2) the architecture of the target processor,

3) and the WCET estimation tool for this processor.

### 2.4.1 Static Code Analysis with Understand

Understand™[Inc16] is a commercial static code analysis tool. It handles large software project with more than 1 million lines of code. The results of the analysis are stored in a separate database. An APIs, for several programming languages, allows access to this database to create individual code analysis.

Understand is used in this thesis to analyse the case study, described in section 2.1.3, and reconstruct an AUTOSAR compliant application thereof. The reconstruction is conducted in three steps. First, SW-Cs are created based on the file names of the source code. Therefore, Understand provides a graph of the application's architecture that shows the hierarchy and dependencies between files. This graph is used for generating the SW-Cs. Files with the same name, except for the file extension, are merged into the same SW-C.

Second, runnables are identified in the task bodies and associated with a SW-C; depending on the runnable's location in a file. Therefore, the CFG is extracted with Understand from every task separately. A runnable is a function that is called from within the task body and that is not called in a Boolean condition. The task itself specifies whether the runnable executes with a fixed period or sporadic. Server-runnables are identified by an analysis of each runnable's call tree; also with Understand. A function is a server-runnable, if it holds an internal state, static variables or counter, or it is called by more than one runnable.

Third, the communication between components and runnables is identified by analysis of each runnable's call tree. The access to global variables is interpreted as sender-receiver communication. Understand's database also contains this information. A new AUTOSAR sender-receiver interface is created, for every identified global variable, and added to the application's VFB model. Moreover, one provide-port and one require-port are added to the communicating SW-C and connected with each other. The description of the model is stored as ARText, which is already introduced in section 2.1.2.

Furthermore, precedence constraints between runnables are derived from the data dependencies and the control within a task. Therefore, Understand's CFG and the results from the data dependency analysis are used. The resulting DAG is used in chapter 4 for scheduling runnables of the same task.

## 2.4.2   parMERASA Multi-core Processor Architecture

Knowing the target architecture is essential for embedded systems software development. It is important to know the timing behaviour of the platform to guarantee that all tasks finish before their deadline. However, components such as caches, pipelines, branch prediction, and other speculative components complicate the estimation of the execution time. For this reason, the analysable parMERASA processor [Ung+13; PQC12; Pao+09] is considered as multicore ECU target platform in this thesis. The approach is however applicable to any other architecture.

Each core has a private instruction scratchpad, a data cache, and is connected to an on-chip SDRAM memory device through a *network-on-chip (NoC)*. The core is assumed to exhibit no timing anomalies [LS99; Rei+06], a counter-intuitive timing behaviour in which the local worst-case does not entail the global worst-case. The NoC has a wormhole-based tree topology [AIS09; Roc+12] with three simple pipelined 2-to-1 routers; thus, each core requires only two hops to reach the memory. Each router uses a round-robin arbitration policy, which makes $\text{lat}_{tree}$ independent from the number of cores.

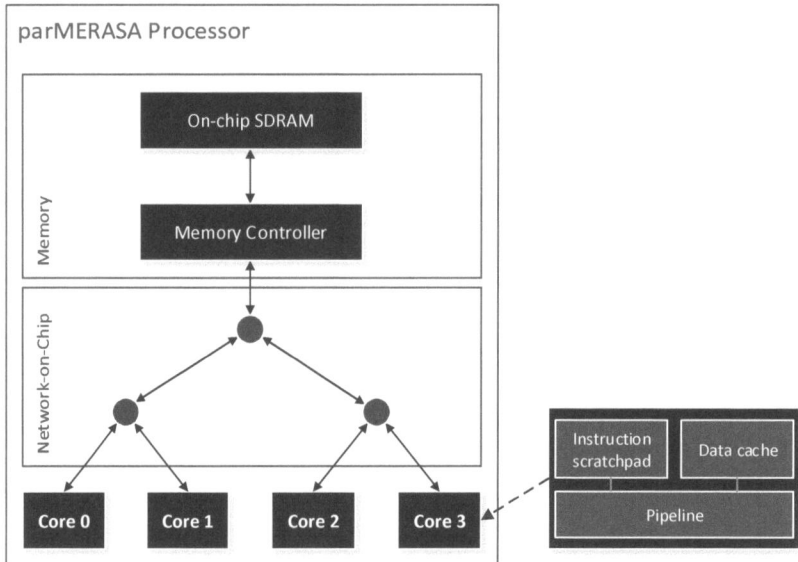

Figure 2.6: Overview about the parMERASA processor's architecture.

In a wormhole NoCs, *fragments of a message (flits)* are transmitted to the next hop as soon as a place is free in the receiver buffer. That means messages are transmitted piecewise and reassembled at the destination node, allowing variable message sizes and simplifying the buffer management. Moreover, only the header flit experiences latency and all other flits of the message immediately follow afterwards.

The NoC and the memory interface are sources of interferences. A pre-computed *upper bound delay (UBD)* bounds the maximum access delay to shared resources. The traversal time of a packet for one hop is denoted as $\text{lat}_{tree}$. The access latency of the memory is denoted as $\text{lat}_{mem}$. The maximum delay, which a one request can suffer on a processor with $m$ identical cores, computes as:

$$\text{UBD} = \text{lat}_{tree} + (m-1) \cdot \text{lat}_{mem} \tag{2.16}$$

### 2.4.3 Static Worst-Case Execution Time Analysis

Timing analysis [Wil+08] is the process of deriving execution-time bounds or estimates for the execution of a task. A key issue in timing analysis is determining a trustworthy upper bound for the execution time of a task; that is the WCET.

All WCET estimates for runnables in this thesis are derived with the *Open Toolbox for Adaptive WCET Analysis (OTAWA)* [Bal+11; ORS13; ORS14]. OTAWA is static timing analysis tool set that uses a model of the target processor, the source code, and the compiled executable to calculate a trustworthy upper bound for the execution time of a task. Static timing analysis techniques rely on the construction of a cycle-accurate model of the system and a mathematical representation of the analysed code.

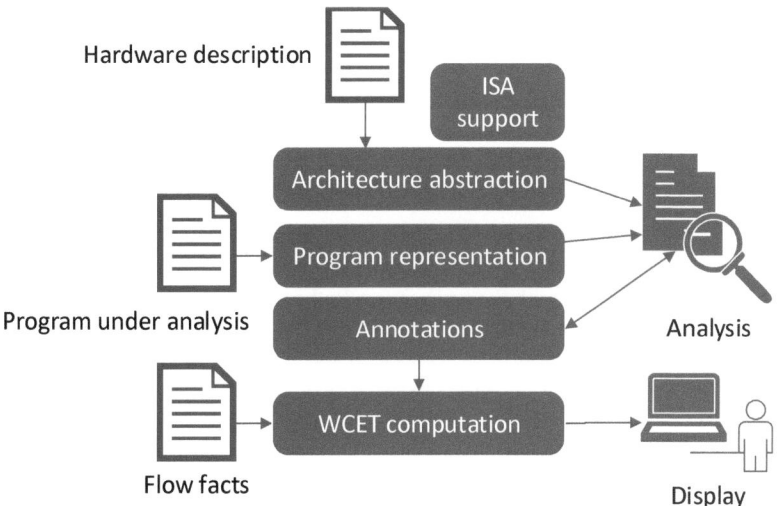

Figure 2.7: Overview about the OTAWA.

Figure 2.7 gives an overview about the functional components in OTAWA. The *instruction set architecture (ISA) support* hides the details of the processor architecture and the *program representation* abstracts the binary under analysis from the analysis. The *architecture abstraction* reads the hardware description to allow for precise estimation of WCET of instruction sequences. Determining the WCET involves a number of *analysis* steps in the appropriate order. Properties of the code can be expressed with *annotations*. The flow fact files provide information about the control flow in the program and loop bounds. The WCET is determined by representing the possible branches of the program through *integer linear programming (ILP)*. The IPET method [LM95] is used for solving the set of equations with lp_solve [Ber+16].

OTAWA was extended in the context of the parMERASA project to support the less pessimistic architecture of the processor described in the previous section. Defining the UBD for a request to the processor's communication subsystem and memory represents the multicore environment. Hence, the WCETs of runnables are time-composable. That means the timing behaviour is independent of simultaneously executed or runnables or tasks, insensitive to the core allocation, and independent of sharing the cache state with other tasks.

### 2.4.4 Erdős-Rényi Model

The evaluation in chapter 6 is partly conducted with randomly generated task graphs. They have a fixed number of nodes (representing tasks) and edges (representing inter-task data dependencies). The model of Paul Erdős and Alfréd Rényi [Erd59] describes a way of generating such random graphs. An Erdős-Rényi graph is formally defined as follows:

**Definition 2.7 (Random Graph $G_{n,N}$):** *A random graph $G_{n,N}$ is a directed graph with n nodes and N edges, where the edges between nodes are chosen at random among all possible edges.*

The graphs are generated with the open source Python library NetworkX [LAN+16]. NetworkX supports the creation, manipulation, and study of the structure, dynamics, and functions of complex networks. It also provides the required functions to create random graphs according to the Erdős-Rényi Model.

## 2.5 Summary of Background

This chapter provided the fundamentals that are essential to understand the mechanisms in the following chapters. The standardised software architecture and methodology AUTOSAR was described basically, domain specific wording was introduced, and methods for migrating legacy software to AUTOSAR were presented. Finally, the case study for experiments, a diesel EMS, was described.

A brief overview about software parallelization described the fundamentals about subtask decomposition and dependency analysis. Moreover, relevant graph concepts were described. These graphs build the foundation for further analysis and parallelization steps.

Subsequently, the extraction of parallelization constraints from automotive software was described. Data dependencies between runnables of the same period, simple precedence constraints, and between runnables with different periods, periodic extended precedence constraints, were formally defined. Different semantics for modelling the end-to-end latency and a model for end-to-end paths were formally introduced.

The last section in this chapter described the considered processor architecture and employed tools. Understand was introduced as static code analysis tool and the OTAWA tool suite was presented for deriving WCET estimated for the target platform (the parMERASA processor). The Erdős-Rényi model is used to generate random task graphs for the quantitative analysis.

The next chapter defines the objectives in this thesis first and reviews current state-of-the-art approaches for embedded software parallelization, afterwards.

# 3 | State of the Art and Problem Analysis

"I suppose it is tempting, if the only tool you have is a hammer, to treat everything as if it were a nail."

Abraham Maslow, 1966

This chapter reviews state-of-the-art approaches, which are relevant to automotive software parallelization. Therefore, functional and non-functional objectives for migrating automotive legacy software to *AUTomotive Open System ARchitecture (AUTOSAR)* multicore *electronic control units (ECUs)* are derived in section 3.1. To what extent existing mapping and scheduling approaches achieve these objectives is subject to a discussed in section 3.2. As these discussions will show, predictability is not achieved to a sufficient degree. Consequently, the scope of consideration is widened and approaches for predictable interprocessor communication are discussed in section 3.3. Finally, section 3.4 summarises the main deficiencies of state-of-the-art approaches and draws conclusions for automotive software parallelization.

## 3.1  Objectives

This section describes the objectives for automotive software parallelization in greater detail. They are split into functional and non-functional objectives. The functional objectives define the functionality of the parallelization approach and are based on the fundamental approach for software parallelization (explained in section 2.2). The non-functional objectives impose constraints on this functionality. They are based on the specific properties of automotive control software (explained in section 2.1) and include demands for mechanisms that ensure correct execution at runtime of the parallel program. Moreover, they include different aspects such as quality of the resulting parallel schedule or runtime mechanism, process-related constraints, and limitations from automotive software standardisation.

These objectives guide the review of state-of-the-art approaches and build the foundation for a parallelization approach that is suitable for automotive legacy applications.

### 3.1.1 Functional Objectives

The functional objectives for parallelizing automotive control software are defined as follows.

a) *Subtask decomposition* — Subtask decomposition of the legacy application is twofold and can be distinguished in the *extraction of precedence constraints* and the *extraction of latency constraints*. The former one is required to define a partial order for the execution of runnables and the latter one is needed to define an upper bound for the end-to-end latency of relevant sensor/actuator paths. The combination of both builds the foundation for maintaining the application semantics during the parallelization process.

b) *Mapping and Scheduling* — A static mapping of either complete tasks (*task-level parallelization*) or parts of each task separately (*runnable-level parallelization*) to cores must be defined for one hyperperiod. The computed schedule must be *feasible*, which means no task misses a deadline. Previously identified parallelization constraints, regarding precedence and end-to-end latency, must be respected. Processor specific properties must be taken into account; for example the *worst-case execution time (WCET)* of a runnable.

### 3.1.2 Non-functional Objectives

The previously defined objectives are common to software parallelization. However, automotive software has strict real-time constraints, runs on a platform with limited resources, and must produce output in a specific order and time. Furthermore, the AUTOSAR standard defines a development process, the software architecture, and limits configuration possibilities. This imposes constraints on the parallelization of automotive control software, which must not be considered by general purpose parallelization approaches. Hence, the non-functional objectives must reflect these special side constraints.

a) *Predictable interprocessor communication* — The interprocessor communication in the parallelized application must be predictable. A real-time system is predictable [Hen08; Axe+14], if its behaviour is deterministic, i.e. all events, especially future events, are predetermined. Important for automotive control software is a specific data-flow that traverses multiple task instances from a sensor to an actuator. The order in which these tasks are traversed matters. Consequently, a parallelized automotive legacy application is predictable, if the order in which data traverse task instances is predetermined.

b) *Robustness* — Generally, a system is robust, if it maintains certain performance levels even under circumstances that deviate from the normal operating environment [HS07]. An important robustness measure for automotive control software is the latency between sensor and actuator (explained in section 2.3.2). Hence, a parallelized automotive application is robust, if the worst-case latency (*first-in-last-out (FILO)* latency) is less than or equal to the FILO latency in the reference system.

c) *Data consistency* — The access to shared memory locations must be conducted in a way that data corruption is avoided. Concretely, simultaneous access to the same memory location (cf. equation (2.2) on page 21) from program portions on more than one core must be prevented. Furthermore, lost updates, a variable change by a task without recognizing concurrent changes by another task, must be avoided.

d) *Efficiency* — Efficiency for automotive software parallelization is twofold. First, the target platform is an embedded controller with limited computational power and on-chip memory. That means the available resources must be used in an efficient manner and the parallelism in the application must be exploited as much as possible. The target is a reduction of the processor's energy consumption to the greatest possible extent. Either by reducing the processor's clock rate (such that deadlines are still kept and idle intervals are filled) or a core's operations are suspended (sleep mode) during idle times. Second, the overhead, this is the time for synchronization and communication between cores, must be kept at a minimum to shorten the execution time as far as possible.

e) *Scalability* — Automotive control software typically comprises a large amount of runnables interacting with each other. Hence, the parallelization approach must be able to handle large applications that are of common practical size (several hundred runnables). The number of cores in the target ECU must not impose restrictions on applicability of the approach.

f) *Low cost* — Re-validating the functional correctness of the parallelized control software is associated with an undesirably high expenditure of human labour and must therefore be kept at a minimum level.

Automotive control software is developed and described according to the AUTOSAR [AUT14a] standard. For this reason, it is necessary to consider the standard in the development of a new parallelization strategy to ensure its acceptance.

g) *Compliance* — The parallelization strategy is compliant to AUTOSAR, if the mapping distributes runnables, the scheduler uses *operating system (OS)*-Applications, and AUTOSAR communication interfaces are used. That means the communication between cores must be transparent to the application, i.e. encapsulation in *run-time environment (RTE)* calls.

h) *Portability* — A central accomplishment of AUTOSAR is its independence from a concrete hardware architecture. Thus, a parallelization approach is portable, if the approach is applicable to any AUTOSAR compliant application. Furthermore, it must be possible to use any AUTOSAR *basic software (BSW)* for executing the parallelized application on the target ECU.

i) *Minimal standard modification* — A parallelization approach beyond the state of the art potentially requires extensions of the existing AUTOSAR standard. The associated expenditure, for adaptation of the OS, RTE, and *virtual function bus (VFB)*, required to implement the proposed techniques in AUTOSAR must be kept at a minimum level.

Existing techniques for subtask decomposition (section 2.2.1) already provide the functionality that is required for automotive software parallelization. Therefore, they are not further discussed in the following. Their specific use is mentioned in the discussion of the individual approach.

Methods for mapping and scheduling, predictable interprocessor communication, and maintaining data consistency in embedded multicore processors are subject to current research. Therefore, they are discussed in the following section, whereas the non-functional objectives guide the comparison.

Software parallelization has been addressed by the research community for several decades. Thus, an exhaustive description of all existing approaches goes beyond the scope of this thesis. Only approaches most relevant to this thesis are explained and literature for further reading is cited.

## 3.2 Mapping and Scheduling

Based on the objectives in section 3.1, this section reviews state-of-the-art approaches for mapping and scheduling, which are used for the parallelization of embedded software. They can be categorized in two groups: *reconfiguring approaches* decompose the application into runnables and reconfigure the runnable-to-task mapping. *Preserving approaches* keep the original runnable-to-task mapping and distribute complete tasks or runnables. A qualitative comparison and a discussion of the described approaches conclude this section.

### 3.2.1 Reconfiguring Parallelization Approaches

Reconfiguring approaches define a new application configuration, an assignment of runnables to tasks and priorities to tasks, rather than defining a schedule. Therefore, different scheduling policies are used. Davis et al. [DB11] survey hard real-time scheduling policies for multiprocessor systems. Most relevant policies for automotive software are *fixed priority (FP)* preemptive, *rate monotonic (RM)*, and *earliest deadline first (EDF)*. They are not subject of the discussion. The reconfiguring parallelization approaches are presented in chronological order of their publication.

### 3.2.1.1 Farhang Nemati et al.

The approach of Farhang Nemati et al. [NBN09b; NBN09a; NNB10] minimizes the blocking-time, from other tasks, with a *best-fit decreasing* allocation heuristic.

The partition algorithm is applicable to real-time systems that use FP scheduling for a periodic task set and where synchronization of shared resources is accomplished with the *Multiprocessor Priority Ceiling Protocol (MPCP)* [Raj91]. The accesses time to a critical section is limited by an appropriate definition in the AUTOSAR OS. Thus, these properties cover a large fraction of automotive software.

*Global critical sections (GCSs)* potentially lead to higher blocking time. Hence, the primary goal of the partitioning algorithm is the reduction of GCSs. Tasks that share resources are mapped to the same partition. The secondary goal is a reduction of ratio and time of holding global resources. A task is preferably grouped into the same partition with another task that requests the same resource more often and for a longer time than other tasks. The potential remote blocking overhead that a task can introduce in another task is referred to as *attraction*.

The heuristic executes in two steps. First, the weight for each task is calculated. It depends on the utilization and parameters that potentially lead to remote blocking by other tasks. Then, tasks that share resources (also indirectly) are grouped into a *macrotask*. If a macrotask is too large for a single core, it is marked as *broken*. Eventually, weights of macrotasks are calculated and tasks are collected in one list in decreasing order of their weights. The list is denoted *mixed list*, because it contains tasks and macrotasks. Afterwards, two different variations of the best-fit decreasing heuristic are executed in a parallel way on the mixed list.

1.) The first variant considers in every allocation step only unassigned tasks. A task at the head of the mixed list is allocated to the first core possible. The tasks of broken macrotasks are first sorted in decreasing order of attraction and afterwards allocated to the processor that fits the largest amount. A new processor is added, if none of the existing can carry the task. This process repeats until the mixed list is empty

2.) The other variant considers in every allocation step only already assigned tasks. A task at the head of the mixed list is allocated to the first core possible. The tasks of broken macrotasks are mapped to a concatenated list of processors, which is first sorted in decreasing order of attraction with already mapped tasks from the macrotask. Like the other variant, a new processor is added if none of the existing processors can carry the task and the process continues until the mixed list is empty. The best solution from the two parallel runs is selected as output of the algorithm.

The MPCP guarantees data consistency for data shared between tasks. However, the execution order in which tasks enter the critical sections can be arbitrary. Thus, the sensor/actuator data-flow potentially differs from the data-flow in the original single-core ECU. A re-validation is required in this case.

### 3.2.1.2 Aurélien Monot et al.

The approach of Aurélien Monot et al. [Mon+10] also use a worst-fit decreasing bin-packing heuristic for the allocation of runnables. The relation between runnables is represented as a graph, in which nodes are runnables and a node's weight is the WCET of the runnable. An edge in the graph *only* reflects whether two runnables can execute in a parallel way or not.

The approach assumes that an application can be separated in independent runnable cluster. Hence, this approach reduces the allocation problem to the bin-packing problem. This means a cluster of dependent runnables is mapped to a core.

One *dispatcher task* per core executes the runnables according to a schedule table. The *worst-fit decreasing* works in four steps:

1.) Dependent runnables are grouped in clusters.

2.) Runnables with locality constraint (must execute on a specific core) are allocated.

3.) The clusters are ordered in decreasing order by their utilization.

4.) Clusters are assigned to the least loaded core.

The runnables are started by the dispatcher task based on predefined activation times. Each table is executed with a fixed period and is divided in slots of equal size. Runnables are assigned to slots based on their period with a least-loaded heuristic in two steps:

1.) Runnables are sorted in increasing order of their period.

2.) Runnable is allocated in increasing order of their period, starting in the least loaded core.

As a result, each core executes one tasks that activates a set of runnable at predefined points in time, similar to *Offene Systeme und deren Schnittstellen für die Elektronik in Kraftfahrzeugen (OSEK)*/AUTOSAR schedule table. A fundamental disadvantage of this approach is the assumption that large amounts of independent runnables or clusters exist. A separation (as required by the approach) is unlikely to be made for a single application, because the amount of data dependencies is high (see section 2.1.3). This approach is therefore ideal for multiple independent applications that are integrated on the same multicore ECU, see [Mon+12]. Furthermore, the execution order of runnables can be arbitrary and thus the sensor/actuator data-flow potentially differs from the data-flow in the original single-core ECU. A re-validation is required under this approach.

### 3.2.1.3  Kathrin Scheidemann et al.

Kathrin Scheidemann et al. [SKS10a; SKS10b] presented in 2010 one of the first multicore case studies with a real automotive application. A BMW *engine management system (EMS)*, with 200 runnables, is parallelized for the execution on a dual-core processor. The article was published in an industry-specific German magazine, but it is discussed here, because of its relevance to this thesis. The article investigates two approaches for distributing runnables to cores: *multilevel graph partitioning* and *list scheduling*.

**Multilevel Graph Partitioning**—Multilevel graph partitioning [HL95] is used for grouping runnables into cores, whereas the optimization target is an equal processor utilization. The runnables are grouped so that the accumulated WCET per group is as even as possible. Additionally, the allocation is optimized for minimal communication cost between the groups. The graph is partitioned, so that the weight of cut edges between the disjoint even sized subsets is minimal.

Lasalle et al. [LK13] provide a good introduction to multilevel graph partitioning. The optimization problem is solved with a *simplify & conquer* approach, which initially was used by multi-grid methods for solving systems of partial differential equations. The process has three distinct phases.

1.) *Coarsening* — The original graph $G_0$ is used to generate a series of increasingly coarser graphs $G_1, G_2, \ldots, G_m$.

2.) *Initial partitioning* — A partitioning $P_m$ of the much smaller graph $G_m$ is generated with a more expensive algorithm.

3.) *Uncoarsening* — The initial partition is used to derive partitioning of successive finer graphs. Therefore, the partition $G_{i+1}$ is projected to the partition $G_i$ and followed by partitioning refinement whose goal is to reduce the edge-cut by moving vertices among the partitions.

The article compares the following allocation strategies using the multilevel graph partitioner METIS [KK98].

1.) *Free allocation of runnables* — In this allocation strategy, all runnables are treated as separate entities and the partitioning considers no further relations but communication and WCET. A free allocation of runnables distributes the load almost equal, but it also increases the total load by 22%.

The authors suspect the higher memory latency and the poor spin-lock's efficiency as root cause for this high overhead. The article points out that implicit communication guarantees data consistency (with spin-locks), but the data-flow can still change. The execution order of runnables becomes non-deterministic and differs from the former sequential execution. Like in the previously discussed approaches, Nemati et al. and Monot et al., a re-validation is required.

2.) *Allocation of runnable groups* — This allocation strategy groups runnables, if they were in the same task in the legacy application and if they communicate with each other. This method is proposed to overcome the shortcomings of a free runnable allocation. The graph partitioning strategy is applied to these groups, in the same fashion like in the free allocation strategy. Grouping runnables reduces the degree of freedom for the partitioning, but it allows a deterministic execution of runnable groups without further synchronization. The results show an unbalanced workload and a total increased load of 29%.

Overall, the total load on the processor is strongly increased, the core load is unbalanced with both strategies. Thus, graph partitioning seems to be no appropriate choice for the parallelization of automotive control software.

**List scheduling**—Scheidemann et al. investigated a list scheduling method that uses a barrier for the synchronization between cores, to fulfil precedence constraints between runnables. Algorithm 3.1 shows the two fundamental steps of list scheduling according to Oliver Sinnen [Sin07b]. First, all runnables (nodes) are sorted according to a priority rule and precedence constraints. The article does not describe the applied priority rule. Moreover, it appears like processed runnables are treated as equal, because the scheduling is repeated several times; for every set of runnables with the same priority in the original application's configuration.

Second, the runnables are allocated in the order as specified by the list $L$. Therefore, a free processor is selected that allows for the earliest finish time of the runnable. Synchronization point (barrier) are inserted after all runnables of a task are allocated, or if the duration since the last barrier is larger than the biggest runnable's WCET (cooperative scheduling). However, the article does not explain how the processor is selected.

```
1 (Part 1) Sort nodes in n ∈ V into list L according to priority rule and
     precedence constraints.
2
3 (Part 2) For each unprocessed n ∈ V
4    (a) Find processor m ∈ Proc that allows the earliest finish time of n.
5    (b) Schedule n on m.
```

Algorithm 3.1: Fundamental list scheduling heuristic

For the implementation of the schedule, each legacy task is decomposed into one subtask per core and the runnables are distributed to these tasks. At runtime, the OS triggers their start synchronously.

This approach allows parallel execution of large groups of runnables. Consequently, the processor load is more balanced. This approach does not require spin-locks, because barriers already guarantee data consistency. Moreover, explicit communication can be used. It is more efficient.

List scheduling heuristics are fundamental for parallel scheduling and one would expect a reduction of the processor load. The authors, however, reported contradictory results. They expected a load reduction of 18%, but the measurements showed an increased load instead. The authors see the reason for this increased load in the slow implementation of barriers. Important details of the method and the implementation are unpublished. This makes it hard to judge the performance of the approach.

Nevertheless, the approach has the advantage of maintaining the data-flow from the original single-core ECU, if the precedence constraints consider intra- and inter-task data dependencies.

### 3.2.1.4   Peter Gliwa et al. and Henia et al.

The work by Gliwa et al. [Gli+11] proposes an iterative model-based allocation of runnables. First, the communication overhead is calculated. The, so called, *communication overhead analysis* considers the interprocessor communication with runnables on other cores and the overhead by hardware and operating system for the data exchange.

The original application's configuration and the communication overhead analysis are combined with the WCET analysis to create a model of the application. A schedulability analysis is conducted with the *symbolic timing analysis for systems (SymTA/S)* [Hen+05] approach and the runnable to core allocation is iteratively optimized.

In a manual step, the runnable that access a variable most frequently are identified. Both are placed in the same core-local memory to reduce the access time to the variable.

SymTA/S is a compositional analysis methodology approach based on formal scheduling analysis techniques and symbolic simulation. The busy window technique, proposed by Lehoczky [Leh90], is used for component level analysis and scheduling analysis. Here, methods from real-time research can be used without further changes of the SymTA/S's internal model. The end-to-end latency of task chains is calculated as the sum of local worst-case response times. Further details are described in the paper of Henia et al. [Hen+05] and a performance analysis is conducted by Perathoner et al. [Per+07].

The approach described by Gliwa et al. targets at providing precise input data for SymTA/S to reduce pessimism in the analysis. Therefore, processor characteristics of Infineon processors are considered. However, bus collisions are ignored and the analysis with SymTA/S provides information about the system performance only, but it does not provide a concrete mapping. The results of the analysis are then used to optimize the mapping.

### 3.2.1.5  Ernest Wozniak et al.

Wozniak et al. [Woz+13] formulate the runnable-to-task mapping as an optimization problem. Two techniques are presented for solving the problem. The first technique is based on mixed integer linear programming, which provides an optimal solution when the solver terminates without an error. A central disadvantage of this approach is its limited scalability. Integer programming is NP-hard and that means finding a solution for an application of realistic size requires unacceptable long time.

Therefore, the authors propose a second technique, which is an evolutionary algorithm that optimizes the end-to-end latency and the memory consumption. Holland [Hol75] and Goldberg [Gol89] first introduced the concept of evolutionary algorithms in 1975 and 1989, respectively. The basic scheme of an evolutionary algorithm looks as follows:

1.) Generate initial population $\mathcal{P}$

2.) Compute *fitness* for all *individuals* $I \in \mathcal{P}$

3.) For $G = 1 \dots N$ or a time limit:

   1.) Produce a set of children $\mathcal{C}$ by *crossover* of $\mathcal{P}$

   2.) Apply *mutation* to $\mathcal{C}$

   3.) Compute fitness for $\mathcal{C}$

   4.) $\mathcal{P} = \mathcal{P} \cup \mathcal{C}$

   5.) Reduce size of $\mathcal{P}$ by *selection*

In the approach of Wozniak et al., each individual represents a specific deployment configuration. The genes of the individual encode the mapping of a signal (allocation to a bus and the message) and the mapping of a runnable (allocation to a ECU, mapping to a task, and position within the task). Thus, one individual encodes a complete system configuration in its genes.

The fitness of an individual is evaluated with a weight function that is computed from the weighted sum of the end-to-end latency, the memory consumption, the bus throughput, and the runnable deadlines. Maximizing the weighted sum for this multicriteria optimization problem can result in an imbalance among the different criteria. For example, a configuration with a high end-to-end latency can be rated good, if the same configuration has a low memory consumption.

### 3.2.1.6   Hamid Faragardi et al.

The work by Hamid Faragardi et al. [Far+14b] proposes an approach based on simulated annealing for minimizing the overall communication cost. In the first step, different simulated annealing meta-heuristics are used to generate a mapping of runnables to tasks. In the second step, an EDF utilization test is performed to check for deadline misses. Therefore, the method generates independent task sets. Otherwise, the utilization test could not be applied here.

A refinement function guides the search towards a solution, which allows merging of previously generated task sets. The mapping considers end-to-end latency constraint in the form of *transactions*: a *directed acyclic graph (DAG)* of runnables and a deadline. The approach treats all transactions as independent and periodic. A runnable is duplicated, if it is shared by at least two transactions.

An undirected graph represents the communication within the application. Nodes represent runnables and edges are labelled with the data rate per hyperperiod between adjacent nodes. The data rate depends on the mapping and the task set structure:

a) Runnables are mapped to the same task (minimal cost).

b) Runnables are mapped to different tasks on the same core.

c) Runnables are mapped to different cores (maximum cost).

The evolutionary algorithm called *Systematic Memory Based Simulated Annealing (SMSA)* considers each transaction as one task, with a deadline equal to the transaction deadline. SMSA calculates a mapping of transactions to cores. A cost function is used to judge the quality of a given mapping, including missed deadlines and communication cost.

a) *SMSA with Feedback Refinement (SMSAFR)* — An improvement of SMSA is the extension by a refinement function, which merges tasks that communicate with each other. Two tasks are merged, if they have the same period and at least one runnable in the one task communicates with another runnable in the other task. Merging tasks reduces the communication cost, because runnables in one task can communicate through the local cache. This optimization step can be conducted before or after the evaluation of each individual.

b) *SMSA with Utilization-Based Refinement (PUBRF)* — Faragardi et al. propose an improvement of SMSAFR in [Far+14a], which uses a utilization-based refinement function. The communication cost model is extended.

The problem formulation of PUBRF considers four possible values for the communication cost:

a) Runnables are mapped to the same task (cost are minimal).

b) Runnables are in different tasks on the same core.

c) Runnables are on separate cores with a share L2 cache.

d) Runnables are mapped to separate cores without a shared cache (maximum cost).

The utilization-based refinement function merges two tasks, if the processor utilization is reduced. Furthermore, merging tasks with different periods is allowed. PUBRF is implemented as a MAX-MIN ant system to find solutions in shorter time.

A disadvantage of this approach is its low efficiency. A runnables is duplicated, if it belongs to more than one transaction. This is an impractical assumption, because runnables are highly connected and this would result in many code duplications that easily exceed the on-chip memory of the controller. Therefore, the approach is considered as inefficiency.

### 3.2.1.7 Martin Lowinski et al.

The recent work of Martin Lowinski et al. [LZG15] addresses the problem of clustering a control application that is actually one cluster. The knowledge of a domain expert is used to relax data dependencies between runnables in a machine-assisted iterative approach. Data dependencies are evaluated according to different criteria and potentially uncritical ones are recommended to the domain expert for relaxation.

An allocation is calculated with a bin-packing heuristic after the feedback from the expert. This process repeats until the application is distributed in a way that the variation of the execution time per partition is within a predefined range. Unfortunately, concrete details on the bin-packing are not explained in the article and a schedule is not generated. Hence, the article only describes mapping approach and further properties, like the end-to-end latency, cannot be derived without further steps.

### 3.2.1.8 Comparison of Reconfiguring Parallelization Approaches

In the following, the reviewed reconfiguring mapping and scheduling approaches are comprehensively compared and discussed. The approaches are qualitatively compared in the table 3.1 against the objectives defined in section 3.1. The tables list the particular characteristics, all functional and non-functional objectives, and they indicate if the approaches satisfy (✓), partially satisfy (○), or do not satisfy (✗) the objective. A question mark (?) is put whenever no judgement is possible based on the published material. The following abbreviations are used in the table:

▷ End-to-end (EE)

▷ Evolutionary algorithm (EA)

▷ Graph partitioning (GP)

▷ List scheduling (LS)

▷ Mixed integer linear programming (MILP)

The reconfiguring approaches discussed in this section define a new application configuration based on the constraints extracted from the legacy application. Mapping and scheduling are seen as complementary steps in the parallelization process. First, a mapping of runnables to cores is defined in such a way that the interprocessor communication is minimized. Second, a new system configuration is synthesised that satisfies the given constraints.

The works of Nemati et al. [NBN09b], Monot et al. [Mon+10], Scheidemann et al. (graph partitioning free and graph partitioning group) [SKS10a; SKS10b], and Gliwa et al. [Gli+11] consider data dependencies only as mutual exclusive condition, without respecting the order. Interpreting the communication between runnables in an undirected way only allows for an arbitrary serial execution order. As a result, the internal data-flow of the application is changed and that means it differs from the original execution on the single-core ECU. This requires a costly re-validation of the functional correctness. The associated expenditure of human labour is undesirably high (non-functional requirement *low cost*).

Contrarily, the approaches of Scheidemann et al. (list scheduling), Wozniak et al. [Woz13], Faragardi et al. [Far+14a; Far+14b], and Lowinski et al. [LZG15] consider directed precedence constraints. However, only Wozniak et al. and Faragardi et al. consider end-to-end latency constraints. Wozniak et al. consider the sum of response times, the time between the release of the runnable until it finishes, of a sequence of runnables and signals. Calculating the latency in this way omits the duration between the completion of one element and the activation of the next element in the sequence. This can lead to an underestimation, if the computed value represents an upper bound on the end-to-end latency. For this reason, this approach is not considered.

In contrast, Faragardi et al. consider the end-to-end latency of a chain with an associated deadline (transaction). The configuration is optimized to schedule all elements of the transaction before this deadline. Such an approach is good when a system is optimized to keep latency constraints. This is the case here and the approach can be considered. For this reason, this is the only approach that can guarantee robustness.

| | | Nemati et al. | Monot et al. | Scheidemann et al. (GP free) | Scheidemann et al. (GP group) | Scheidemann et al. (LS) | Gliwa et al. and Henia at el. | Wozniak et al. (MILP) | Wozniak et al. (EA) | Faragardi et al. | Lowinski et al. |
|---|---|---|---|---|---|---|---|---|---|---|---|
| **Functional Objectives** | Subtask decomposition | o | o | o | o | o | o | o | o | ✓ | ✓ |
| | ▷ Precedencies | o | o | o | o | ✓ | o | ✓ | ✓ | ✓ | ✓ |
| | ▷ EE Latency | ✗ | ✗ | ✗ | ✗ | ✗ | ✗ | o | o | ✓ | ✗ |
| | Mapping | ✓ | ✓ | ✓ | ✓ | ✓ | ✓ | ✓ | ✓ | ✓ | ✓ |
| | Scheduling | o | ✓ | o | o | o | ✗ | o | o | o | ✗ |
| **Non-functional Objectives** | Predictable interprocessor com. | ✗ | ✗ | ✗ | ✗ | o | ✗ | ✗ | ✗ | ✗ | ✗ |
| | Robustness | ✗ | ✗ | ✗ | ✗ | ✗ | ✗ | ? | ? | ✓ | ✗ |
| | Efficiency | ✓ | ✓ | ✓ | ✓ | ? | ✓ | o | o | ✗ | ? |
| | Data consistency | ✓ | ✓ | ✓ | ✓ | ✓ | ? | ✓ | ✓ | ✓ | ? |
| | Scalability | ✓ | ✓ | ✓ | ✓ | ? | ✗ | ✗ | ✓ | ✓ | ✗ |
| | Low cost | ✗ | ✗ | ✗ | ✗ | o | ✗ | o | o | ✗ | ? |
| | Compliance | ✓ | ✓ | ✓ | ✓ | ✓ | ✓ | ✓ | ✓ | ✓ | ✓ |
| | Portability | ✗ | ✗ | ✗ | ✗ | ✓ | ✗ | ✗ | ✗ | ✓ | ✓ |
| | Minimal standard modification | ✓ | ✓ | ✓ | ✓ | ✓ | ✓ | ✓ | ✓ | ✓ | ✓ |

Table 3.1: Qualitative comparison of reconfiguring parallelization approaches.
Legend: satisfied (✓), partially satisfied (o), unsatisfied (✗), or unknown (?).

The reconfiguration in two steps makes the mapping heuristic important for the performance and additional metrics are used to optimize the mapping for specific constraints. The approaches of Nemati et al. (best-fit) and Monot et al. (worst-fit) use bin-packing heuristics. Heuristics like this are good to balance the load, but a bin-packing heuristic can only be used if runnables, or complete tasks, can be treated as independent or if precedence constraints are respected.

Wozniak et al. use an evolutionary algorithm and Faragardi et al. use simulated annealing for combining and optimizing multiple criteria at once. Both have a good scalability and can be used for large applications with many constraints. However, the duplication of runnables makes the approach of Faragardi et al. inefficient. The use of a weighted sum metric in the approach of Wozniak et al. can result in an imbalance among the different criteria. Thus, a ranking with a weighted sum metric is no ideal choice.

Graph partitioning, as proposed by Scheidemann et al., also seems to be no appropriate choice for the parallelization of automotive control software. The reason for this is the total load on the processor is strongly increased. Efficiency and scalability of Scheidemann et al. (list scheduling) cannot be evaluated here, because the reason for the contradiction between expectations and the results remains unclear.

Most of the approaches, exceptions are Gliwa et al. and Lowinski et al., are only applicable to a target system with specific properties. They rely on a core local FP or EDF scheduling. This strongly limits the use (portability) of the approaches.

All approaches are compliant to AUTOSAR and no further modifications of the standard are required for their use. This gives a good indication about AUTOSAR's capabilities for parallel execution. The review showed deficiencies in the state-of-the-art approaches and thus extensions are potentially required to fulfil the objectives in this thesis.

**Summary**—Bin-packing heuristics are a good way to balance the load over cores on the condition that precedence constraints between runnables and tasks are respected. Evolutionary algorithms or simulated annealing are good to combine multiple optimization criteria, as they are found in automotive software parallelization. However, a weighted sum is no appropriate optimization metric. A good way of considering end-to-end latency constraints is a chain of runnables and an associated deadline. Scheduling the runnable in the chain before the deadline guarantees an upper bound on the latency. Directly generating a system configuration limits the use of an approach needlessly. Instead, a better alternative is generating a *configuration independent schedule*, which only contains start and finish times of runnables or tasks, and implementing it with the mechanisms that are available on the target platform. Section 3.2.2.1 discusses a method for generating configuration independent schedules.

## 3.2.2  Preserving Parallelization Approaches

Preserving approaches keep the original runnable-to-task mapping and are further divided in two groups: *task-* and *runnable-level parallelization*. Under the first approach, tasks are the unit of scheduling and they are distributed to available cores. Under the second approach, a task body is distributed with different levels of granularity to cores and the original schedule is kept. Again, the parallelization approaches are presented in chronological order of their publication.

### 3.2.2.1  Sönke Hartmann

The work of Sönke Hartmann [Har98; Har02] describes an evolution algorithm for solving the *resource-constrained project scheduling problem (RCPSP)*. The RCPSP is a classical scheduling problem with the objective of minimizing the *schedule length (makespan)*. Concretely, a set of jobs $\mathcal{J} = \{1, \ldots, J\}$ must be distributed on a set of limited renewable resources $K^\rho$ with constant per-period availability $R_k^\rho$ for resource $k$. Precedence relation, represented by the set pred$_j$ for job $j \in J$, constrain some jobs. The request of a job $j$ for resource $k$ is denoted as $r_{j,k}$. The processing time of job $j$ is denoted as $p_j$. Hence, the RCPSP is identical to the mapping and scheduling of runnables or tasks to cores, whereas the runnables represent the jobs and the processor represents the renewable resource.

Using an evolution algorithm to solve a concrete problem means to define a fitness function, define the genome of an individual, and operators for a crossover, mutation, and selection. The definitions for the evolution algorithm proposed by Hartmann are briefly explained in the following.

**Representation of individuals**—The evolution algorithm does not directly work on the solution of the scheduling. Instead, the solution is encoded as activity list $\lambda = (j_1, \ldots, j_J)$ and transformed by a *schedule generation scheme (SGS)* into a schedule $S = (\text{st}_1, \ldots, \text{st}_J)$ that assigns a start time $\text{st}_j$ to each activity $j$. Either a serial or a parallel SGS [Kol96] is used. The former one schedules jobs in the order as defined by the activity list, where each activity is assigned the earliest precedence and resource feasible start time. The latter one computes a decision point at which an activity to be scheduled is started. At this point, a set of eligible activities is determined and successively scheduled until none is left. This process repeats until all activities are scheduled. Consequently, an individual is encoded as $I = (\lambda, SGS)$. In the initial population the SGS is chosen randomly and the activity list is constructed with a variant of a rule based sampling heuristic [Kol96].

**Crossover**—The crossover merges two individuals. Two random numbers $1 \leq q_1 < q_2 \leq J$ are drawn to merge the activity lists. The daughter's activity list takes the positions $1, \ldots, q_1$ from the mother, $q_1 + 1, \ldots, q_2$ from the father (already selected activities are not considered again), and the remaining positions are taken from the mother again. The activity list of the son is generated analogously. That means the first and the third part are taken from the father and the second part is taken from the mother. The daughter inherits the SGS from the mother and the son from the father.

**Mutation**—The activity list is traversed from left to right and an activity is shifted to the right with a probability $p_{mutation}$. The SGS is changed with the same probability.

**Selection**—The fitness for a scheduling problem is the makespan. The individuals are sorted by their fitness and the ones with the lowest makespan are selected for survival of the iteration.

A comprehensive evaluation of heuristics for the RCPSP in [HK00] and [KH06] reported that the method is among the best performing meta-heuristics for solving the RCPSP. An advantage of the approach is its versatility. It can be used for scheduling of runnables without modification. The result is a configuration independent schedule that can be implemented with any scheduling policy. Contrarily, the use for the task scheduling for a hyperperiod is possible, if the earliest start time of a task (depending on the ticks of a real-time clock) is considered.

### 3.2.2.2 Daniel Cordes et al.

Daniel Cordes et al. [CMM10] describe an automatic parallelization process, in which the application is analysed and represented with a *hierarchical task graph (HTG)*, also as described in section 2.2.2. Node weights represent measurement-based execution times and edge weights represent communication cost.

The parallelization of the annotated HTG is done recursively, with depth-first-search. Nodes are combined to an input set for an *integer linear programming (ILP)* and a solver is used to calculate a mapping of child nodes to cores. The results of the solver are combined until the root node is reached. This ensures the scalability even for large applications.

The ILP solver minimizes the critical path by splitting a node into three sections: sequential, parallel, and sequential. The solution can contain different levels of granularity, because every child node contains parallel sets with different execution times. Platform specific task creation overhead or communication cost can be considered.

Using different levels of granularity is a benefit because idle times are minimized, but it is also a drawback because the computational complexity grows with the task size. The integration in AUTOSAR is impossible, as a runnable-to-task mapping is required and a task can only span one core.

### 3.2.2.3 David August et al.

The book chapter of David August et al. [Aug+11] provides a good overview about automatic parallelizing compiler. The described techniques focus on extracting parallelism from loops. As already stated in section 2.2.2, a dependency analysis is conducted first. Afterwards, a *program dependence graph (PDG)* is constructed from the *control dependence graph (CDG)* and the *data dependence graph (DDG)* (definition 2.2). The compiler applies several methods for optimization and parallelization to the PDG and generates source code afterwards. Synchronization is achieved by constructing a control flow, with high level language statements like while- or for-loops, which executes instructions in a parallel way. The most widely used techniques are:

▷ DOALL and DOACROSS [Hur+97]

▷ DOPIPE [Dav81] and decoupled software pipelining [Ott+05]

▷ Parallel stage decoupled software pipelining [Ram+08]

▷ Speculative parallel stage decoupled software pipelining [Vac+07]

Although, there is a wide range of techniques, they cannot be used for the parallelization of automotive control software. Loops are rare and speculative approaches increase the energy consumption. Several possibilities are computed in a parallel way and only the relevant one result is used. All other computations are superfluous and wasted energy. Moreover, the WCET of a speculation is higher than without, because the time for a roll-back must be considered.

Apart from this, speculation relies on data dependencies that *do not* manifest at runtime and to shorten the computation time. Nevertheless, the WCET must be considered for the scheduling. Hence, loop-level parallelization techniques are not expected to provide significant performance improvements for automotive software.

### 3.2.2.4 Yohei Kanehagi et al.

Kanehagi et al. [Kan+13] demonstrated the use of the Fortran compiler *optimally scheduled advanced multiprocessor (OSCAR)* [Kas+92; Kas+95] for the parallelization of single tasks of an EMS. Therefore, OSCAR has been extended to support a special C dialect, which is close to MISRA-C. The compiler relies on the decomposition of the task as *macro-flow graph (MFG)*, as described in section 2.2.2. A method called the *earliest executable condition (EEC)* is applied to identify parallel *macro tasks (MTs)*. Concretely, the EEC for a MT is the time, when all control and precedence relations with predecessors are satisfied. The calculation of this point in time is based on the average processing time of operations. That means the processing time must be provided as input data for the compiler. To this end, OSCAR uses a list scheduling heuristic to minimize the length of the critical path within the task.

OSCAR does not distribute runnables directly. Instead, a complete task is first disassembled with different levels of granularity and the parts are distributed to the available cores. Smaller parts are automatically agglomerated and OpenMP synchronization operations are inserted. The task execution is synchronously triggered on all cores (via the processors interrupt system). Thus, task execution can follow the scheduling from the original application's configuration, where tasks execute one after another and only one task at a time. The integration in AUTOSAR is impossible, as a runnable-to-task mapping is required and a task can only span one core. Moreover, the compiler for the embedded system must be able to process OpenMP pragmas.

### 3.2.2.5 Comparison of Preserving Parallelization Approaches

In the following, the reviewed preserving parallelization approaches are comprehensively compared and discussed. The approaches are qualitatively compared in the table 3.2 against the objectives defined in section 3.1. The tables list the particular characteristics, all functional and non-functional objectives, and they indicate if the approaches satisfy (✓), partially satisfy (○), or do not satisfy (✗) the objective. A question mark (?) is put whenever no judgement is possible based on the published material.

Preserving approaches keep the original application and thus apply to a wider range of software (portability) than the reconfiguring approaches, which are discussed in the previous section. Preserving approaches guarantee the same data-flow, as in the original application's configuration for the single-core. Thus, the validation effort is drastically reduced (low cost).

Precedence constraints are used to extract a predictable synchronized multicore schedule. End-to-end latency constraints are, however, not respected, but this is not a disadvantage. The data-flow within a task and the task scheduling remain identical after the parallelization. Although, the task WCET is reduced and this means the end-to-end latency is either equal or smaller than in the original application's configuration for the single-core.

All approaches define a static mapping and a schedule for runnable-level parallelization with different levels of granularity. Moreover, they are efficient and scalable.

In addition, the list scheduling of Hartmann describes a general scheduling heuristic. The approach is thus compliant to AUTOSAR and could be used to define a task-level parallelization schedule for a hyperperiod. However, the ticks of a real-time clock and deadlines of task instances must be respected in this case, for example with an appropriate problem formulation or transformation. Unfortunately, existing literature does not provide any approaches in this regard.

| | | Hartmann | August et al. | Kanehagi et al. | Cordes et al. |
|---|---|---|---|---|---|
| **Functional Objectives** | Subtask decomposition | ○ | ○ | ○ | ○ |
| | ▷ Precedencies | ✓ | ✓ | ✓ | ✓ |
| | ▷ Latency | ✗ | ✗ | ✗ | ✗ |
| | Mapping | ✓ | ✓ | ✓ | ✓ |
| | Scheduling | ✓ | ○ | ○ | ○ |
| | ▷ Runnable-level | ✓ | ✓ | ✓ | ✓ |
| | ▷ Task-level | ✓* | ✗ | ✗ | ✗ |
| **Non-functional Objectives** | Predictable interprocessor com. | ✓ | ✓ | ✓ | ✓ |
| | Robustness | ✓ | ✓ | ✓ | ✓ |
| | Data consistency | ✓ | ✓ | ✓ | ✓ |
| | Efficiency | ✓ | ✗ | ✓ | ✓ |
| | Scalability | ✓ | ✓ | ✓ | ✓ |
| | Low cost | ✓ | ✓ | ✓ | ✓ |
| | Compliance | ✓ | ✗ | ✗ | ✗ |
| | Portability | ✓ | ✓ | ✓ | ✓ |
| | Minimal standard modification | ✓ | ✗ | ✗ | ✗ |

Table 3.2: Qualitative comparison of preserving parallelization approaches.
Legend: satisfied (✓), partially satisfied (○), unsatisfied (✗), or unknown (?).

All approaches guarantee predictable interprocessor communication and data consistency by construction, which makes the parallel program robust.

The parallelizing compiler proposed by August et al. and Kanehagi et al. as well as the ILP approach if Cordes et al. generate OS independent synchronized source code, but in a way that is not supported by AUTOSAR. A task is spread over multiple cores and AUTOSAR does not support this kind of multicore usage. According to the standard, a task is statically assigned to an OS-Application, which in turn is mapped to a core.

Enabling such parallelization requires an extension of the standard in a way that *software-components (SW-Cs)* can be distributed over cores. The start and termination of tasks needs synchronization. The error handling must span multiple cores and react across the borders of a single core. Therefore, these approaches are a suboptimal choice for the parallelization of automotive control software.

**Summary**—Preserving parallelization approaches fulfil most of the functional and non-function objectives in this thesis. The central advantage of these approaches is the low cost, because no re-validation is required.

Two of the four approaches use a list scheduling heuristic and they report a high efficiency and scalability. This makes the list scheduling a promising candidate heuristic for runnable-level parallelization.

The methods can be extended for task-level parallelization, if the problem formulation is adjusted or transformed to respect real time. Again, one of the approaches proposes an evolution algorithm to maintain scalability. Its high efficiency makes this approach a promising candidate for the task-level parallelization in a hyperperiod.

Nevertheless, deficiencies exist in the compliance with AUTOSAR. Parallelizing compiler and the ILP-based approach distribute a task with different levels of granularity, which is not supported.

## 3.2.3   Discussion and Summary

This section reviewed state-of-the-art approaches for mapping and scheduling for the parallelization of embedded software. They are now compared against each other and conclusions, for a parallelization approach for automotive control software, are drawn.

Reconfiguring approaches define a new application configuration based on the constraints extracted from the legacy application. Mapping and scheduling are seen as complementary steps and conducted one after another. The new system configuration is compatible with the AUTOSAR standard. This is not the case for all preserving parallelization approaches.

Contrarily, preserving approaches keep the original task set (runnable-to-task mapping etc.), which defines a correct system configuration. The task properties remain unchanged, but the tasks, or their content, are executed in a parallel way. Task-level parallelization approaches distribute complete tasks to cores and runnable-level parallelization distributes a task body with different levels of granularity to cores and the original schedule is kept. They guarantee the same data-flow, as in the original application's configuration for the single-core.

Interprocessor communication is handled in different ways. Reconfiguring approaches execute tasks in a parallel way and use data consistency protocols to synchronize the access to shared memory locations. Maintaining approaches consider precedence constraints and add synchronization points in the execution. None of the approaches is ideal for automotive software parallelization. Data consistency protocols prevent simultaneous manipulation of the same memory location, but they do not always enforce the same order of manipulations from tasks. This can lead to an unexpected task interleaving, which changes the sensor/actuator data-flow. Consequently, a re-validation of the functional correctness is required, if tasks are executed in a parallel way. Precedence constraints force serialization of task execution, because tasks are typically not independent from each other (see section 2.1.3). This prevents parallel execution.

Removing or changing the inter-task data dependencies results in an unpredictable data-flow, because it is not guaranteed any more that input data are completely produced when the receiver starts execution. Therefore, a fundamental requirement for the migration of a legacy application from to a multicore ECU is the *definition of a predictable and reproducible data-flow*, i.e. the order in which tasks communicate. Additionally, this eases the validation and testing on the new platform.

Still, using the original task set as parallelization constraint is a reasonable way to maintain the application semantic. As a result, the advantages of preserving over reconfiguring approaches are their portability, they apply to a wider range of software, their cost is lower, no re-validation is required, and the parallel program is more robust.

The review allows for the following conclusions. Bin-packing heuristics are a popular and good way to balance the load over cores. List scheduling is a promising candidate heuristic for scheduling of dependent runnables (runnable-level parallelization) and tasks (task-level parallelization). Evolutionary algorithms or simulated annealing are good to combine multiple optimization criteria and to maintain scalability. A good way of considering end-to-end latency constraints is a chain of runnables and an associated deadline. Generating a configuration independent schedule is better than directly generating a system configuration. Finally, extensions of the AUTOSAR standard are necessary to fulfil the objectives in this thesis.

**Concluding** — reconfiguring approaches define an efficient system configuration and they are all compliant to AUTOSAR, but a re-validation of the functional correctness is required and their applicability is limited. Preserving approaches fulfil most of the requirements, but not all are compatible with AUTOSAR. Thus, a new method for the parallelization of automotive control software is required that incorporates the insights from both categories.

Furthermore, none of the approaches proposes a satisfying mechanism for *predictable interprocessor communication*. Either, the access to shared memory locations is unpredictable or data dependencies force frequent serialization of the task scheduling. Therefore, the next section discusses methods and concepts for predictable interprocessor communication, which allow exploiting task-level parallelism.

## 3.3 Predictable Interprocessor Communication and Data Consistency

The review in the previous section showed that none of the approaches provides a *predictable interprocessor communication* for parallel execution of tasks. For this reason, this section first discusses the interprocessor communication in AUTOSAR. Afterwards, alternative approaches are compared and discussed with respect to predictability and reproducibility.

The cores of a multicore processor perform calculations independent of each other, but they share resources such as the bus, memory, or other peripherals. That means the parallel execution on multiple cores requires a coordination of accesses to these shared resources to avoid unforeseen computational interleaving and thus *data races* (concurrent access to the same shared memory location from at least two cores). Otherwise, inconsistent data might be the result or the data-flow between a sensor and an actuator might break. Costly re-validation of the functional correctness is the consequence.

It is reasonable to use the original task set as parallelization constraint to maintain the application semantic (see section 3.2.3). Thus, the target is to achieve the same sensor/actuator data-flow (see section 2.3.2) as in the original execution on the single-core ECU. Regardless of which data-flow paths an application contains, they have to be identical in all multicore ECUs (reproducible). That means tasks must access a shared variable always in the same order.

### 3.3.1 Interprocessor Communication in AUTOSAR

AUTOSAR provides the *inter-OS-application communicator (IOC)* for inter-partition (a partition is statically assigned to a core) communication. The IOC guarantees data consistency for the data transmitted through it. Concurrent calls to the IOC are not allowed (not reentrant). A major disadvantage of this approach is its low efficiency. Each call must be encapsulated in spin-locks to prevent simultaneous changes to the same memory location. This is necessary, because the state on the other core is unknown. The case study in [SKS10a] reported a high overhead due to communication through the IOC. An alternative option would be asynchronous communication (AUTOSAR implicit communication). This idea is discussed in more detail in the following. Therefore, a distinction is made between two scenarios:

a) Communication between sporadic and periodic tasks.

b) Communication between tasks with different release periods.

The time when a *sporadic* and a *periodic* task communicate is generally unknown, as it depends on an external unforeseen event (e.g. the camshaft position in case of $\tau_1$). The tasks are executed independently from each other already in the single-core ECU and this is known to produce correct output. The sporadic task must execute immediately after the event and the periodic task executes with fix period to miss no deadline (the task does not wait for input from a sensor). Hence, no strict order of execution (precedence) can be determined, i.e. the data-flow is in general neither predictable nor reproducible. Consequently, the asynchronous nature of AUTOSAR implicit communication can be used to decouple the tasks on the multicore ECU and allow parallel execution.

The simple and extended precedence constrained imposed from explicit and implicit communication define the execution order of two *periodic* tasks. For the task set in figure 2.2 it is easy to see that the extended precedencies cause sequential execution of all periodic tasks. A high number of extended precedencies is not a particular characteristic of this use case, but it is a typical property of automotive control software. That means performance improvements of multicore ECUs cannot be exploited, as long as such a high number of precedence constrains must be respected by a scheduling policy.

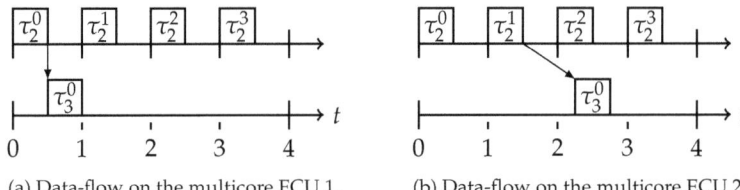

(a) Data-flow on the multicore ECU 1.  (b) Data-flow on the multicore ECU 2.

Figure 3.1: Example for scheduling on two multicore ECUs with implicit communication. The data-flow is not reproducible.

Always using implicit communication at task level allows parallel execution due to its asynchronous nature. However, in this case the data-flow depends on the scheduling on the target multicore ECU; concretely, the actual start of a task. This is illustrated in figure 3.1 with an exemplary scheduling of the two tasks $\tau_2$ and $\tau_3$, from figure 2.2, on two multicore ECUs.

A system can have different valid sets of precedence constraints. The start time $st_3^0 = 0.5$ on ECU 1 is valid, because the task finished before its deadline, and the resulting data-flow is $\tau_2^0 \rightsquigarrow \tau_3^0$. Contrarily, the start time $st_3^0 = 2.25$ on ECU 2 is also valid and the resulting data-flow is $\tau_2^1 \rightsquigarrow \tau_3^0$. Both scheduling policies place $\tau_3^0$ before its deadline, but the data-flow is different on both platforms. The consequence is, each implementation for a multicore ECU produces a different output. That is, the data-flow paths in ECU 1 and ECU 2 are not identical as they are supposed to be (section 3.1).

Guaranteeing the same output, independent from the actual start of a task, is essential to define a reproducible and predictable data-flow in the multicore ECU. Defining the same data-flow for all target multicore ECUs makes the system behaviour reproducible and it can be tested easier. The current mechanisms in AUTOSAR do not allow for predictable and reproducible execution on a multicore. This motivates for an analysis of mechanisms that guarantee predictability.

## 3.3.2 Deterministic Multithreading

*Deterministic multithreading (DMT)* [Lu+15] is a technique for parallel execution of multithreaded applications on commodity hardware platforms. The execution is constraint, so that the application always executes with the same thread interleaving and thus produces the same output. Approaches for DMT are categorized in:

a) *Weak DMT* guarantees a *deterministic order of all lock acquisitions* for a given program input.

b) *Strong DMT* guarantees a *deterministic order of all memory accesses* to shared data for a given program input.

A description of approaches for weak and strong DMT as well as schedule memorization is provided in the following. Afterwards, a discussion in regard of the objectives is conducted.

### 3.3.2.1 Weak Deterministic Multithreading

Kendo is an approach for weak DMT proposed by Olszewski et al. [OAA09] that implements a subset of the POSIX Threads API. Threads are allowed to continue execution only if other threads have executed more instructions. The concept of *deterministic logical time (DLT)* is used to track progress of threads. The DLT is constructed from independent monotonically increasing *deterministic logical clocks (DLCs)* [Lam78]; one per thread. The clocks are updated independently and never based on the progress of other threads.

An event on thread 1 is said to occur at an earlier DLT than an event in thread 2, if thread 1 has a lower DLC than thread 2 at the time of the events. An event can be of arbitrary nature, as long as they are repeatable in every run. However, it is desirable to track events as closely as possible to physical time to achieve a good load-balancing, but not mandatory. The authors propose the performance counters of the Linux operating system for this purpose.

The DLT is used to compute a load-balanced interleaving of synchronization accesses to shared data via locks. This interleaving is repeatable. The deterministic acquisition of locks is based on the concept of a *turn*. It is a thread's turn (only one at a time), if

1) All threads with smaller ID (assigned at creation time) have greater DLCs, and

2) All threads with larger ID have greater or equal DLCs.

A thread increments its DLC as it spins on a contested lock to prevent deadlocks. A queue is used to guarantee fairness among threads by employing a first-come first-served ordering.

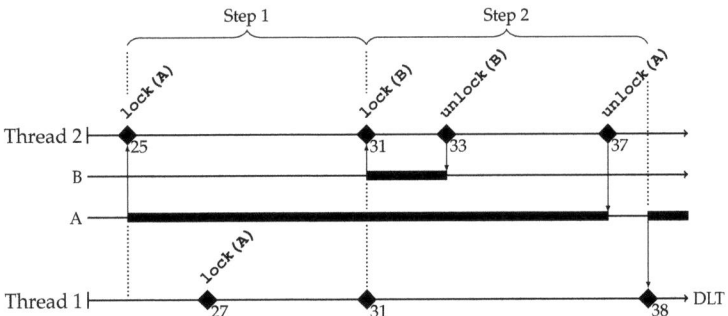

Figure 3.2: Lock acquisition with Kendo.

Figure 3.2 shows two threads that share the resource *a*. Thread 1 acquires *a* at DLT 25 and thread 2 is therefore unable to lock *a* at DLT 27. Thread 2 increments its DLT, while it waits, commonly denoted as *spinning*, on the lock to allow progress in thread 1 (acquire lock for resource *b* at DLT 31) and hence prevent a deadlock. This process continues until thread 1 releases *a* at DLT 37 and thread 2 can acquire the lock at DLT 38.

The concept of *lazy reading* is used to guarantee deterministic reading of global shared variables without acquiring a lock. Users can specify a tolerance window for the age of the value. Larger tolerance makes the lazy read faster, at the expense of returning an older value. Concretely, for lazy reading each task maintains an internal logical clock. A write-instruction is encapsulated in a lock and the value is paired with a logical write-time. The receiver task has user-defined tolerance window for the age of input data. Thus, the read operation can be performed without acquiring a lock and a larger tolerance makes the read faster.

### 3.3.2.2 Strong Deterministic Multithreading

The survey by Bergan et al. [Ber+11] gives an overview about strong DMT approaches, which use a so called *lockstep quanta*, in which each thread is isolated. The quantum ends with a global barrier, after which threads communicate with each other deterministically. Figure 3.3 illustrates the phases. Thread 1 finishes before thread 2 in this example, but communication is delayed until both have finished. A global barrier synchronizes the threads and the communication is performed afterwards, following different strategies. Four different deterministic communication strategies are described in literature: data-ownership tracking, transactional memory with ordered commit, non-speculative store buffering with ordered commit. Furthermore, a distinction between software-only and hardware-supported approaches is made.

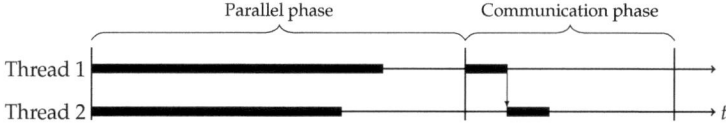

Figure 3.3: Lockstep quantum and communication phase in strong DMT systems.

A major drawback of strong DMT is the large synchronization overhead. Lu et al. [Lu+14] address this issue. A combination of Kendo and the *lazy release consistency* memory model [Amz+96] is proposed, to renounce global barriers, but guarantee strong determinism. Release consistency is a memory consistency model for distributed shared memory systems, in which visibility of changes to shared data to other threads can be delayed until a synchronization point. A thread must *acquire* shared data before modification and *release* them afterwards, making the enclosed instructions a critical section. Lazy release consistency enforces consistency at the time of an acquire operation. The opposite is the eager release consistency model [Car94] that enforces consistency at the time of a release. Kendo is used to ensure that all synchronization operations happen in a deterministic order. A memory modification of thread 1 is made visible in thread 2 if and only if the modification happens before the executing instruction in thread 2.

### 3.3.2.3 Schedule Memorization

Cui et al. introduce with TERN [Cui+10] and its successor PEREGRINE [Cui+11] the idea of schedule memorization. An execution trace records the order in which `pthread_mutex_lock` and `pthread_mutex_unlock` are called, when a program runs for the first time on an input. The trace is relaxed into a *hybrid schedule*, which comprises mem-schedules, a deterministic schedule for shared memory accesses, and *sync-schedules*, schedules with synchronization operations, afterwards. A mem-schedule guarantees strong determinism, but can incur high overhead.

On the contrary, a sync-schedule has a low overhead, but only weak determinism is guaranteed (deterministic for race free program sections). The authors assume that data races occur only within minor portions of an execution and a *mem-schedule* is thus used only used for these parts of the execution.

PEREGRINE uses *determinism-preserving slicing* to generalize schedules for a wider range of inputs. This is a precondition slicing technique [Cos+07] that combines static and dynamic analysis techniques to remove unnecessary filter conditions. *Schedule-guided simplification* is used to precisely analyse a program according to a specific schedule. The program is simplified first, then standard alias analysis is performed on the simplified program to get more precise results. For example, functions are cloned to separate the results for each thread instead of merging them.

### 3.3.2.4  Discussion of Deterministic Multithreading

In the following, the reviewed approaches are comprehensively compared and discussed. The approaches are qualitatively compared in the table 3.3 against the objectives defined in section 3.1. The table lists relevant non-functional objectives and it indicates if the approaches satisfy ( ✓ ), partially satisfy (○), or do not satisfy (✗) the objective. A question mark (?) is put whenever no judgement is possible based on the published material.

| | Weak DMT | Strong DMT | Schedule memorization |
|---|:---:|:---:|:---:|
| Robustness | ○ | ✓ | ○ |
| Efficiency | ✗ | ✗ | ✗ |
| Scalability | ✗ | ✗ | ✗ |
| Low cost | ✗ | ✓ | ✗ |
| Compliance | ✗ | ✗ | ✗ |
| Portability | ✗ | ✗ | ✗ |
| Minimal standard modification | ✗ | ✗ | ✗ |

Table 3.3: Qualitative comparison of methods for predictable interprocessor communication based on DMT.
Legend: satisfied  (✓), partially satisfied  (○), unsatisfied  (✗), or unknown (?).

A common shortcoming of all deterministic multithreading approaches is the high runtime overhead (up to 10 times for strong [Ber+11] and 2.6 times for weak [SA14]

DMT approaches). DMT approaches are typically implemented on a Linux operating system. This limits the portability and it makes the migration to AUTOSAR a hard task.

Weak deterministic systems provide a deterministic order of synchronization operations. Kendo provides an interface for thread synchronization and, hence, the programmer must take care about the software decomposition. An artificial clock is used for ensuring a deterministic order, which is not necessarily bound to real time. To prevent data races (concurrent access to the same shared memory location from at least 2 threads) all shared memory accesses must be protected by locking, at the cost of high locking overhead. Otherwise, the execution is non-deterministic in this case. Unfortunately, automotive applications use many shared variables and they are accessed frequently. Thus, using Kendo for automotive applications is impractical and inefficient.

Strong deterministic systems are the only DMT approaches that always achieve the same data-flow. This is achieved by separating computation from communication. Threads compute their results in isolation and the communication afterwards always follows the same pattern. This makes the concept of *deterministic lazy release consistency* a potential concept for deterministic parallel execution in automotive software.

Schedule memorization is based on the assumption that data races are rare. This may be true for workstation programs, but not for automotive applications. Thus, schedule memorization techniques would use inefficient mem-schedules for large parts of the program. Determinism-preserving slicing is insufficient to guarantee reuse of tested schedules in all cases. Thus, the execution becomes non-deterministic occasionally. Bergan et al. [BCG13] address this issue. However, the approach uses expensive symbolic execution instead. Ultimately, the delay introduced by the replayer is unacceptable high for an automotive embedded system with reaction times of up to few microseconds.

DMT approaches achieve general-purpose deterministic execution. Most solutions provide POSIX-like APIs or rely on special hardware support. These approaches are well suited for migrating lock-based legacy programs to multicore architectures. However, they introduce high overhead and they are not suitable for the migration or design of real-time systems.

### 3.3.3  Time-Triggered Architecture

The *time-triggered architecture (TTA)* [Kop+95] origins in the Cyber-Physical Systems Group at Technical University of Vienna lead by Prof. Kopetz. Continuous research made the concept to one of the most important design principles for *cyber-physical system (CPS)* [PKS14]. A TTA [KB03] spans the system as a whole, including control software, controller, sensors, actuators, communication infrastructure, etc.

Restrictive architectural rules are enforced to reduce the number of possible system states and guarantee determinism. Critical events are scheduled at particular points in time. This makes TTAs applicable to large scale distributed systems, in which communication is trigger according to a *synchronized time* and a schedule.

TTA models the time based on Newtonian physics. Real time progresses along a dense timeline from the past to the future. The sparse time model is used to consistently order the events on the basis of global time. That means the continuum of time is divided into an infinite sequence of alternating durations of activity and silence. The activity interval must be larger than the precision of the clock synchronization. All events that occur within an interval are considered to happen at the same time.

The TTA can be used to model complete distributed real-time computer systems that are composed of nodes (self-contained units composed of host computer and communication controller). Nodes are connected through replicated broadcast channels. A set of relevant state variables (*real-time entities*) models the system behaviour. The real-time images (a temporally accurate picture of a real-time entity) are updated through the network interface periodically. The communication system is independent, a priori-defined, and follows a TDMA scheme.

The TTA represents a high-level system design methodology for complex and potentially large CPS. Such systems are deterministic, analysable, robust (fault-tolerant), composable, and allow easy safety assessment (for certification or *Automotive Safety Integrity Level (ASIL)* requirements). Thus, TTAs find their predominant usage in safety-critical systems. However, the concepts can also be applied to automotive software parallelization, because determinism is a central requirement for parallel execution.

### 3.3.3.1 Logical Execution Time

The work of Kirsch and Sokolova [KS12] describes the *logical execution time (LET)* as the time it takes between reading program input until writing program output, regardless of the time it takes to execute the program in between. The LET is a real-time programming abstraction. Conceptually, a LET program execution has three steps: read the program input (in zero time), then execute, and finally write the output (in zero time) exactly when the time has elapsed since reading input. Hence, communication logically happens instantaneously at fixed points in time and the program executes within a time window with a deadline represented by the LET.

When the execution of a program finishes before the deadline, writing the output is delayed until the deadline. This makes the deadline a logical upper and lower bound for the execution. Thus, using a faster processor does not result in lower response time, but in decreased core utilization.

Henzinger et al. [HHK01] introduced the high-level programming language Giotto in 2001. An extension called xGiotto, with support for asynchronous events, is described by Ghosal et al. [Gho+04]. The work by Belau et al. [BHS12] describes a method for the transformation from AUTOSAR to Giotto. The elements of the SW-C model are set in relation to elements in Giotto, for instance a require-port in AUTOSAR is represented by an in port or sensor in Giotto. Afterwards, LETs are assigned to runnables corresponding to the required update frequency, for example five milliseconds.

### 3.3.3.2 OASIS Model

OASIS [Dav+98; Lou+02] was a research project whose outcome was a model and a runtime environment for safety-critical applications. The model is based on the TTA and comprises rules and methods for the design and implementation of parallel programs with deterministic and predictable behaviour. The target is to proof functional properties (safety, liveness, and timeliness) based on the system specification.

An application is defined as a finite number of independent tasks (called *agents*). OASIS follows implements an object-oriented paradigm, in which data and computations are encapsulated in a task. Thus, the task is the exclusive owner and the only entity allowed to writing data within it. The decomposition into tasks expresses processes that can execute in a parallel way. The number of tasks is fixed and the algorithms must be bound by known time limits.

OASIS relies on a clock provided by the TTA. Hence, the progress of a task is independent from the hardware platform. The shared time base guarantees a synchronization at particular points in time. Tasks can communicate with each other in a time-triggered fashion, according to the TTA concept. A task is composed of a certain number of instructions, which can be chained depending on internal conditions of the task or external conditions of the environment. Each instruction is associated with an interval of time for its execution, which is specified in the tasks *program code*. The communication in OASIS is non-blocking and either takes place periodically (via temporal variables) or via message boxes. Each temporal variable produces a timestamped data-flow, including pairs of value and time. A task can make values visible to others by declaring a certain point in time as publication time. The value of the variable is observable by others, from this specific point in time on, but it cannot be modified.

A real-time clock $H_i$ is associated with task $\tau_i$ and represents a set of physical instants at which input or output data can be accessed by $\tau_i$. The union of all real-time clocks $H_\Omega$ includes all observable instants of the system and is defined as:

$$H_\Omega = \bigcup H_i \tag{3.1}$$

The clock $H_i$ can be derived from the global clock $H_\Omega$ with the factor $K_i$ and a shifting $\Delta_i$ as follows:

$$H_i = K_i \cdot H_\Omega + \Delta_i \tag{3.2}$$

That means in OASIS the coexistence of multiple time scales is allowed, whereas a TTA has only one time scale. Thus, asynchronism is possible and application design becomes easier.

A key feature of OASIS is the possibility to manipulate the progress of a task with the ADV-instruction. The code is split in a part before the instruction, the one which is processed at this point in time, and a part after the instruction (processed after the next instant). The instruction ADV(k) means that the next instant is the current instant plus $k \cdot H_\Omega$ periods. Consequently, series of instructions with precedence relation can be executed in sequence. The earliest start time and deadlines can be specified in a straightforward manner. Figure 3.4 shows an example for constraint execution with the OASIS ADV instruction. The earliest start of instruction_2 is constraint by start and the deadline is defined by end. Thus, the formal duration of instruction_2 is equal to end - start. This formal duration is hardware independent and always the same. Hence, the design guarantees predictability and it makes timing properties visible in the implementation.

```
1  foo() {
2      instruction_1;
3      advance(start);
4      instruction_2;
5      advance(end);
6  }
```

Figure 3.4: Exemplary use of the OASIS advance instruction.

This programming language shown in figure 3.4 is called ΨC [Cha+04]. It allows a combination of a formal description of different real-time tasks, in which algorithmic parts (in ANSI C) are combined with an observable temporal behaviour described in a declarative way.

### 3.3.3.3 PharOS Automotive Operating System

Chabrol et al. [CAD09] and Aussagès [Aus+10] transferred the concepts of OASIS to the automotive domain. PharOS is a complete framework for the design, implementation, and execution of safety-critical applications. It guarantees freedom from interference by construction ("safe by construction"). Therefore, temporal and spatial partitioning mechanisms are provided.

In contrast to OASIS' ADV operation, the possibilities for describing temporal constraints are improved. *Time-constrained automata (TCA)* [Lem+11] are used for describing the temporal constrains of an application, also supporting dynamically changing time scales. PharOS supports the timing constraints before(d), after(d), advance(d), and the no-constraint for the ΨC language. They are translated with a source-to-source compiler into regular C code, whereby timing constraints are replaced by calls to the scheduler. The implementation of PharOS is strict in the sense that timing budgets are supervised and a task is stopped if processing takes more time than considered in the design. This is an advantage, on the one hand, because a task can never exceed its time budget and other tasks can start in time. It is a disadvantage, in the other hand, because a critical task can be stopped, if the reserved time budget is too short. The work of Lemerre et al. [LO12] proofed that PharOS is deterministic.

Hence, the communication between tasks in PharOS is deterministic. A message is formally sent when the consecutive `before(d)` statement is reached and the message cannot be received before the preceding `after(d')` statement has passed ($d' > d$). Moreover, the implementation ensures independence of send time and reception order.

One peculiarity of PharOS is that sporadic tasks cannot communicate with each other directly. Messages take a detour through a time-triggered task. The processor's memory protection mechanism (*memory management unit (MMU)* and *memory protection unit (MPU)*) are used to realize spatial isolation and fault containment. Each task owns a private memory partition containing several segments with various privileges. The whole system is layered to achieve a protection between OS and application.

The practicability of PharOS is shown by Chabrol et al. in [Cha+13]. A powertrain controller is implemented upon PharOS. A particular property of such systems is a sporadic task, which executes synchronous to the angular position of the camshaft or the crankshaft.

### 3.3.3.4 Discussion of Time-Triggered Architectures

In the following, the reviewed approaches are comprehensively compared and discussed. The approaches are qualitatively compared in the table 3.4 against the objectives defined in section 3.1. The table lists relevant non-functional objectives and it indicates if the approaches satisfy ($\checkmark$), partially satisfy ($\circ$), or do not satisfy ($\times$) the objective. A question mark (?) is put whenever no judgement is possible based on the published material.

The TTA is a well understood concept and already proven in use with safety critical embedded systems (robustness). This comes at the cost of overprovisioning computation, memory, and communication resources (efficiency). Although, case studies with OASIS and PharOS proved efficiency for embedded systems.

The programming language *Giotto* implements the LET concept for periodic task sets and its successor *xGiotto* is extended for supporting also sporadic tasks. Both are designed for education and scientific research in the first place. Thus, they do not scale and this makes them unattractive for the use with large automotive software.

|                              | LET/xGiotto | OASIS Model | PharOS/PsiC |
|------------------------------|:-----------:|:-----------:|:-----------:|
| Robustness                   | ✓           | ✓           | ✓           |
| Efficiency                   | ○           | ○           | ○           |
| Scalability                  | ✗           | ✓           | ✓           |
| Low cost                     | ✗           | ✓           | ✓           |
| Compliance                   | ✗           | ✗           | ✗           |
| Portability                  | ✗           | ✗           | ✗           |
| Minimal standard modification| ✗           | ✗           | ✗           |

Table 3.4: Qualitative comparison of methods for predictable interprocessor communication based on a TTA.
Legend: satisfied  (✓), partially satisfied  (○), unsatisfied  (✗), or unknown (?).

Nevertheless, the LET provides a useful concept for guaranteeing deterministic execution and a predictable data-flow. That means it should be considered for the parallelization.

OASIS and PharOS rely on a proprietary programming language and tools to implement their approaches. The design methodology differs heavily from the AUTOSAR methodology. That means the integration of the concepts in the standard is accompanied with high effort.

### 3.3.4   Discussion and Summary

This section reviewed methods for interprocessor communication between parallel executed tasks that provide a predictable and reproducible data-flow. They are now compared against each other and conclusions, for a parallelization approach for automotive control software, are drawn.

The mechanisms defined in the AUTOSAR standard focus on providing data consistency in the first place and they introduce a high overhead. Using asynchronous communication instead can be used to decouple sporadic tasks from periodic tasks, but it results in an unpredictable data-flow when used between periodic tasks. Thus, alternative approaches were reviewed.

Strong DMT provides general-purpose determinism on conventional architectures. A synchronized artificial clock, the DLT, is used to control the execution order of threads.

Similarly, TTAs synchronize the execution of threads based on a real-time clock. The computations are decoupled from the communication in both approaches, lockstep quanta in strong DMT and LET in a TTA.

The disadvantage of a TTA, in this regard, is the strict time budget for a LET interval. A task can be terminated, if the time budget is exhausted. This issue does not appear in an artificial clock, because it has no budget. However, the DLT must be linked to real time to make them compatible with automotive software parallelization; and the time budget for the LET must be defined large enough to avoid unintended behaviour. The low efficiency of DMT makes the latter option the preferred approach.

Weak DMT approaches propose an interesting method for reducing the waiting time for other threads: lazy reading. A lazy read explicitly requests an older input value to continue execution instead of waiting for latest results. Especially, programs that frequently poll a variable perform significantly better, but at the cost of working on a less up-to-date value. Similarly, temporal variables, used by OASIS and PharOS, maintain a value history with associated timestamps. A producer can publish data at a specific point in time and a receiver can request the value of a specific point in time. This makes it possible to receive a consistent "picture", when all variable values are observed from the same point in time, regardless of partial value updates afterwards. Automotive software is generally robust and reading an older input value is valid, if the end-to-end latency is smaller than or equal to the worst acceptable one.

Concluding, the review allows for the following conclusions. The duration of a LET interval must be greater than or equal to the WCET of the runnables that are executed within it. Otherwise, the sensor/actuator data-flow can break. A predictable data-flow can be achieved by a separation of computation and communication. Timestamps can be used to order values logically and independent from their computation. Lazy reading can speed-up the computation, but it must be possible to derive the data-flow, the end-to-end latency, and guarantee an upper bound on the latency. The timing constraints of PharOS (before, after, advance, no-constraint) are ideal synchronization operations to control the runnable and task execution based on a synchronized clock. Thus, a complete toolchain is not required for the implementation.

## 3.4 Summary of State of the Art

This chapter reviewed state-of-the-art approaches for automotive software parallelization. For this, section 3.1 lists a set of functional and non-functional objectives, taking the properties of legacy automotive embedded control software and the AUTOSAR standard's methodology into account. Subsequently, state-of-the-art approaches were explained, compared against the objectives, and conclusions were drawn for a parallelization approach for automotive control software.

### 3.4.1 Summary

Section 3.2 reviewed state-of-the-art approaches for mapping and scheduling for the parallelization of embedded software. Reconfiguring approaches define a new application configuration, which is efficient and compatible with the AUTOSAR standard. However, a re-validation of the functional correctness is required and their applicability is limited.

Contrarily, preserving approaches keep the original application's configuration and the tasks, or their content, are executed in a parallel way. Task-level parallelization approaches distribute complete tasks to cores. Runnable-level parallelization distributes a task body with different levels of granularity to cores and the original task schedule is kept. They maintain the same data-flow and fulfil most of the requirements, but not all of them are compatible with AUTOSAR. Furthermore, the proposed interprocessor communication mechanisms either access shared memory locations is an unpredictable order or data dependencies force frequent serialization of the task scheduling.

Thus, section 3.3 discussed mechanisms for interprocessor communication, which produce a predictable and reproducible data-flow and allow for parallel execution. Strong DMT and TTAs separate computation from communication to ensure determinism. However, the DLT in DMT must be linked to real time to make them compatible with automotive software parallelization; and the time budget for the LET windows in a TTA must be defined large enough to avoid unintended behaviour. Weak DMT provides an interesting method, lazy reading, for improving parallel performance, but this demands for clear rules for transforming the sensor/actuator data-flow and the transformation must be set in relation to the original application's configuration. Thus, a new method for the parallelization of automotive control software is required that incorporates the insights from the reviewed approaches.

### 3.4.2 Conclusions for Automotive Software Parallelization

The review allows for drawing the following conclusions for automotive software parallelization. A fundamental insight results from the comparison of mapping and scheduling approaches. Generating a configuration independent schedule is better than directly generating a system configuration. Using the original task set as parallelization constraint for this is a reasonable way to maintain the application semantic, because no re-validation of the functional correctness is required. Thus, the parallel program is more robust and the migration cost is lower.

Parallelization constraints can be derived from the original application's configuration, described in section 2.3. Simple precedence constraints are derived on the granularity of runnables, from the original task implementation. The original task priority assignment is considered to derive extended precedence constraints. Latency constraints are derived for relevant end-to-end chains by taking task periods as upper bound into account.

Generally, a predictable data-flow can be achieved by a separation of computation and communication with the concept of logical execution times (LETs). The duration of a LET interval must be greater than or equal to the WCET of the runnables that are executed within it. Otherwise, the sensor/actuator data-flow can break. Timestamps can be used to order computed values logically and independent from their computation.

The parallelization should be divided in runnable- and task-level parallelization, because appropriate methods exist already for former one. They can be made compliant to AUTOSAR, if they consider runnables as *unit of scheduling (UoS)*. The timing constraints of PharOS (before, after, advance, no-constraint) can be used to control the runnable and task execution based on a synchronized clock.

Task-level parallelization can define LETs for tasks, based on the original application's configuration, to make the interprocessor communication on task-level predictable Here, lazy reading can speed-up the computation. Therefore, the communication between tasks must be classified whether relaxation and thus parallel execution of the tasks is valid. This requires a transformation of the single-core data-flow, in such a way that an identical data-flow is guaranteed for all multicore ECUs. Moreover, the end-to-end latency for critical data-flow chains must be computed to guarantee an upper bound on the latency.

A combination of runnable- and task-level parallelization techniques is required to compute a hyperperiod schedule and thus derive the reduction of the processor's clock rate. Therefore, task- and runnable-level parallelization can be combined in a divide & conquer manner. Each task is separately parallelized and the overall schedule is combined from parallelized tasks. The end-to-end latency and the processor's clock rate can be used to judge the quality of the solution, instead of a weighted sum approach. The target is a minimal processor's clock rate that guarantees a strict upper bound on the latency.

The review showed that bin-packing heuristics are a popular and good way to balance the load over cores. List scheduling is a promising candidate heuristic for scheduling of dependent runnables (runnable-level parallelization) and tasks (task-level parallelization). Evolutionary algorithms or simulated annealing are good to combine multiple optimization criteria and to maintain scalability. A good way of considering end-to-end latency constraints is a chain of runnables and an associated deadline.

# 4 | Runnable-level Parallelization

> "Computers are good at following instructions,
> but not at reading your mind."

> Donald Knuth, 1984

This chapter presents two runnable-level parallelization strategies for automotive control software that consider runnables (and not tasks) as the *unit of scheduling (UoS)*. The analysis in section 3.2 showed that AUTOSAR-specific approaches re-arrange runnables in new tasks and this requires a re-validation of the functional correctness, because the order in which runnables process data is changed. Alternative approaches are not compliant to AUTOSAR. It is therefore necessary to introduce a new method that considers *the runnable* as UoS and respects the communication between runnables defined by the original application's configuration as constraint.

Thus, a first proposal named *RunPar* [Pan+14] is developed as collaborative work in the context of the FP7 research project parMERASA. The author of this thesis contributed in formulating the problem, analysing the use case, and conducting experiments. RunPar distributes the runnables of the same task to cores and it keeps the original application's configuration (runnable-to-task mapping and scheduling). Thus, the application performance is improved, the sequential execution of tasks is kept, and consequently no re-validation of the functional correctness is necessary.

The analysis of RunPar showed that large idle intervals on a core can be introduced, if a task contains a long critical path. Consequently, a new *AUTomotive Open System ARchitecture (AUTOSAR)* structure named *Supertask* is proposed in [Keh+16], which further exploits runnable-level parallelism and still maintains the original data-flow of the application. Runnables from (originally) consecutive scheduled tasks are grouped into a Supertask and then scheduled with RunPar, whereas inter-task data dependencies are respected.

The first part of this chapter describes the parallelization with RunPar and the construction of a Supertask. The second part of this chapter evaluates and compares both approaches.

# 4.1 Allocation of Runnables

This thesis proposes a complete runnable-level parallelization strategy that maintains the original single-core application configuration, which is carried out as follows:

1) *Extraction of the runnable dependence graph (RDG)* — the source code of each task is analysed separately and data dependencies between runnables are identified. Simple precedence constraints (definition 2.3) are derived and represented in the form of a *directed acyclic graph (DAG)*, which is denoted as RDG.

2) *Partitioned scheduling of Runnables* — A static schedule for the execution of runnables is derived for each task with the partitioned scheduler *RunPar*.

3) *Construction of Supertasks* — All possible task activation patterns are derived from the original application's configuration. Tasks with the same activation time are combined in one Supertask, whereas inter-task data dependencies are derived on runnable-level. A static schedule is derived with RunPar.

4) *Implementation* — The parallel static schedule is implemented in AUTOSAR with the concept of *logical execution times (LETs)* (section 3.3.3).

The next section first introduces the notations and the problem formulation for this chapter. The steps from the list above are explained in more detail afterwards.

## 4.1.1 Notations and Problem Formulation

Runnable-level parallelization means to distribute runnables of the same release period to a set of cores, whereas precedence constraints between these runnables must be respected. A *program dependence graph (PDG)*, as described in section 2.2.2, is ideal to represent data dependencies. The target here is a partitioning of runnables. Hence, it is enough to represent the data dependencies on the granularity of runnables. For this reason, the graph representation is denoted as RDG and defined in definition 4.1.

**Definition 4.1 (Runnable Dependence Graph (RDG)):** *The DAG $G_i = (V_i, E_i)$ represents the precedence constraints between runnables of the same release period in a task $\tau_i$. Each node $V_i$ represents a runnable. The edge $(q, r) \in E_i$ means q precedes r ($q \rightarrow r$), with $q, r \in V_i$. A worst-case execution time (WCET) estimate $c_r$, expressed in time units, further characterises each runnable $r \in V_i$.*

Automotive control software is a real-time application according to definition 2.1. However, this definition does not capture the dependencies between runnables. Thus, a RDG extends the properties of a task. The resulting AUTOSAR application is defined as follows.

**Definition 4.2 (AUTOSAR application $\mathcal{A}$):** *The AUTOSAR application $\mathcal{A}$ consists of a set of n tasks:*

$$\mathcal{A} = \{\tau_i \mid 1 \le i \le n, i \in \mathbb{N}\}. \tag{4.1}$$

*The real-time attributes $(\pi_i, T_i, G_i = (V_i, E_i), C_i, O_i, D_i)$ characterise each task $\tau_i \in \mathcal{A}$.*

- ▷ *$\pi_i$ is the priority.*
- ▷ *$\tau_i$ is instantiated periodically with period $T_i$.*
- ▷ *$G_i$ is the RDG of task $\tau_i$ according to definition 4.1.*
- ▷ *$C_i$ is the WCET of the task expressed in time units, i.e. the sum of runnable WCETs of $\tau_i$:*

$$C_i = \sum_{r \in V_i} c_r \tag{4.2}$$

- ▷ *$O_i$ is the release time of the first instance of the task, i.e. the offset with respect to the start time of the system.*
- ▷ *$D_i \le T_i$ is the relative deadline of the task; they are implicitly defined, i.e. $D_i = T_i$.*
- ▷ *The release time of $\tau_i^p$ is $o_i^p = O_i + pT_i$.*
- ▷ *The absolute deadline of $\tau_i^p$ is $d_i^p = o_i^p + D_i$.*

Definition 4.2 also covers sporadic tasks, if they are considered as periodic task with their maximal possible frequency. Definition 4.3 defines the problem of partitioning the tasks of an AUTOSAR application to $m$ identical cores.

**Definition 4.3 (Static partitioning $\Phi$):** *Let m be the number of identical cores of a target processor. Let $G_i$ be the RDG for a task $\tau_i$ in the AUTOSAR application $\mathcal{A}$. The static partitioning of $G_i$ onto m identical cores is represented by*

$$\Phi_i = (\varphi_1, \ldots, \varphi_m) \tag{4.3}$$

*where each $\varphi_k \in \Phi_i$, $1 \le k \le m$, denotes a subset of runnables $\varphi_p \subseteq V_i$ that are mapped to core k. Thus, the WCET of the partitioned task $\tau_i$ is defined as*

$$C_i^\Phi = \max_{k=1,\ldots,m} \left\{ \sum_{r \in \varphi_k} c_r \right\} \tag{4.4}$$

The WCET of a static partitioning is the maximum WCET over all allocations. As a result, cores cannot have idle intervals. RunPar schedules an artificial runnable in the length of the needed idle interval to fill the gap. Thus, the definition still applies.

The static partitioning of a task $\tau_i \in \mathcal{A}$ must fulfil different constraints to be valid. First, the allocation must be precedence feasible (constraint 4.1).

**Constraint 4.1 (Precedence feasibility):** *Let $\Phi_i = (\varphi_1, \ldots, \varphi_m)$ be a static partitioning for a task $\tau_i$ in the AUTOSAR application $\mathcal{A}$. Let $\mathrm{st}_r$ denote the start time of a runnable $r \in V_i$ as defined by $\Phi_i$. The partitioning $\Phi_i$ is precedence feasible, if for all $(k, \ell) \in E_i$*

$$\mathrm{st}_\ell > \mathrm{st}_k + c_k \tag{4.5}$$

That means all predecessors of a runnable $r \in V_i$ finish before $r$ starts. The second condition that a static partitioning must fulfil is given by constraint 4.2.

**Constraint 4.2 (Unique allocation of runnables):** *Let $\Phi_i = (\varphi_1, \ldots, \varphi_m)$ be a static partitioning for a task $\tau_i$ in the AUTOSAR application $\mathcal{A}$. A runnable $r \in V_i$ is assigned to maximal one core, if for any two $\varphi_k, \varphi_\ell \in \Phi_i$*

$$\varphi_k \cap \varphi_\ell = \varnothing, \quad k \neq \ell \tag{4.6}$$

That means each runnable can be allocated to one core only. Consequently, the partitioning of a task divides its RDG in maximal $m$ subgraphs; one per core.

**Definition 4.4 (Subgraphs of partitioning $\Phi_i$):** *Let $G_i$ be a RDG for a task $\tau_i$ in the AUTOSAR application $\mathcal{A}$. Let $\Phi_i = (\varphi_1, \ldots, \varphi_m)$ be a static partitioning for $\tau_i$. $\Phi_i$ partitions $G_i$ into maximal $m$ subgraphs $G_i^k = (V_i^k = \varphi_k, E_i^k), 1 < k < m$. An edge $(k, \ell) \in E_i$ is also in $E_i^k$, if $k, \ell \in G_i^k$.*

The execution of a runnable consumes processor capacity. Definition 4.5 defines the utilisation that a runnable consumes from the available processor capacity.

**Definition 4.5 (Utilization of a runnable $r$):** *Let $\tau_i$ be a task in the AUTOSAR application $\mathcal{A}$. The utilization $u_r$ of the runnable $r \in V_i$ with WCET estimate $c_r$ is*

$$u_r = \frac{c_r}{T_i}, \quad 0 \leq u_r \leq 1 \tag{4.7}$$

Each core has a limited computational capacity that cannot be exceeded. The allocation of a runnable to a core increases its utilisation and the limit is given by constraint 4.3.

**Constraint 4.3 (Processor capacity constraint):** *Let $\Phi_i = (\varphi_1, \ldots, \varphi_m)$ be a static partitioning for a task $\tau_i$ in the AUTOSAR application $\mathcal{A}$. Let $G_i^k$ be the subgraph of the RDG $G_i$ on core $k$. The cumulative utilization of allocated resources for core $k \in \{1, \ldots, m\}$ is*

$$u_\Sigma^k = \sum_{r \in V_i^k} u_r \leq 1 \tag{4.8}$$

That means the total capacity of a processor is limited to 1.

## 4.1.2 Extraction of the Runnable Dependence Graph

Figure 4.1 shows the source code of an artificial, but representative, implementation of two AUTOSAR tasks $\tau_1$ and $\tau_2$. The discussion in section 2.3 showed that the concrete execution order from the original application's configuration is important. One cannot derive the execution order for runnables that communicate in a bidirectional way and execute with the same period straightforward. Thus, the control flow of the legacy task is used to define a correct execution order of runnables for the parallelization, because this configuration is known to lead to correct functional behaviour.

```
1 void Task_1() {
2    Runnable_1();
3    Runnable_2();
4    Runnable_3();
5 }
```

```
1 void Task_2() {
2    Runnable_4();
3    Runnable_5();
4    Runnable_6();
5 }
```

(a) Source code of $\tau_1$.    (b) Source code of $\tau_2$.

Figure 4.1: Exemplary task implementation.

Existing analysis techniques are sufficiently mature to be used for the analysis of automotive control software (see section 2.2.2). The source code of automotive applications considered in this thesis follows the MISRA-C [Mot+08] guidelines, which only uses a subset of the C programming language. For example, these guidelines recommend avoiding recursion or floating-point variables in the controlling expression of loops. These guidelines help to facilitate code safety, reliability, and simplification of source code analysis. Consequently, there is no urgent need for new analysis techniques to enable parallelization of automotive control software.

The extraction of precedence constraints between runnables requires analysis on the granularity of high-level language statements, because the access to shared variables within runnables provides information about the communication in the application. Subsequently, these data dependencies are aggregated per runnable and the RDG (definition 4.1) is derived.

Figure 4.2 shows an example the task set composed of

$$\tau_1(\pi_1 = 2, T_1 = 10, G_1 = (V_1 = \{1, 2, 3, s, e\}, E_1 = \{(s, 1), (s, 2), (1, e), (2, 3), (3, e)\}),$$
$$C_1 = 4, O_1 = 0, D_1 = 10)$$

and

$$\tau_2(\pi_2 = 1, T_2 = 20, G_2 = (V_2 = \{4, 5, 6, s, e\}, E_2 = \{(s, 4), (4, 5), (4, 6), (5, e), (6, e)\}),$$
$$C_2 = 5, O_2 = 0, D_2 = 20)$$

imposed by the task implementation figure 4.1

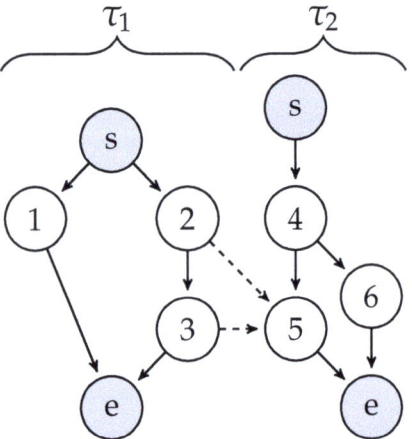

Figure 4.2: RDG for the tasks $\tau_1$ (left) and $\tau_2$ (right) from figure 4.1.

The RDG guarantees that the data-flow within a task is kept. However, the tasks must be executed in the correct order to produce the data-flow from sensor to actuator through the complete application. For this reason, the concrete task scheduling of the original application's configuration (figure 4.3) is taken into account. As a result, the task implementation and the scheduling define this data-flow through the runnables of the application. Based on the analysis in section 2.3, the general assumption is that the tasks in the original system were scheduled with a *rate monotonic (RM)* non-preemptive policy. Hence, the priority of $\tau_1$ is higher than the priority of $\tau_2$ ($\pi_1 > \pi_2$).

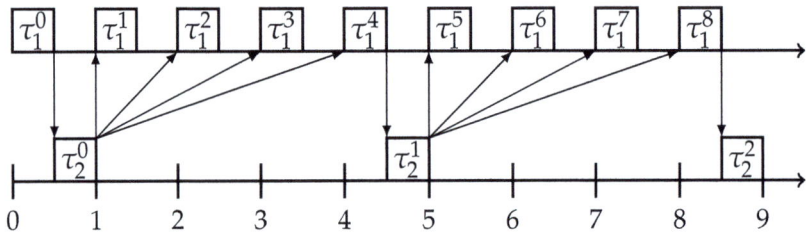

Figure 4.3: Task schedule on the single-core *electronic control unit (ECU)*.

The dashed lines in figure 4.2 represent inter-task data dependencies. These are $2 \rightarrow 5$ and $3 \rightarrow 5$. They can be derived based on the data dependencies between the runnables in combination with the scheduling in figure 4.3.

### 4.1.3 The RunPar Allocation Algorithm

Structural partitioning is a fundamental design characteristic of AUTOSAR applications (see section 2.1). A *software component (SW C)* (and task) is statically assigned to one core. Hence, partitioned multicore scheduling [DB11] is ideal for automotive software.

This section introduces the partitioned scheduler RunPar [Pan+14], which was developed in the collaborative FP7 research project parMERASA. The author of this thesis mainly contributed in formulating the problem, analysing the case study, static WCET analysis of a diesel *engine management system (EMS)* use case, and conducting experiments.

**Definition 4.6 (RunPar($\mathcal{A}$, $m$, Prio, $H^D$, $H^I$)):** *Given the AUTOSAR application $\mathcal{A}$ (definition 4.2). RunPar computes for all $\tau_i \in \mathcal{A}$ a static partitioning $\Phi_i$ (definition 4.3) for m identical cores, constraint by the RDG $G_i$ (definition 4.1) using the priority rule Prio, the bin-packing heuristic $H^D$ for dependent runnables, and the bin-packing heuristic $H^I$ for independent runnables.*

```
 1  (Classify runnables.) Set V_i^D ← {r | r ∈ V_i, deg(r) > 0} and set
        V_i^I ← {r | r ∈ V_i, deg(r) = 0}.
 2
 3  (Sort runnables.) Sort runnables in V_i^D and V_i^I in decreasing order by priority
        rule Prio.
 4
 5  (Allocate dependent runnables.) For each unprocessed r ∈ V_i^D with indeg(r) = 0
 6      (a) Select core k ← binpack(r, H^D, 0).
 7      (b) Allocate r to φ_k.
 8
 9  (Allocate successors.) For each unprocessed r ∈ V_i^D whose predecessors are already
        scheduled
10      (a) Select a predecessor p from Φ_i, which produces maximal cumulative
            utilization u_max.
11      (b) Set the earliest start time st_r ← ft_p.
12      (c) Select core k ← binpack(r, H^D, st_r).
13      (d) If u_Σ^k < u_max: allocate idle interval to φ_k.
14      (e) Allocate r to φ_k.
15
16  (Allocate independent runnables.) For each r ∈ V_i^I
17      (a) If some φ_k ∈ Φ_i contains an idle region j for r, resize j.
18          Otherwise, select core k ← binpack(r, H^I, st_r).
19      (b) Allocate r in a free slot on φ_k.
20
21  (Return.) Return Φ_i.
```

Algorithm 4.1: The RunPar allocation algorithm

Basically, RunPar can be used with any bin-packing heuristic or priority rule. The following explanations mention suitable methods. They are compared against each other in the evaluation section of RunPar in section 4.2.2. Algorithm 4.1 lists the pseudo-code for RunPar. Runnables are allocated under constraints 4.1 to 4.3. Runnables from different tasks are not executed in a parallel way, instead task execution follows the single-core scheduling.

### 4.1.3.1 Runnable classification

The most flexible runnables, regarding schedulability, are the ones that do not communicate with other runnables of the same task. These runnable can execute at an arbitrary point in the parallelized task and dependencies are still guaranteed. They are ideal to fill idle intervals that arise from scheduling of runnables under precedence constraints. As a result, RunPar identifies them and defers them to the end of the scheduling process.

If a runnable does not communicate with other runnables of the same task, then no edge is found in the RDG $G_i = (V_i, E_i)$ of the task $\tau_i$, see definition 4.2. For the runnable $r \in V_i$ the function indeg($r$) returns the number of ingoing edges of $r$ (indegree), i.e. the number of predecessors in $G_i$. The edge from the starting node to the runnable $(s, r)$ is not counted. Likewise, the function outdeg($r$) returns the number of outgoing edges of $r$ (outdegree), i.e. the number of successors in $G_i$. The edge from the runnable to the terminal node $(r, e)$ is not counted. The function deg($r$) returns the runnables node degree; the sum of outdegree and indegree.

RunPar classifies all runnables in $V_i$ in *dependent* ($V_i^{\mathcal{D}}$) and *independent* ($V_i^{\mathcal{I}}$) (line 1). A runnable is classified as dependent, if the runnable has degree deg($r$) > 0. The runnable is independent otherwise. Independent runnables are deferred and scheduled at the end.

Communication with other tasks or with past instances of the same task is possible, but such data dependencies must not be taken into account. The reason is, the application scheduling (sequential execution of tasks) already guarantees these dependencies. The inter-task data dependencies will however be taken into account when constructing Supertasks, as will be explained in section 4.1.4.

### 4.1.3.2 Priority rule

The runnables in $V_i^{\mathcal{D}}$ and $V_i^{\mathcal{I}}$ are sorted according to a priority rule Prio (line 3). Considering the critical path for parallelization provides the best overall guidance towards bottlenecks in parallel programs [HM92]. Several criteria can be used for prioritizing runnables during allocation: deadline, period, frequency, or utilization.

None of these criteria considers the critical path, because they provide an indicator per runnable that is independent from data dependencies (precedence constraints) with other runnables. For this reason, RunPar computes the *combined utilization* per runnable, which is the maximum sum of utilizations of successor nodes. For example, the combined utilization of runnable 4 from figure 4.2 is $c_4 + \max\{c_5, c_6\}$. Runnables 5 and 6 compute their combined utilization in the same way. Hence, RunPar prioritises runnables on the critical path.

### 4.1.3.3 Allocation

The runnables are allocated in decreasing order of their priority, as the lists $V_i^{\mathcal{D}}$ and $V_i^{\mathcal{I}}$ define. As a first step, dependent runnables without a predecessor are allocated (line 5). The target core is selected according to the allocation strategy $H^{\mathcal{D}}$ (line 6). The assignment of the runnable to the target partition is done in line 7.

Bin-packing heuristics are ideal to find an allocation of objects (runnables) to a limited number of containers (cores) in short time. Considering a *worst-fit (WF)* decreasing heuristic seems to be an intuitively good choice, because always the least loaded core is selected; the one with the smallest $u_\Sigma^k$. The use of a WF heuristic guarantees a better runnable-to-core load balance, which most likely provides more parallelism among runnables with respect to other heuristics, such as *first-fit (FF)* decreasing heuristics. This hypothesis is later investigated in experiments in section 4.2.2.

As a second step, the successors of already scheduled runnables are processed, if all predecessors are already scheduled (line 9). In line 10, RunPar pre-computes the cumulative utilization of all possible allocations of predecessors $p$ and selects the one producing the maximal value ($u_{\max}$). The finish time of $p$ (ft$_p$) defines the earliest start time (st$_r$) for the allocation of the runnable (lines 11 and 12). If necessary, an idle interval is inserted (line 13) before the allocation of the runnable (line 14). The steps 10 - 14 are repeated until all runnables in $V_i^{\mathcal{D}}$ are scheduled.

As a third and last step, independent runnables are allocated in line 16. RunPar checks, whether a runnable fits within an idle region (line 17) and adjusts the size of the region in this case. Otherwise, the heuristic $H^{\mathcal{I}}$ is used to select a core in line 18. Finally, the runnable is allocated to the previously selected core in line 19. RunPar returns the solution $\Phi_i$ for task $\tau_i$ in line 21.

#### 4.1.3.4 Example for RunPar

Figure 4.4 shows an example for the allocation with RunPar, with configuration $H^{\mathcal{D}} = H^{\mathcal{I}} = $ worst-fit and Prio = combined utilization. The task set composed of $\tau_1$ and $\tau_2$ is scheduled according to the precedence constraints defined in figure 4.2. Both tasks are scheduled separately and executed consecutively to guarantee the inter-task data dependencies. Runnable 2 is allocated as first to core 0, because it has the highest combined utilization.

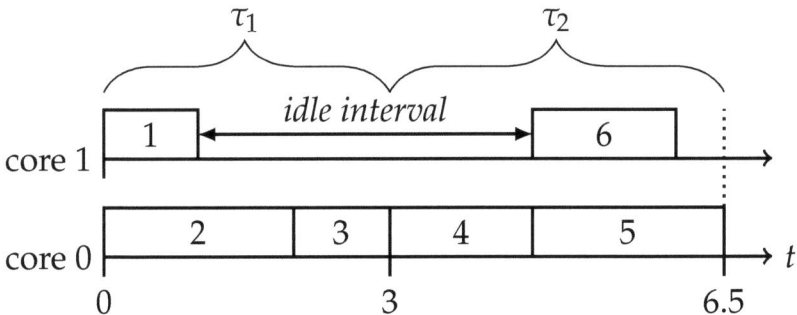

Figure 4.4: Exemplary schedule with RunPar.

### 4.1.4 Construction of a Supertask

This section presents a mechanism for utilizing idle intervals of consecutively executed tasks: the *Supertask*. The motivation behind the Supertask concept is that the sequential execution of parallelized tasks might produce large idle intervals (see figure 4.4). Hence, these intervals should be utilized, unless runnables are subject to data dependencies.

There are two reasons for this large gap in figure 4.4: first, precedence constraints $(2, 3), (4, 5), (4, 6)$ prevent an earlier execution of runnables 3, 5 and 6. Second, consecutive task execution ($\tau_1 \rightarrow \tau_2$) shifts the execution of runnable 4 beyond runnable 3, although no precedence constraint exists. Therefore, this section proposes to combine tasks into one Supertask structure, whereby inter-task data dependencies are transformed to simple precedence constraints of the Supertask. This allows for parallel execution of runnables from both tasks, guaranteeing the same order as in the original task set, and idle intervals are filled.

**Definition 4.7 (Supertask construction):** *Let $\tau_a$ and $\tau_b$ be two consecutively scheduled tasks ($\tau_a \rightarrow \tau_b$) in the AUTOSAR application $\mathcal{A}$. The Supertask $\tau_{a.b}$ has the following real-time attributes:*

$$
\begin{aligned}
\tau_{a.b} = (&\pi_{a.b} = \max(\pi_a, \pi_b), \\
&T_{a.b} = \mathrm{lcm}(T_a, T_b), \\
&G_{a.b} = (V_{a.b} = V_a \cup V_b, E_{a.b} = E_a \cup E_b \cup E^{inter}), \\
&C_{a.b} = C_a + C_b, \\
&O_{a.b} = \mathrm{lcm}(T_a, T_b), \\
&D_{a.b} = \mathrm{lcm}(T_a, T_b))
\end{aligned}
\tag{4.9}
$$

The edge set $E^{inter}$ represents inter-task data dependencies and they are identified by dependency analysis, whereby the original execution order of tasks defines the control flow: $\tau_a \rightarrow \tau_b$ (see section 2.2.2 and section 4.1.2). However, the number of combined tasks can be larger than two. Therefore, the process is repeated several times.

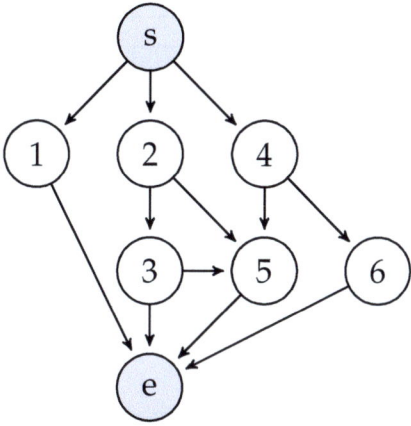

Figure 4.5: RDG for Supertask $\tau_{1.2}$.

Figures 4.5 and 4.6 show an example for a Supertask, which is based on the RunPar example in figure 4.2. $\tau_1$ and $\tau_2$ are combined into

$$\tau_{1.2} = (\pi_{1.2} = \max(2,1) = 2,$$
$$T_{1.2} = \text{lcm}(10,20) = 20,$$
$$G_{1.2} = (V_{1.2} = \{1,2,3,s,e\} \cup \{4,5,6,s,e\},$$
$$E_{1.2} = \{(s,1),(s,2),(1,e),(2,3),(3,e)\}) \cup \{(s,4),(4,5),(4,6),(5,e),(6,e)\})$$
$$\cup \{(2,5),(3,5)\}),$$
$$C_{1.2} = C_1 + C_2 = 9,$$
$$O_{1.2} = 20,$$
$$D_{1.2} = 20))$$

(4.10)

The runnables 2, 3, and 5 represent the critical path of $\tau_{1.2}$. They are allocated first; to core 0. Runnable 4 can execute immediately after runnable 1, followed by runnable 6. Overall, Supertasks reduce the utilization of a subset of tasks executed within a given cycle. In the example, the idle interval is filled and the total execution time is reduced from 6.5 to 5.

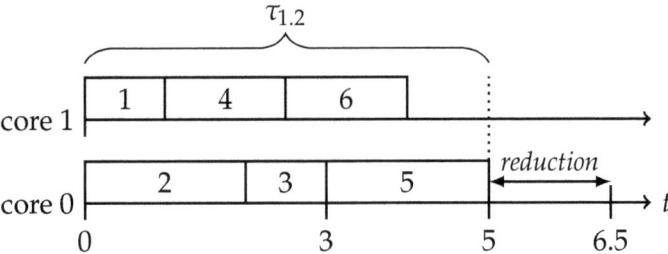

Figure 4.6: Example for a Supertask with RunPar.

## 4.1.5 Implementation

This section describes the implementation of RunPar and Supertasks in embedded system with AUTOSAR software architectures. In addition, it discusses the impact on the standard and necessary (although minimal) extensions of the standard.

### 4.1.5.1 Implementation of a Static Partitioning Φ

RunPar defines a time window for the execution of a runnable in the length of its WCET. This concept is also known as LET (see section 3.3.3 for details). There are generally two AUTOSAR-compliant ways to implement the static partitioning $\Phi_i$:

1) *Schedule tables* are used to trigger the start of each runnable. Therefore, each task instance is replaced with one runnable schedule table per core that defines the starting point, and the order of each runnable that forms the task. An expiry point triggers the start of one runnable and the offset to the next expiry point is equal to the WCET of the activated runnable.

2) The `advance`-instruction from OASIS (also described in section 3.3.3) is used to guarantee that each runnable always executes with its WCET. Therefore, the original task is replaced with one per core that contains the runnables that execute on this core and `advance`-instruction are inserted after each runnable.

### 4.1.5.2 Implementation of Supertasks

The extension of the previous methods for a Supertask is straightforward. A Supertask extends the schedule table by a new entry. Similar to tasks, each Supertask has its own starting point, the order in which it is activated, and an associated runnable schedule table are derived with RunPar. The implementation of the allocation solution $\Phi_i$ is done analogous to RunPar. The Supertask is activated at $pT_{a,b}$ instead of the original tasks. Supertasks do neither change the runnable-to-task mapping nor the single-core task scheduling. The tasks and the execution order of tasks remain the same.

For example, the Supertask in figure 4.6 is activated with a period of 4ms. At runtime, the AUTOSAR *operating system (OS)* task scheduler checks first, if a Supertask must be executed in the current cycle. If this is the case, the AUTOSAR OS schedules runnables that form the Supertask as defined by RunPar (or any other runnable-level scheduler), preventing execution of those tasks already executed within Supertasks.

### 4.1.5.3 Handling of Interrupts

A consequence of the parallelization with LETs is a guaranteed execution window that cannot be interrupted by other tasks. However, automotive control software typically contains sporadic tasks, like the crank-angle task in an EMS. They require a quick response after an interrupt. Therefore, this section explains a method for a cooperative scheduling policy to handle interrupts, for preempting a LET-based task or Supertask during its execution. The largest response time is equal to the longest runnable WCET in the application. This holds true as long as there are no scheduling anomalies [But11].

Let $\tau_p$ be a periodic task and let $\tau_s$ be a sporadic task. Both are parallelized on runnable-level. At some point in time, an interrupt $I_s$ triggers the execution of $\tau_s$ during the execution of $\tau_p$. This situation is handled in a co-operative manner, as shown in figure 4.7. At the time of the interrupt, the latest finish time $ft^{max}$ and the earliest finish time $ft^{min}$ among all running runnables are determined. In the example, these values are $ft^{min} = ft_1$ and $ft^{max} = ft_3$. All runnables that finish execution until $ft^{max}$ are still executed. That means a short runnable could be started after the interrupt, if it terminates before or at $ft^{max}$. The core $k$ idles for the duration $\Delta_k$ until $\tau_s$ starts.

$\tau_p$ relinquishes control to the scheduler at $ft^{max}$ and $\tau_s$ starts synchronously on all cores. This can be guaranteed by the mechanism in [BKU14]. The parallel execution on all cores guarantees the data dependencies within the interrupted task without additional overhead. Moreover, $\tau_s$ can execute runnables in a parallel way and finish earlier.

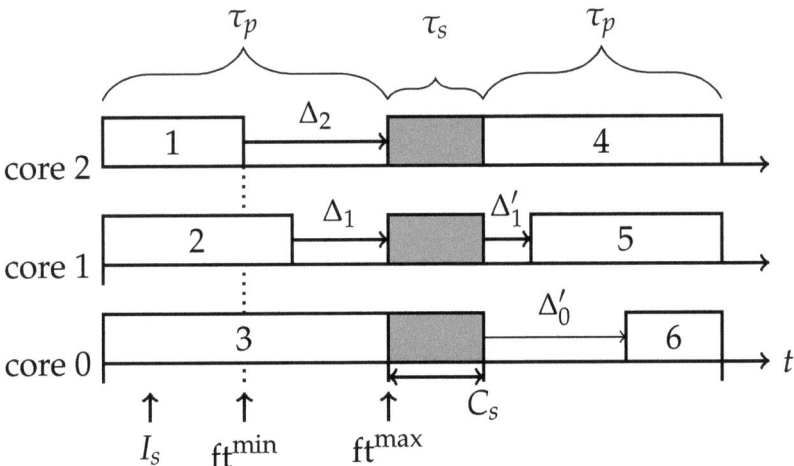

Figure 4.7: Interrupt of a task or Supertask.

The original task interleaving is restored after $\tau_s$ by injecting idle intervals of duration $\Delta'_c$. Hence, shifting the start time $st_r$ of a runnable $r$ to the future start time

$$st'_r = st_r - ft^{min} + C_s \qquad (4.11)$$

Overall, the total overhead for the interrupt $I_s$ is computed by the function

$$\text{overhead}(I_s) = C_s + 2 \cdot C_{\text{context}} + \max\{\Delta_0, \cdots, \Delta_{k-1}, \Delta'_0, \cdots, \Delta'_{k-1}\} \qquad (4.12)$$

, where $C_{\text{context}}$ represents the WCET for one context switch.

Hence, Supertasks are compatible with sporadic tasks, but the overhead depends on the largest WCET of a runnable. Considering a sporadic task as periodic task, with maximum frequency, results in the longest response time. Therefore, no experiments are conducted as there is no gain in knowledge expected.

#### 4.1.5.4   Impact on AUTOSAR

The AUTOSAR standard does not directly support runnable-level parallelization and thus extensions are required. An OS-Application is assigned to one core (see section 2.1.1). This is insufficient for the efficient implementation of parallelized tasks. Hence, a fundamental extension is the support for multicore assignments to an AUTOSAR OS-Application. The consequences of this extension are:

1) *Software-Components must be distributed over cores.* One SW-C is assigned to one core. If the component contains multiple runnables that can execute in a parallel way, the component needs to be allocated to multiple cores. Otherwise, the SW-C must be decomposed, which is associated with additional cost.

2) *The start and termination of tasks must be synchronized.* For this, schedule tables can be used. Alternatively, the method presented in [BKU14] can be applied to systems based on PharOS [Aus+10].

3) *The error handling must span multiple cores and react across the borders of a single core.* The *fault detection, isolation, and recovery (FDIR)* requires an extension at the application level [AUT14b]. During the *detection* all cores executing a part of the runnable must synchronize about the occurrence of a fault (or error). When a fault has been detected the *isolation* performs a damage assessment and damage control. Subsequently, the root cause (and the core) causing the fault are detected. In the last step *recovery* actions are initiated on all cores that execute parts of the parallelized runnable. Hence, every core of the OS-Application must at least be able to detect and isolate an error. Furthermore, the standard needs extension at *basic software (BSW)* level, for example the error hooks.

There are two alternatives for the mapping of a runnable to a core:

1) A core is specified when the task is assigned to an OS-Application. All runnables mapped to the task are assigned to the same core automatically.

2) The task is assigned to multiple cores and the core is specified during the runnable-to-task mapping.

The main advantage of the first alternative is the low impact on the methodology, because the method of the runnable-to-task mapping can remain unchanged.

## 4.2   Evaluation of Runnable-level Parallelization

This section evaluates the concept of a Supertask in three steps: first, a qualitative analysis is conducted in which the non-functional objectives from section 3.1.2 are discussed. Thereupon, research questions are derived and subsequently investigated in experiments. The experiments in section 4.2.2 are conducted to find an ideal configuration for RunPar, which is then used for scheduling the runnables of Supertasks in section 4.2.3.

## 4.2.1 Qualitative Analysis and Resulting Research Questions

This section discusses the RunPar and Supertasks in the context of the functional and non-functional objectives defined in section 3.1. Research questions for the quantitative evaluation are derived whenever necessary.

### 4.2.1.1 Functional Objectives

*Subtask decomposition* — RunPar is a method for runnable-level parallelization that respects precedence constraints between runnables in the form of a RDG. The extraction of latency constraints is not required for this approach, because the application's semantic is maintained on the multicore ECU and the task's WCET is shortened.

*Mapping and Scheduling* — RunPar is a static mapping and scheduling heuristic, which specifies the execution order, the core, and an individual time window for the execution of a runnable. Based on the RDG, each task is parallelized separately by defining a partial order for the execution of the task's runnables. The task uses all available cores for the execution and they are scheduled like in the original configuration for the single-core. Supertasks further consider the original single-core scheduling to merge consecutively executed tasks before they are parallelized. A hyperperiod schedule is composed from the separately parallelized tasks, which is further explained in chapter 6.

### 4.2.1.2 Non-functional Objectives

*Predictable interprocessor communication* — RunPar achieves a predictable interprocessor communication by defining a LET window for the execution of a runnable. The start and finish time of these intervals is derived from the RDG and the runnable's WCET. Thus, runnables can use the same communication mechanism as before. Executing tasks in the same order as in the single-core ECU results in the same data-flow on the multicore ECU.

*Robustness* — Runnable-level parallelization with RunPar or Supertasks does not increase the end-to-end latency of sensor/actuator data-flows in the application. The reason for this is the parallelization reduces the WCET of a task, but the activation and scheduling are identical to the execution on the single-core ECU. Thus, the worst-case latency is less than or equal than in the original system.

*Data consistency* — Considering precedence constraints between runnables prevents simultaneous access to the same memory location. The access to shared memory locations always takes places in the same order, because tasks are executed in the same order and the runnables within the task are executed with the same predefined schedule. Thus, also lost updates are impossible with this approach.

*Efficiency* — RunPar reduces the overall processing time by distributing runnables of a task to cores. RunPar can use any bin-packing heuristic or priority rule. This imposes the following research question:

⋄ *Which bin-packing heuristic and priority rule provide the highest degree of parallelism for automotive control software, if the application contains many data dependencies?*

Furthermore, a Supertask is a promising solution for filling idle intervals between consecutively scheduled tasks. The WCET of a Supertask is shorter than a separately parallelized task set. However, many data dependencies are a typical characteristic of automotive software. They limit the possibilities for parallel execution. Hence, this leads to the following research question:

⋄ *Can Supertasks further reduce the WCET of consecutively scheduled tasks in automotive control software, if the application contains many data dependencies?*

Nevertheless, data dependencies limit the achievable degree of parallelism and this imposes the question:

⋄ *How many cores can be utilized with parallelized automotive control software, if the application contains many data dependencies?*

The runtime overhead with RunPar is low. Either the AUTOSAR OS directly handles synchronization, when schedule tables are used, or tasks use an efficient synchronization operation, like the `advance`-instruction.

*Scalability* — Partitioned scheduling is an NP-complete problem [GJ90] and thus finding an optimal schedule in reasonable time is hard. Therefore, deriving a solution with a heuristic like RunPar is a typical way to address this challenge. To proof the practicability of RunPar and Supertasks, experiments should be conducted with an application that has the properties of a real automotive control application.

*Low cost* — The robustness of RunPar is in favour of the cost for migrating the application, because the end-to-end latency has potentially a value that is equal to or smaller than in the former sequential execution. Hence, no re-validation of the functional correctness is necessary.

*Compliance, portability, minimal standard modification* — The main advantage of the proposed approach for task-level parallelization is its compliance with AUTOSAR. The generated solution can easily be implemented with schedule tables or with a *time-triggered architecture (TTA)* and both, RunPar and Supertasks, can be used with any AUTOSAR compliant application. However, simple but not mandatory extensions of the AUTOSAR standard would ease the integration.

*Summary of non-functional objectives* — RunPar constructs a predictable and robust parallel program, in which data consistency is guaranteed. The runtime overhead is low and a re-validation is unnecessary. RunPar is compliant to AUTOSAR although optional extensions of the standard would guarantee the same behaviour on any target platform after porting. However, the discussion of non-functional objectives could not assess efficiency of the approach. An ideal configuration and the maximal achievable parallelism, under many data dependencies, need to be investigated quantitatively. Consequently, experiments are conducted in the next two sections to find an ideal configuration for RunPar and to investigate improvements with Supertasks.

The *speed-up* quantifies how much faster the parallel execution finished. It is used as metric for the performance evaluation and defined in the following.

**Definition 4.8 (Speed-up):** *Let $G_i$ be a RDG for a task $\tau_i$ in the AUTOSAR application $\mathcal{A}$ (definition 4.2). Let $\Phi_i = (\varphi_1, \dots, \varphi_m)$ be a static partitioning for $\tau_i$ (definition 4.3). Let $C_i$ be the WCET of $\tau_i$ and let $C_i^{\Phi}$ be the WCET of $\tau_i$ according to $\Phi_i$. The speed-up from parallelization of task $\tau_i$ is*

$$\frac{C_i}{C_i^{\Phi}} \qquad (4.13)$$

An investigation of the impact on the minimal processor's clock rate is not conducted at this point, because a schedule for a hyperperiod is needed for this. The construction of such a schedule requires further mechanisms that are described and investigated in chapter 6.

## 4.2.2 RunPar

As preparation for the evaluation of Supertasks, this section first looks for an ideal bin-packing heuristic and priority rule for RunPar. The experiments are conducted with the diesel EMS use case described in section 2.1.3, because the application contains numerous runnables, which frequently communicate with each other (also via inter-task communication). The analysis tool described in section 2.4.1 is used to identify the data dependencies between runnables. Based on this, the RDGs are constructed for each task as described in section 4.1.2. The WCET for each runnable is statically derived with OTAWA (section 2.4.3). The necessary static analysis of the use case for this has been conducted in the context of Becerril-Sandoval's Master's thesis [Bec14].

An exemplary RDG is shown in figure 4.8 for $\tau_{10}$, which is executed every 96 milliseconds. The task is composed of 23 runnables (white coloured nodes) and constraint by 24 precedence constraints (solid edges). Dashed edges denote control flow with the start node ($v_s$) and the finish node ($v_t$). This example illustrates the complexity of a real application and the limitations imposed by data dependencies well.

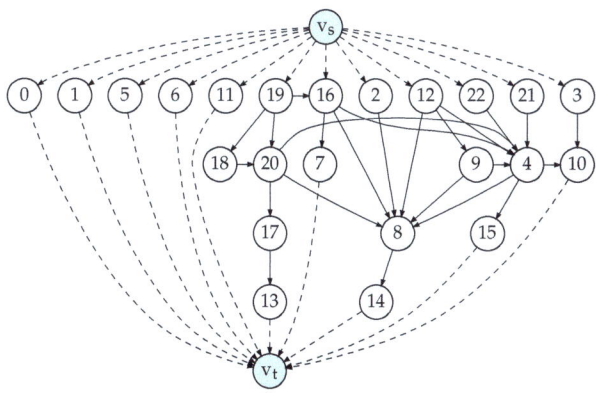

Figure 4.8: The RDG for the $\tau_{10}$ ($T_{10} = 96$ ms).

The RDG properties of the complete application are listed in table 4.1. The number of runnables and precedence constraints varies widely. Particularly interesting are the tasks $\tau_1$, $\tau_5$, and $\tau_6$.

The task $\tau_1$ is activated by a sensor at the camshaft of the engine and takes places several times per revolution. The sensor also reads the current position (in degrees of a complete engine stroke), with the consequence that the number of processed runnables varies with the position. In the worst-case 69 runnables are processed.

The only task without precedence constraints is $\tau_4$, because it consists of one runnable only. Hence, runnable-level parallelization only improves the performance when $\tau_4$ is combined with other tasks into a Supertask.

The largest task in the use case is $\tau_6$. The task contains 254 runnables, which are constraint by 1350 precedence constraints.

### 4.2.2.1 Experiment Configuration

Each task from table 4.1 is separately parallelized with RunPar. For the crank-angle task, the largest possible case (for WCET) is parallelized. Table 4.2 lists the two target platform configurations that are used for the evaluation.

| Task | $\tau_1$ | $\tau_2$ | $\tau_3$ | $\tau_4$ | $\tau_5$ | $\tau_6$ |
|---|---|---|---|---|---|---|
| No. Runnables | 69* | 21 | 36 | 1 | 80 | 254 |
| No. precedence constraints | 181* | 8 | 90 | 0 | 102 | 1350 |
| **Task** | $\tau_7$ | $\tau_8$ | $\tau_9$ | $\tau_{10}$ | $\tau_{11}$ | $\tau_{12}$ |
| No. Runnables | 44 | 31 | 23 | 23 | 47 | 9 |
| No. precedence constraints | 62 | 97 | 23 | 24 | 209 | 1 |

Table 4.1: Properties of the RDG for each task from the use case (section 2.1.3).

| Parameter | Proc$_2$ | Proc$_4$ |
|---|---|---|
| Cores | 2 | 4 |
| Data cache size | 256 KB | |
| Cache latency | 1 cycles | |
| lat$_{tree}$ | 1 cycles | 2 cycles |
| lat$_{mem}$ | 10 cycles | 10 cycles |
| UBD (equation (2.16) page 32) | 11 cycles | 32 cycles |

Table 4.2: Processor setup for the evaluation of RunPar and Supertasks.

The setup considers lat$_{tree}$ = 1 cycles for the two-core processor and lat$_{tree}$ = 2 for a four-core processor, i.e. a message traverses one and two routers, respectively. The memory latency is lat$_{mem}$ = 10 cycles. This configuration provides an *upper bound delay (UBD)*= 11 cycles for the two-core and UBD= 32 cycles for the four-core processor.

RunPar computes a valid allocation $\Phi_i$ using the priority rule Prio, the bin-packing heuristic $H^D$ for dependent runnables and $H^I$ for independent runnables. To find an ideal configuration for RunPar, the tasks listed in table 4.1 are parallelized with the setups defined in table 4.3. RunPar is executed with worst-fit and first-fit bin-packing heuristics, in combination with utilization and combined utilization as priority rule. Best-fit and next-fit are variants of the worst-fit and first-fit, which would produce similar results. Thus, they are not considered here. Setups 1 to 4 apply the same heuristic to dependent and independent runnables, whereas setups 5 to 8 apply different heuristics.

#### 4.2.2.2 Expectations

Intuitively, the combined utilization seems to be a good choice, because the critical path is considered implicitly. For the bin-packing, a worst-fit decreasing seems to be an intuitively good choice, because always the least loaded core is selected. Thus, the expectation is that configurations with combined utilization as priority rule and worst-fit as bin-packing heuristic perform best.

| Param. | $S_1$ | $S_2$ | $S_3$ | $S_4$ |
|--------|-------|-------|-------|-------|
| $H^D$ | first-fit | worst-fit | first-fit | worst-fit |
| $H^I$ | first-fit | worst-fit | first-fit | worst-fit |
| Prio | utilization | utilization | combined utilization | combined utilization |
| Param. | $S_5$ | $S_6$ | $S_7$ | $S_8$ |
| $H^D$ | first-fit | worst-fit | first-fit | worst-fit |
| $H^I$ | worst-fit | first-fit | worst-fit | first-fit |
| Prio | utilization | utilization | combined utilization | combined utilization |

Table 4.3: Investigated heuristics and priority rules.

### 4.2.2.3 Results

Figure 4.9 shows the average and maximum WCET speed-up for the setups in table 4.3. As expected, the setups that allocate dependent runnables with worst-fit ($S_2, S_4, S_6, S_8$) provide a higher average speed-up than first-fit. Hence, worst-fit is the superior allocation strategy for this application and this matches with the expectations.

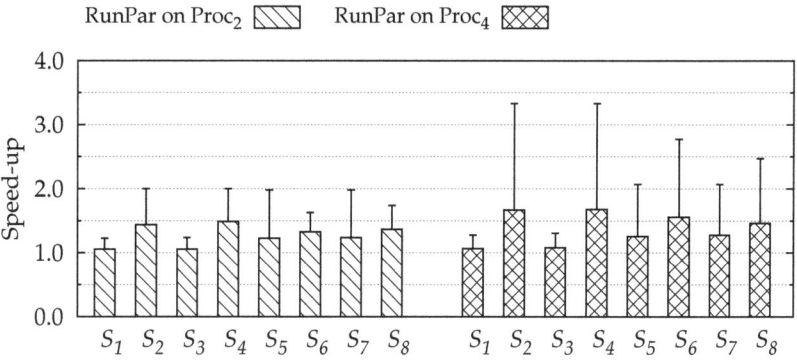

Figure 4.9: Average and maximum speed-up of RunPar for setups 1 to 8 on two cores (left) and four cores (right).

Surprisingly, using the combined utilization as priority rule only provides a small improvement over the utilization in the average case only. This observation is unexpected, because the combined utilization indirectly considers the critical path and thus seems to be the superior rule. However, RunPar considers precedence constraints and hence combined utilization and utilization deliver similar results. Thus, they are equivalent priority rules. However, our findings confirm $S_4$ as best choice for the EMS, due to its slightly better average performance ($S_2$ vs. $S_4$). Therefore, detailed results are presented for $S_4$ and this configuration is used for all future experiments.

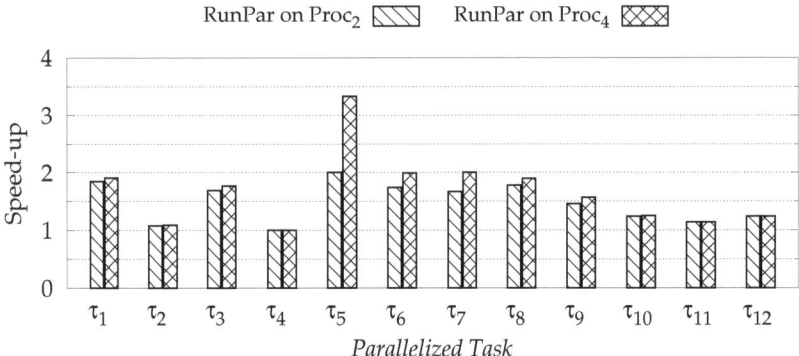

Figure 4.10: Speed-up of RunPar for setup 4 on two cores and four cores in comparison.

Figure 4.9 already illustrated that the benefit of four cores over two cores is only small. To investigate this in more detail, figure 4.10 shows the speed-up per task with the best setup (4) on tow cores and four cores in direct comparison. $\tau_5$ profits from the additional cores and the speed-up increases from 2.0 times faster to 3.3 times faster execution, but the benefit in all other cases is comparably small. $\tau_6$ contains a high number of runnables. This indicates that the large amount of precedence constraints limits the parallelism and this motivates for the concept of a Supertask. However, the expected advantages need to be validated by experiments in the next section.

### 4.2.3  Comparison with Supertask

This section investigates the impact of data dependencies on the exploitation of idle intervals with Supertasks. Inter-task communication must be respected as precedence constraints when tasks are merged. This might again cause serialization such that no benefit is taken from the Supertask structure. Therefore, a comparison between separate parallelization of tasks and parallelization with Supertasks is conducted.

All possible Supertasks (23) that can occur at runtime in the original application's configuration of the use case are listed in table 4.4, including the number of tasks composing them. The tasks are, in a first step, combined in a Supertask and afterwards parallelized with the ideal configuration of RunPar. That is, a worst-fit bin-packing heuristic is used to allocate dependent and independent runnables. The runnables are processed depending on their combined utilization.

| Nr. | Supertask | Nr. Tasks | Nr. | Supertask | Nr. Tasks |
|-----|-----------|-----------|-----|-----------|-----------|
| 1 | $T_{2.3}$ | 2 | 13 | $T_{2.3.5.6.8.9.10}$ | 7 |
| 2 | $T_{2.4}$ | 2 | 14 | $T_{2.3.7.4.5.6.8.9}$ | 8 |
| 3 | $T_{2.3.5}$ | 3 | 15 | $T_{2.3.7.4.5.6.8.10}$ | 8 |
| 4 | $T_{2.3.7.4}$ | 4 | 16 | $T_{2.3.5.6.8.9.11.12}$ | 8 |
| 5 | $T_{2.3.5.6}$ | 4 | 17 | $T_{2.3.5.6.8.9.10.11}$ | 8 |
| 6 | $T_{2.3.7.4.5}$ | 5 | 18 | $T_{2.3.7.4.5.6.8.9.11}$ | 9 |
| 7 | $T_{2.3.5.6.8}$ | 5 | 19 | $T_{2.3.7.4.5.6.8.9.10}$ | 9 |
| 8 | $T_{2.3.7.4.5.6}$ | 6 | 20 | $T_{2.3.5.6.8.9.10.11.12}$ | 9 |
| 9 | $T_{2.3.5.6.8.9}$ | 6 | 21 | $T_{2.3.7.4.5.6.8.9.11.12}$ | 10 |
| 10 | $T_{2.3.5.6.8.10}$ | 6 | 22 | $T_{2.3.7.4.5.6.8.9.10.11}$ | 10 |
| 11 | $T_{2.3.7.4.5.6.8}$ | 7 | 23 | $T_{2.3.7.4.5.6.8.9.10.11.12}$ | 11 |
| 12 | $T_{2.3.5.6.8.9.11}$ | 7 | | | |

Table 4.4: Investigated Supertasks.

#### 4.2.3.1 Expectations

The Supertask combines runnables from consecutively scheduled tasks and this makes it possible to execute a runnable earlier, if no precedence constraint exists in the RDG. Hence, the combination of tasks provides more scheduling possibilities than in the separate parallelization case (for example, $\tau_4$ has always the same execution time, because it contains only one runnable). Thus, the expectation is that Supertasks benefit from additional cores. That means four cores should provide a better performance than tow cores. The higher the improvement with Supertasks is the smaller is the impact of inter-task data dependencies.

#### 4.2.3.2 Results

Figure 4.11 shows the speed-up with processor $Proc_2$ (table 4.2) and setup $S_4$ (table 4.3). The x-axis denotes the Supertask and number of combined tasks increases from the left to the right side. As expected, the results show an equal or better scalability for Supertasks over the separate task parallelization in any case. The improvement from task interleaving ranges between 5% and 35%. The minimum speed-ups are a 1.15 times faster and a 1.13 times faster execution with Supertask 2, which contains a task having only one runnable ($\tau_4$).

The maximum speed-up with separate parallelization is a 1.7 times faster execution. This value increases with Supertasks to a 2.0 times faster execution, which means an efficiency of 100%. The over maximum speed-ups are a 1.85 times faster and a 2.65

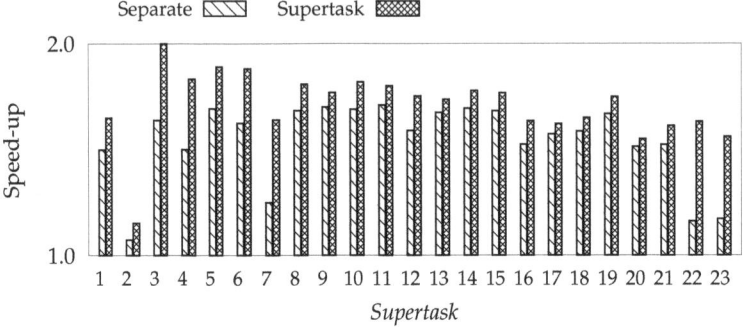

Figure 4.11: Speed-up on two cores.

times faster execution of Supertask 10, which also provides the highest improvement (46%) when the number of cores changes from two to four. The average speed-up improved from a 1.56 times faster to a 1.71 times faster execution with Supertask.

The same experiment is conducted for the processor $Proc_4$. Figure 4.12 shows the results of the experiment. Similar to the two-core processor case, Supertasks obtain a better scalability than separate task parallelization in all cases. The improvement ranges between 5% and 43%. The maximum speed-up with separate parallelization is a 1.95 times faster execution and the value increases with Supertasks to a 2.66 times faster execution, which means an efficiency of 66%. The average speed-up improved from a 1.72 times faster to 1.98 times faster execution with Supertasks.

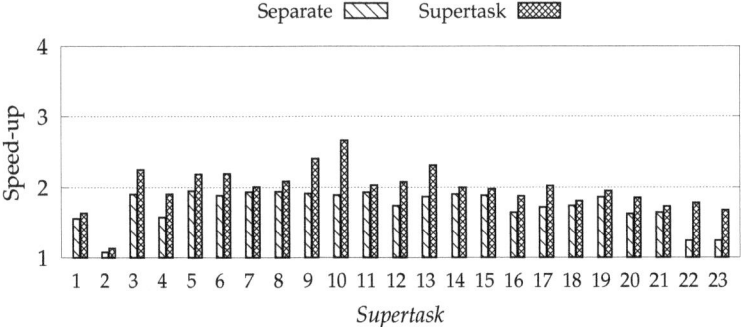

Figure 4.12: Speed-up on four cores.

These results show that Supertasks can utilize idle intervals between consecutively scheduled tasks and they utilize four cores better. Increasing the number of cores results in significantly better performance than with separate parallelization. Especially, a large amount of runnables (Supertasks 22 and 23) profit from merging tasks. The average speed-up increases from a 1.7 times faster execution on two cores to a 1.98 times faster execution on four cores.

However, the high number of precedence constraints between the runnables prevents the Supertask from taking benefit from more than two cores. The average improvement between two and four cores is only 15%. This indicated that a large amount of data dependencies forces serialization within the Supertasks and the ideal number of cores for applications like the EMS use case is two.

## 4.2.4  Discussion of Research Questions

Due to the evaluation of RunPar and Supertasks, it is possible to answer the related research questions from the qualitative discussion in section 4.2.1.

> ◇ *Which bin-packing heuristic and priority rule provide the highest degree of parallelism for automotive control software, if the application contains many data dependencies?*

An initial set of experiment showed that the *combined utilization* as priority rule and a *worst-fit decreasing* heuristic provide the highest degree of parallelism. Unexpectedly, using the utilization provided similar results, with the consequence that they are seen as equivalent priority rules. That mean, the priority rule influences the parallelism marginal, if numerous precedence constraints must be respected.

> ◇ *Can Supertasks further reduce the WCET of consecutively scheduled tasks in automotive control software, if the application contains many data dependencies?*

Supertasks are found to provide better performance than separate task parallelization. The average speed-up improves from a 1.56 times faster to a 1.71 times faster execution on two cores and from a 1.72 times faster to a 1.98 times faster execution on four cores, respectively. That mean, it is possible to fill the idle intervals between consecutively scheduled tasks, although inter-task data dependencies exist. However, the highest achieved speed-up with Supertasks is a 2.66 times faster execution on four cores. The results give an indication about the third research question.

> ◇ *How many cores can be utilized with parallelized automotive control software, if the application contains many data dependencies?*

The efficiency on two cores is high: 77% and 85% with separate and Supertask parallelization (derived from figure 4.11), respectively. In contrast, the efficiency decreases on four cores down to 43% and 49% for separate and Supertask parallelization (derived from figure 4.12), respectively. Thus, runnable-level parallelization is ideal for a few cores, if the application contains many data dependencies.

## 4.3   Summary of Runnable-level Parallelization

This chapter introduced two runnable-level parallelization strategies for automotive control software, whose objective is to maintain the same application configuration to avoid application re-validation. Runnables (and not tasks) are considered as the UoS. The original application's configuration is used to derive precedence constraints within the task. The concept of Supertasks is introduced to increase the level of parallelism already achieved by RunPar. Therefore, consecutively executed tasks are grouped and executed with a period equal to the least common multiple of tasks composing it. Hence, idle intervals between parallelized tasks are utilized and the validation effort after the migration is drastically reduced.

A static schedule for the execution of runnables is derived for each Supertask with the partitioned scheduler *RunPar*. RunPar uses a bin-packing heuristic and a priority rule to assign the longest chain of dependent runnables first. RunPar constructs a predictable and robust parallel program, in which data consistency is guaranteed. The runtime overhead is low and a re-validation is unnecessary. A minimal implementation of RunPar and Supertasks is proposed considering also the implications of interrupt handling. The implementation only requires minimal modifications at operating system level and sporadic tasks are supported. The parallel static schedule is efficiently implemented with the concept of LETs, either directly by the AUTOSAR OS or with an efficient synchronization operation.

The performance evaluation in this chapter was conducted to investigate the efficiency, scalability, and practicability of the runnable-level parallelization with RunPar and Supertasks. Therefore, a complex diesel EMS with several hundred runnables and thousands of data dependencies is used. RunPar was evaluated to find an ideal configuration. Here, the combined utilization in combination with a worst-fit decreasing heuristic provided the best results. The evaluation of the Supertask concept showed that four cores are better utilized than with a separate parallelization of tasks. However, these results show that a high number of data dependencies prevent the efficient parallelization with more than two cores.

Consequently, these results motivate for investigating the inter-task communication further and search for ways to reduce their impact. Thus, the next chapter proposes a method that relaxes inter-task data dependencies and executes complete tasks in a parallel way, whereas a deterministic and predictable data-flow is ensured.

The way how sporadic tasks are scheduled imposes the question, if this could lead to a significant performance degradation. Although, the frequency of sporadic tasks can be high, but the WCET of the sporadic task is comparably small. The use of multiple cores can shorten this time. Thus, the investigation of systems with high system load from sporadic tasks remains as a possible future work.

# 5 | Task-level Parallelization

"The true rule is, *don't communicate*
except when you have to."

_____

Michael Resch, 2009

This chapter introduces a strategy for task-level parallelization for automotive control software. The analysis of interprocessor communication mechanisms in section 3.3 showed that *AUTomotive Open System ARchitecture (AUTOSAR)* does not enforce a predictable and reproducible communication when tasks are executed in a parallel way.

However, determinism can be achieved with other mechanisms by decoupling computation from communication, for example based on a synchronized clock (a *time-triggered architecture (TTA)* [KB03] with *logical execution time (LET)* [KS12]). Using this concept for task-level parallelization of automotive control software requires a relaxation of inter-task data dependencies for a complete task period. Otherwise, tasks still must execute in a serial way. Temporal variables or lazy reading can be used for this, if their usage is coordinated in such a manner that a predictable and reproducible data-flow is created.

Further analysis of existing mapping and scheduling approaches in section 3.2 showed that none of the existing approach uses lazy reads or temporal variables to migrate an AUTOSAR application to a multicore *electronic control unit (ECU)*. The main deficit of existing task-level parallelization is the lack of a mechanism that guarantees a predictable communication with the consequence that tasks can be scheduled freely within their period.

Therefore, this chapter introduces *timed implicit communication (TIC)* [Keh+15] that decouples dependent tasks and allows parallel execution of producer and consumer tasks. The same data-flow is guaranteed on all multicore ECUs. This is realized by applying AUTOSAR implicit communication at task-level and shifting the reception of data by one producer period (and bound to the task period). That means the producer task stores data in a buffer and attaches a publication timestamp, which is the end of the current producer period. Afterwards, the consumer task reads from the previous producer instance as compared to the single-core ECU execution by selecting a value with the appropriate timestamp from the buffer. Deriving the communication period from the original application's configuration for the single-core ECU reduces the validation effort. This guarantees the same communication pattern regardless of the employed multicore task scheduling.

The first part of this chapter describes the approach for task-level parallelization in more detail and the second part evaluates it.

# 5.1 Timed Implicit Communication

The task-level parallelization with TIC is carried out as follows:

1) *Extraction of periodic extended precedence constraints* — The inter-task data-flow is derived from the original application's configuration for the single-core and described as repetitive pattern. This is explained in section 5.1.2.

2) *Multicore scheduling* — A feasible schedule for the multicore ECU is defined. TIC makes it possible to treat task instances that communicate via TIC as if they were independent. This step is therefore not explained further. Possible scheduling policies are described in [DB11].

3) *Transformation of communication and definition of timestamps* — Implicit communication between a *sporadic* task and a *periodic* task does not require any change, because it is generally unknown when the communication takes place (section 3.3.1). Instead, the purpose of using explicit communication here is to guarantee data consistency (prevent data corruption by another task). As a result, implicit communication, as replacement, decouples these tasks.

    Changing the communication from explicit to implicit works well in this case and produces the same valid data-flow as in the execution on the single-core ECU. However, this approach is insufficient when both tasks are periodic. Hence, TIC replaces all implicit and explicit communication *between periodic tasks*. A *publication timestamp* is attached to each produced datum and the receiver gets the appropriate date assigned in such a manner that it reads from the previous producer instance. Section 5.1.3 explains how the data-flow for TIC is determined.

4) *Implementation* — TIC is integrated in the AUTOSAR *run-time environment (RTE)* to be transparent for the application, but it requires storing produced data in a buffer to avoid overwriting. The size of the buffer is limited (the details are discussed in section 5.1.4).

The next section first introduces the notations and the problem formulation for this chapter. The steps from the list above are explained in more detail afterwards.

## 5.1.1 Assumptions and Notations

It is necessary to make fundamental assumptions about the legacy application $\mathcal{A}$ (definition 4.2) to apply TIC. The method only applies to applications for which a feasible schedule (constraint 5.1) exists.

**Constraint 5.1 (Schedule feasibility):** *Let* $\mathcal{A} = \{\tau_i \mid 1 \leq i \leq n, i \in \mathbb{N}\}$ *be a legacy AUTOSAR application according to definition 4.2. A schedule for the application is called feasible, iff*

$$\forall \tau_i^p : \quad o_i^p \leq \mathrm{st}_i^p < \mathrm{ft}_i^p \leq d_i^p, \quad p = 0, \ldots, \infty \tag{5.1}$$

Furthermore, the following assumptions are made.

1) Precedence constraints between tasks can be described as a repetitive pattern according to definition 2.5. This assumption serves as a guarantee for that every data-flow between a sensor and an actuator appeared in the same way in the original single-core ECU.

2) During execution on the single-core ECU input data of a task remained unchanged. This assumption excludes all system configurations that allow higher priority tasks to preempt a running task and update one or more data that are shared by the tasks. The preempted task would continue its calculations on partly updated data otherwise and the data-flow would be unpredictable and not reproducible on the multicore ECU. This assumption does not apply to communication with a sporadic task.

3) The kind of inter-task communication (explicit or implicit) is known. The migration of explicit communication requires an additional step during the implementation. Hence, it is necessary to know the kind of communication in advance.

These assumptions are realistic and they cover a large fraction of automotive software.

### 5.1.1.1 Valid Behaviour with Lazy Reading

To understand when older input values produce valid behaviour, a typical single-core communication pattern is discussed. Figure 5.1a shows a typical preemptive schedule on a single core processor. This configuration has two tasks, which communicate with each other. $\tau_1$ executed with a period of 1 ms and $\tau_2$ executes with a period of 2 ms. The *worst-case execution time (WCET)* of $\tau_1$ is $1/3$ ms and the WCET of $\tau_2$ is 1 ms. In a *rate monotonic (RM)* preemptive every execution of $\tau_2$ is interrupted by the execution of $\tau_1$.

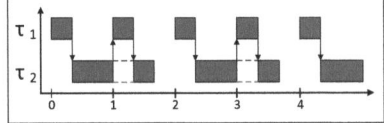 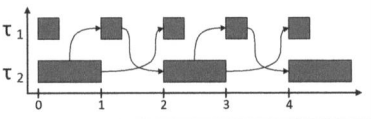

(a) Single-core scheduling example.        (b) Scheduling example with lazy reads.

Figure 5.1: Preemption of $\tau_2$ by the higher prioritised task $\tau_1$ (left) and with lazy reads (right).

The preemption lets both tasks partly work on new and less up-to-date values. $\tau_1$ receives at $t = 3$ new data for all variables that are already updated by the execution of $\tau_2$ and the remaining data are received from the previous execution of $\tau_2$ (finished at $t = 1^2/3$). In the opposite direction, the first part of $\tau_2$ works on the previous input data and the second part of the task works on newer input data. As a result, one can conclude that tasks do not necessarily depend on updated input values of the current computation iteration. A previous (older) input may also produce a valid output and does not lead to a fault behaviour. In other words, it is valid to assume that tasks of automotive software are to some extent robust against less up-to-date input data or delay in the communication. For example, a task polling a temperature sensor does not require the latest value.

Figure 5.1b shows the example from figure 5.1a with lazy reads or temporal variables, where the tolerance window is 2ms and 1ms for $\tau_1$ and $\tau_2$, respectively. Both task can execute in a parallel way, because no data-flow with the concurrently executed task exists any more. Moreover, both tasks receive a consistent set of input data from the other task.

### 5.1.1.2   End-to-end Latency of a Data-flow Path

The target in this chapter is the parallel execution of tasks. This is achieved by a transformation of the data-flow, determined by the periodic extended precedence constraints between them. This can affect the end-to-end latency of critical sensor/actuator chains. The focus here is on the *first-in-last-out (FILO)* latency, described in section 2.3.2, because it represents an upper bound on the reaction time of the controller.

The model for end-to-end path, introduced in section 2.3.2.2, is general and covers arbitrary granularities. Thus, the formalization of a *timed path (TP)* (equation (2.13) on page 30) is adapted to the purpose of this chapter, which is the covered path through task instances from the sensor to the actuator. Thus, a data-flow path through task instances simply represents a TP and is defined as follows.

**Definition 5.1 (Data-flow Path):** *Let $M_{i,j}$ be periodic extended precedence constraints according to definition 2.5. For any $k \in \mathbb{N}$, a data-flow path from $\tau_i$ to $\tau_j$ is a sequence of task instances*

$$P_{i,j} = \tau_{l_0}^{n_0} \tau_{l_1}^{n_1} \ldots \tau_{l_k}^{n_k} \tag{5.2}$$

*, such that $\forall q \in [0, k]$:*

$$(n^{q-1}, n^q) \in M_{l_{q-1}, l_q} \quad \wedge \quad \tau_{l_0}^{n_0} = \tau_i^n \quad \wedge \quad \tau_{l_k}^{n_k} = \tau_j^{n'} \tag{5.3}$$

A single path $\kappa \in \mathrm{TP}_r^{\mathrm{FILO}}$ is from now on represented as a data-flow path through the task instances that $\kappa$ traverses:

$$\hat{P}_{i,j} = \tau_{l_0}^{n_0} \ldots \tau_{l_k}^{n_k} = \tau_i^{n_0} \ldots \tau_j^{n_k} \tag{5.4}$$

The task $\tau_i^{n_0}$ denotes the start task and $\tau_j^{n_k}$ denotes the sink task of the data-flow path. The ^ (hat) indicates that $P$ represents the longest possible path; the FILO path. A superscript $s$ denotes the path in a sequential schedule and a superscript $p$ denotes the path in a parallel schedule. The FILO latency ($\mathrm{FILO}_{i,j}$) is calculated from the start of the path in $\tau_{l_0}^{n_0} = \tau_i^{n_0}$, reading sensor input, and the finish time of the last task in the path $\tau_{l_k}^{n_k} = \tau_j^{n_k}$, writing to the actuator:

$$\mathrm{FILO}_{i,j} = \mathrm{ft}_{l_k}^{n_k} - \mathrm{st}_{l_0}^{n_0} = \mathrm{ft}_j^{n_k} - \mathrm{st}_i^{n_0} \tag{5.5}$$

For better illustration, figure 5.2 shows an artificial single-core schedule example.

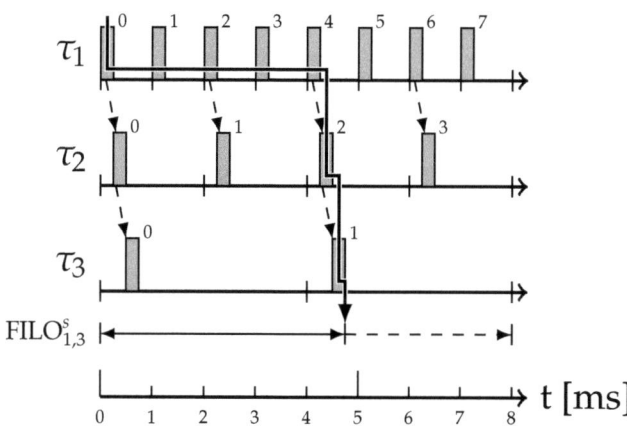

Figure 5.2: $\hat{P}_{1,3}^s$ and $\mathrm{FILO}_{1,3}^s$ on the single-core.

Here, an input datum traverses the task instances in a typical rate monotonic fashion; from the sensor, read in $\tau_1$, to actuator, written in $\tau_5$. The FILO path is taken, if a value change takes place *just after* the sensor read-instruction in $\tau_1^0$. Hence, $\tau_1$ does not process the changed value. The resulting FILO path is

$$\hat{P}_{1,3}^s = \tau_1^0 \, \tau_1^1 \, \tau_1^2 \, \tau_1^3 \, \tau_1^4 \, \tau_2^2 \, \tau_3^1. \tag{5.6}$$

The FILO latency is $\mathrm{FILO}_{1,3}^s = \mathrm{ft}_3^1 - \mathrm{st}_1^0 = T_3 + C_1 + C_1 + C_3$ in this example.

## 5.1.2   Extraction of Extended Precedence Constraints

The inter-task data dependencies are derived in a similar way like for the runnable-level parallelization described in section 4.1.2. The main difference here is that the runnable-to-task mapping remains unchanged during the migration with TIC and this guarantees a correct data-flow within a task. That means it is enough to derive only inter-task data dependencies at this point. The analysis in section 2.3 concluded that dependencies between periodic tasks with different release times are ideally represented as a repetitive pattern. Formally, the extended periodic precedencies in definition 2.5 can be used for this purpose. As proposed in section 2.3, task priorities of the original application's configuration for the single-core are used to derive inter-task data dependencies, because this configuration is known to lead to correct functional behaviour.

Figure 2.2 provides a simplified representation of the inter-task communication for the diesel *engine management system (EMS)* use case used to evaluate the parallelization concepts in this thesis. The task $\tau_1$ in this figure executes after an interrupt from the camshaft sensor (the *crank-angle task*). The tasks $\tau_2$ to $\tau_{12}$ execute with the period denoted by the label close to the node, e.g. task $\tau_2$ has a period of one millisecond. An arrow represents communication between the tasks, which is imposed by the runnables mapped to this task. Thus, communication takes place with different frequencies, but with a repetitive pattern that defines the *extended precedencies*. This use case illustrates the high degree of connectivity between tasks in a real application and this motivates for the decoupling inter-task communication with TIC to improve parallelism.

The number of inter-task data dependencies has a direct impact on the schedulability of an application, because more dependencies reduce the possibilities for parallel execution. Consequently, the objective of TIC is a reduction of inter-task data dependencies for allowing tasks to be scheduled earlier. Thus, they finish earlier and this improves the performance. However, communication cannot be neglected completely as a complete data-flow path from the sensor(s) to the actuator(s) must be established. Instead, the extended periodic precedence constraints are transformed.

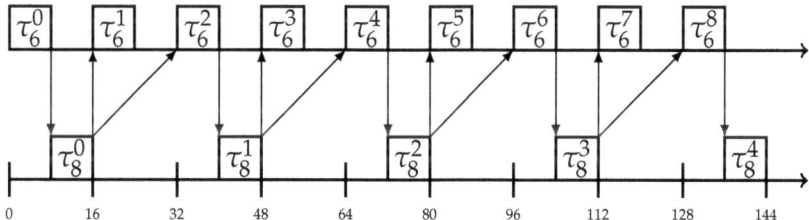

Figure 5.3: Task schedule on the single-core ECU between $\tau_6$ and $\tau_8$.

The transformation with TIC is illustrated with the example in figure 5.3, which is limited to two tasks to maintain readability. In this figure $\tau_6$ (with a period of 16 milliseconds) and $\tau_8$ (with a period of 32 milliseconds) communicate in a bidirectional way. In this configuration $O_6 = O_8 = 0$ and $\tau_6$ has a higher priority in this configuration, because its period is shorter and the resulting extended periodic precedence constraints are:

$$M_{6,8} = \{(0,0)\} \quad \text{and} \quad M_{8,6} = \{(0,1),(0,2)\} \tag{5.7}$$

It must be assumed that the developer's intention with a particular application configuration for the single-core ECU was to define a correct functioning system. That means the extended periodic precedencies of the single-core ECU provide a suitable basis to define the data-flow on the multicore ECU. Furthermore, the assumption is that reading data from an earlier producer instance does not cause harm due to the robustness of automotive software as stated in section 5.1.1.1.


### 5.1.3  Transformation of Communication

Let $\tau_i^n$ and $\tau_j^{n'}$ be periodic tasks with the same release time (but different release periods) and $\tau_i^n \to \tau_j^{n'}$. The task $\tau_i^n$ does not publish produced data until the end of its current period:

$$d_i^n = O_i + (n+1)T_i \tag{5.8}$$

As a result, the receiver task $\tau_j^{n'}$ cannot read data produced by $\tau_i^n$ before $d_i^n$. But, $\tau_j^{n'}$ can read data from the previous instance of $\tau_i^{n-1}$ and therefore execute in a parallel way to $\tau_i^n$.

The motivation for considering task periods is that this characteristic is the same for all platforms. Thus, the data-flow paths are identical on all multicore ECUs. To determine a data-flow path on the multicore ECU in more general terms, it is enough to specify the extended precedencies. Therefore, shifting the reception of data transforms the precedence constraints from the single-core ECU by one producer period:

**Definition 5.2 (Transformed Extended Precedence Constraints):** *Let $M_{i,j}$ be the extended precedencies from the single-core ECU (definition 2.4). The transformed extended precedencies on the multicore ECU $M_{i,j}^{MC}$ are defined as:*

$$M_{i,j}^{MC} = \left\{ (n^*, n') \middle| \begin{array}{l} \exists n : (n, n') \in M_{i,j} \quad \wedge \\ n^* = \max(n \in \mathcal{I}_{p_{i,j}} | d_i^n \leq o_j^{n'}) \end{array} \right\} \tag{5.9}$$

The transformed extended precedencies have the same hyperperiod (the least common multiple of all task periods) as the precedence constraints on the single-core ECU. Hence, the periodic extended precedencies $M_{i,j}^{\prime MC}$ can be derived analogous to definition 2.5 in section 2.3. That means the consumer task instance reads from the latest producer period that ends before the release of the consumer task instance. For all $(n, n') \in M_{i,j}^{\prime MC}$ a publication time $d_i^n$ for $\tau_i^n$ and a read time $o_j^{n'}$ is used for $\tau_j^{n'}$. This guarantees that tasks always consume input data at the beginning of a new period.

### 5.1.3.1    Example for TIC

For illustration purpose, equation (5.9) is applied to the example in figure 5.3 with the extended precedencies defined in equation (5.7) for the single-core ECU. $\tau_6$ publishes data every 16 ms with TIC on the multicore ECU. The data elements are redirected to a buffer with timestamps $d_6^0 = 16$ ms for $\tau_6^0$, $d_6^1 = 32$ ms for $\tau_6^0$ and $\tau_6^1$, respectively. $\tau_8^1$ has a release time of $o_8^1 = 32$ ms and hence data cannot be read from $\tau_6^2$ earlier than $t = 48$ ms. Instead, $\tau_8^1$ reads the data from the previous instance of $\tau_6^2$:

$$\tau_6^2 \leadsto \tau_8^1 \Rightarrow \tau_6^1 \leadsto \tau_8^1 \tag{5.10}$$

As a result, $\tau_8^1$ and $\tau_6^2$ can execute in a parallel way. The data-flows in the opposite direction are defined accordingly and the periodic extended precedencies of equation (5.7) are transformed to:

$$M_{6,8} = \{(1,1)\} \quad \text{and} \quad M_{8,6} = \{(0,3), (0,4)\} \tag{5.11}$$

The result of the migration is shown in figure 5.4, where the execution on a dual-core processor is illustrated. In this example, all task instances can immediately be executed when they are released, because no data dependency must be respected. Moreover, all task instances can be executed in arbitrary order as long as they finish their execution before their relative deadline. The resulting data-flow is identical in any case.

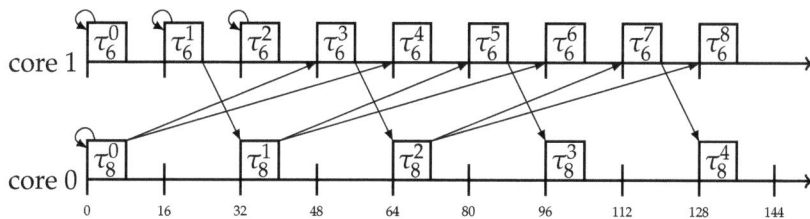

Figure 5.4: Task schedule on the single-core ECU between $\tau_6$ and $\tau_8$.

### 5.1.3.2 Start-up Phase

At application start no data have been produced and a task cannot read buffered data. Thus, the tasks consume a default input value instead. This is indicated by the self-loops at the task instances $\tau_6^0$, $\tau_6^1$, $\tau_6^2$, and $\tau_8^0$. More general, a consumer task instance $\tau_c$ reads a default input value from the producer task $\tau_p$ until:

$$t = \max(O_c + T_c, O_p + T_p) \tag{5.12}$$

For example, for the data-flows $\tau_8 \rightarrow \tau_6$ and $\tau_6 \rightarrow \tau_8$ (in figure 5.4) both tasks read a default value from the buffer for $t \leq 32$. $\tau_6^0$ to $\tau_6^3$ consume the default value, $\tau_6^3$ consumes the value produced by $\tau_8^0$; $\tau_8^0$ reads a default value, and $\tau_8^1$ reads from $\tau_6^1$. This start-up phase applies to all task instance $\tau_i^n$ and $\tau_j^{n'}$ related by precedence constraints

$$(n, n') \in M_{i,j}^{\prime,MC} \tag{5.13}$$

in the range

$$n \leq \frac{\max(O_i + T_i, O_j + T_j)}{T_i} \tag{5.14}$$

for the sender or

$$n' \leq \frac{\max(O_i + T_i, O_j + T_j)}{T_j} \tag{5.15}$$

for the receiver task.

## 5.1.4 Implementation

It is recommended to integrate TIC in the AUTOSAR RTE to avoid changes in the application's source code. The RTE hides the concrete implementation of the communication, but it guarantees a standardised behaviour (see section 2.1 for details). In this case, no further modifications of the application are required, because TIC maintains the data-flow within the RTE. From the application's perspective implicit and explicit communication behave identical to the single-core implementation.

However, within the RTE a mechanism is required to store data with timestamps. A buffering data structure with the following properties satisfies the needs:

1) The read and write access is never blocked (wait-free). This is necessary to prevent tasks from stalling due to simultaneous access to the buffer.

2) The write-operation `write(x, v, p)` stores the value v for the variable x with the publication timestamp p.

3) The read-operation `read(x, r)` returns the value of the variable x with publication timestamp r.

The number of elements in this buffer is a crucial factor for the practicability of TIC. A task produces one new datum per variable and per period. This datum remains in the buffer until all receiver task instances have read it, even if new instances of the producer task were executed.

Let $b_i^n$ denote the time until a datum from the producer task $\tau_i^n$ must be available in the buffer. The receiver tasks of $\tau_i^n$ are determined with the function $\mathrm{rcv}(\tau_i^n)$:

$$\mathrm{rcv}(\tau_i^n) = \{\tau_j \mid (n, n') \in \tau_i \xrightarrow{M_{i,j}} \tau_j\} \tag{5.16}$$

Each datum produced by $\tau_i^n$ must remain available in the buffer until the last receiver task period has finished:

$$b_i^n = \max_{\tau_j^{n'} \in \mathrm{rcv}(\tau_i^n)} (d_j^{n'}) \tag{5.17}$$

Afterwards, the *out-dated* data can be removed or overwritten. At this point, one can take benefit from the predictability of the communication that means the transformed extended precedence constraints, which appear in a repetitive pattern. It is *known in advance* how task instances communicate with each other and thus the buffer usage can be optimized.

For each pair of producer task $\tau_p$ and its associated consumer task $\tau_c$ one can distinguish between the following two cases:

1) $T_p < T_c$: Figure 5.5 illustrates the buffer size for the communication with TIC for the example from figure 5.4, for the case where the producer task has a smaller period than the receiver task. In the worst-case, the buffer stores elements from subsequent invocations until data for all receiver tasks has been produced. A new element is stored, if at least one receiver finishes. Then, an out-dated element is removed or overwritten. But, an additional element is required, because the new element is produced in parallel to the consumer task execution. Thus, the size of the buffer is limited to $|\mathrm{rcv}(\tau_i^n)| + 1$.

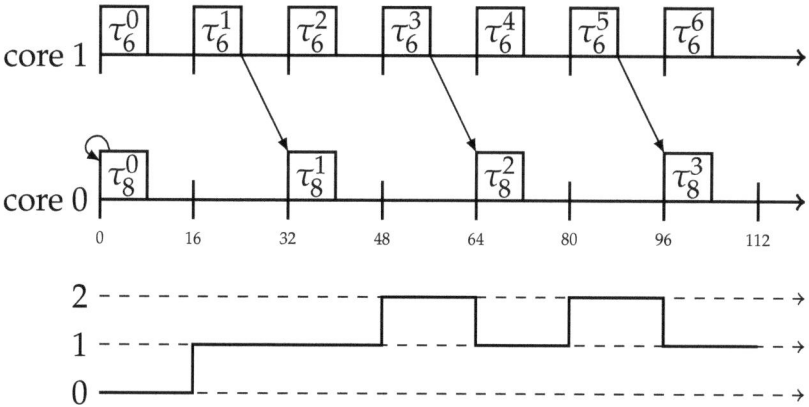

Figure 5.5: The buffer size for the inter-task communication with TIC from $\tau_6$ and $\tau_8$.

2) $T_p > T_c$: Figure 5.6 illustrates the buffer size for the communication with TIC for the example from figure 5.4, for the case where the producer task has a larger period than the receiver task. Two buffer elements are required to hold the values of the previous and the current task instance. Thus, the maximal buffer size is limited to 2 in this case. A third buffer element is required to allow parallel execution of producer and consumer task, when the execution overlaps due to drifting time scales. Such a case appears when the task periods are not whole-numbered multiples of each other, for example between a task with a period of 5 ms and 16 ms (not shown in the figure).

The access time for the buffer varies depending on the implementation and the processor architecture. All buffer accesses can easily be precomputed for a system configuration, in which all task periods are multiples of each other. However, real applications contain odd and even task period and thus overwriteable buffer fields must be identified at runtime of the program. Finding an overwriteable field can be done with binary search [Cor09] with a logarithmic number of comparisons, if the entries are stored in a sorted list. Always appending the latest value to tail of the list can facilitate this.

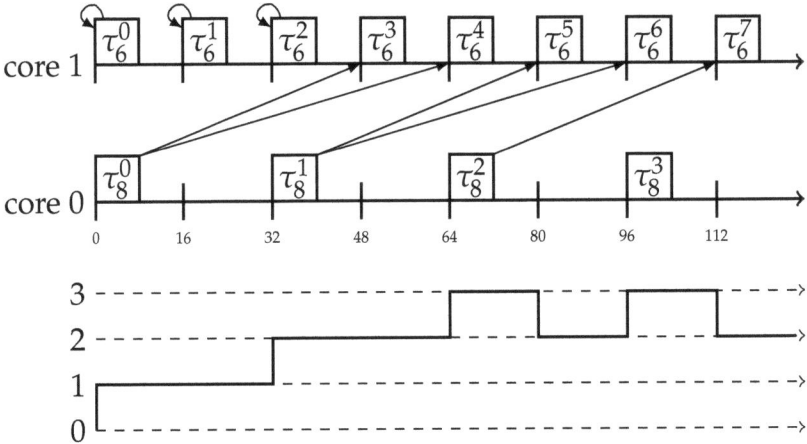

Figure 5.6: The buffer size for the inter-task communication with TIC from $\tau_8$ and $\tau_6$.

Nonetheless, it is no subject of this thesis to optimize the internals of this buffer. Instead, different efficient buffer implementations are considered in the evaluation section. The optimization remains as a future work and is described in more detail in section 7.2.

## 5.2  Evaluation of Task-level Parallelization

This section evaluates TIC in two steps: first, a qualitative analysis is conducted in which the objectives from section 3.1 are discussed. Thereupon, research questions are derived and subsequently investigated in experiments.

### 5.2.1  Qualitative Analysis and Resulting Research Questions

This section discusses TIC in the context of the functional and non-functional objectives defined in section 3.1. Research questions for the quantitative evaluation are derived whenever necessary.

#### 5.2.1.1 Functional Objectives

*Subtask decomposition* — Periodic extended precedence constraints (definition 2.5) define inter-task data dependencies as repetitive pattern. Based on this, TIC transforms the partial order that is imposed by inter-task data dependencies to allow parallel execution of communicating tasks. As a side effect, the end-to-end latency of sensor/actuator chains is increased and its impact on a critical sensor/actuator path (section 2.3.2) must be investigated. This effect manifests when a complete hyperperiod schedule is defined and this is a complex problem that requires a separate approach, which is further explained in chapter 6.

*Mapping and scheduling* — TIC does not calculate a mapping of tasks or a task schedule. Instead, inter-task communication is transformed. This increases the freedom for the task scheduling and this makes it possible to schedule a task at any point in time within its period. Thus, scheduler can treat tasks, which use TIC, as independent and this allows for more mapping and scheduling possibilities.

#### 5.2.1.2 Non-functional Objectives

*Predictable interprocessor communication* — TIC is a method for predictable interprocessor communication that guarantees the same data-flow independent from the task scheduling. The use of timestamps for a datum makes it possible to identify the appropriate value on receiver side and form a predictable data-flow. Thus, further synchronization is not required and any scheduler can be applied.

*Robustness* — Keeping the original runnable-to-task mapping ensures predictability, reproducibility, and an identical data-flow for all target ECU platforms. However, TIC increases the end-to-end latency and this can cause instability of the controller (for example if the controller reacts too slowly on changes).

Generally, the FILO latency for a path with TIC is at least the sum of task periods composing it. However, it is important to remark that the actual value can be smaller or bigger, depending on the finish time of the last task in the data-flow path. As a result, the task scheduling is of great importance for a small latency. Therefore, and despite the benefits of TIC, it requires careful consideration whether inter-task communication uses TIC or not. Consequently, the challenge in the migration with TIC is selecting an appropriate subset of inter-task communication that tolerates a delay. For these reasons, a performance evaluation is impossible in this chapter and chapter 6 later introduces a latency-aware scheduling meta-heuristic that also minimizes the processor's clock rate.

*Data consistency* — Performing computations on a copy of the datum allows simultaneous access to the same variable without corruption. Encapsulating shared functions in client/server-calls prevents lost updates.

*Efficiency* — The execution time of each task increases due to communication with the buffer. The overall impact depends on the number of accesses to the buffer and the efficiency of the concrete implementation. Some buffered communication can be optimized, for example when the task's periods are multiples of each other, while others cannot be optimized. However, it must be investigated whether the gained parallelism can outweigh the overhead of buffer accesses. This leads to the following research question:

⋄ *How does the buffer overhead affect the degree of parallelism, when automotive control software uses TIC?*

Task-level parallelization provides good performance only when multiple tasks must be scheduled, but this is not always the case in a multiperiodic system. In contrast, runnable-level parallelization always provides a speed-up when a task is executed. This imposes the research question:

⋄ *When are task-level and runnable-level parallelization ideally applied to automotive control software to maximize the degree of parallelism?*

Concretely, runnable-level parallelization has shown to provide a high efficiency on two cores. This results from the comparable fine granularity and from the low overhead. TIC in contrast, has a more coarse-grained granularity and introduces additional overhead. This leads to the research question:

⋄ *How performs task-level parallelization with TIC on two and four cores in comparison to task-level parallelization with RunPar or Supertasks?*

*Scalability* — The buffer allocates additional memory to hold historic copies of the same variable. The discussion in section 5.1.4 concluded that the size of the buffer is limited. However, the concrete memory consumption depends on the efficiency of the buffer implementation. Optimizing this buffer is no subject of this thesis and thus further investigations are not conducted. Instead, the experiments are conducted with idealistic and realistic buffer overhead values to reflect a best-case and a worst-case overhead, respectively.

*Low cost* — TIC increases the end-to-end latency of sensor/actuator paths. This requires either a re-validation of the functional correctness or it must be considered by the scheduler. The former one is costly and thus chapter 6 introduces a latency-aware scheduling.

*Compliance, portability, and minimal standard modification* — TIC is compliant to AUT-OSAR, allows current legacy applications to execute tasks in parallel way without any modification at source code level, and it is independent from the workload of the application. However, an extension of the AUTOSAR RTE and standardization is necessary to implement and use the approach, respectively. The associated expenditure is expected to be acceptable.

*Summary of non-functional objectives* — The communication with TIC produces a predictable and reproducible data-flow. The execution of a task is decoupled from the communication with other tasks. TIC is compliant to AUTOSAR and the expenditure for integrating it in the standard is small. However, discussion could not assess the efficiency of the approach and its performance in comparison with the approach for runnable-level parallelization. Therefore, experiments are conducted in the next two sections to investigate the impact of the buffer overhead and compare TIC with the approaches for runnable-level parallelization presented in the previous chapter. Again, the *speed-up* is used as metric (see definition 4.8), because it quantifies how much faster the parallel execution finishes.

Like in chapter 4, no investigation of the impact on the minimal processor's clock rate is conducted, because a schedule for a hyperperiod is needed for this. The construction of such a schedule requires further mechanisms that are described and investigated in chapter 6.

## 5.2.2   Experiment Configuration

TIC is evaluated in two steps. The first set of experiments investigates the impact of the buffer on the performance. Second, task-level parallelization with TIC is compared against runnable-level parallelization with RunPar and Supertasks to investigate when the mechanisms are ideally applied.

The experiments are conducted with same diesel EMS use case described in section 2.1.3 as in the previous chapter, because the tasks frequently communicate with each other. The analysis tool described in section 2.4.1 is used to identify the data dependencies between tasks and identify AUTOSAR client-server communication. A server-runnable typically maintains an internal state, which is changed during invocation and this requires a mechanism to ensure memory coherency. This is out of the scope of the approach in this thesis and to still perform a performance evaluation client-server calls to a server are encapsulated in *ticket-locks* [ORS14]. This blocks other runnables until the execution of the server-runnable has finished. These locks are integrated within the RTE and they are transparent to the client and the server, as well. Thus, no changes of the application are required. Data consistency and data coherency are guaranteed.

Extended periodic precedence constraints are derived based on the TDG shown in figure 5.7 and the original task scheduling equation (5.18). The edges in this graph represent the extended periodic precedence constraints (the labels are omitted to maintain readability). The tasks of this application are not executed in a strict *deadline monotonic (DM)* order in the single-c011 ore ECU. $\tau_7$ ($T_7 = 20$ ms) is directly called from at the end of $\tau_3$ ($T_3 = 4$ ms) and $\tau_{10}$ ($T_{10} = 96$ ms) is called after $\tau_8$ ($T_8 = 32$ ms). Thus, the original task schedule order is:

$$\tau_2 \rightarrow \tau_3 \rightarrow \tau_7 \rightarrow \tau_4 \rightarrow \tau_5 \rightarrow \tau_6 \rightarrow \tau_8 \rightarrow \tau_{10} \rightarrow \tau_9 \rightarrow \tau_{11} \rightarrow \tau_{12} \qquad (5.18)$$

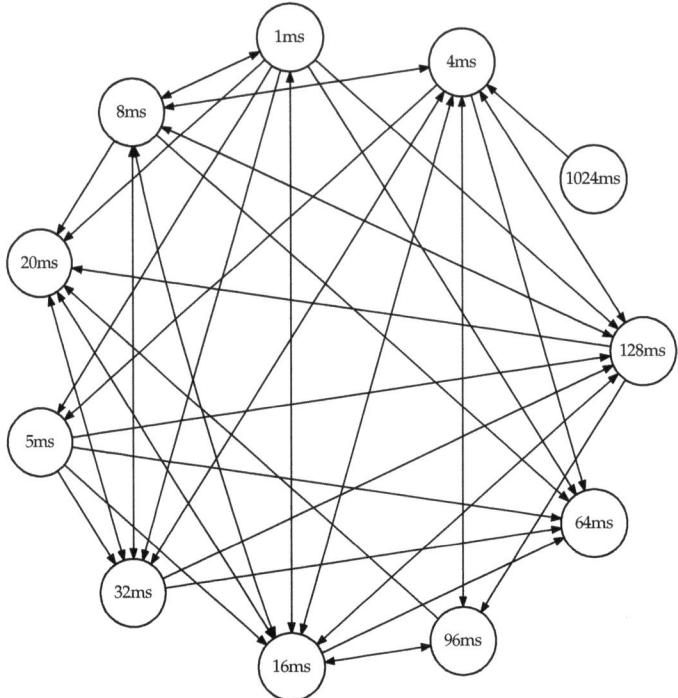

Figure 5.7: The *task dependence graph (TDG)* for the periodic tasks of the EMS use case in section 2.1.3.

The periodic extended precedence constraints can be derived from this and transformed with TIC afterwards. For example, the repetitive pattern $M_{3,7} = \{(5,0)\}$ (from $\tau_3$ with a period of 4 ms to $\tau_7$ with a period of 20 ms) transforms into the repetitive pattern $M_{3,7}^{MC} = \{(4,0)\}$. The WCET for each task and the overhead for a ticket-lock are derived by static analysis with OTAWA (section 2.4.3).

A non-preemptive scheduling scheme is considered on the multicore ECU. For the estimation of the speed-up the *worst-case scenario* is scheduled, i.e. the situation when all tasks have the same release time. That means all tasks shown in figure 5.7 are scheduled with a partitioned scheduler. Chapter 4 described such a method (RunPar). Moreover, the crank-angle task ($\tau_1$) is placed in a separate core to guarantee that interrupts can always be handled with low latency.

Table 5.1 lists the three target platform configurations that are used for the evaluation.

| Parameter | $Proc_4$ | $Proc_8$ |
|---:|:---:|:---:|
| Cores | 4 | 8 |
| Data cache size | 256 KB | |
| Cache latency | 1 cycles | |
| $lat_{tree}$ | 2 cycles | 3 cycles |
| $lat_{mem}$ | 10 cycles | 10 cycles |
| UBD (equation (2.16)) | 32 cycles | 73 cycles |
| $C_{lock}$ | 337 cycles | 538 cycles |

Table 5.1: Processor setup for the evaluation of TIC.

The setup considers $lat_{tree} = 2$ for a four-core processor and $lat_{tree} = 3$ for an eight-core processor, i.e. a message traverses two or three routers, respectively. The memory latency is $lat_{mem} = 10$ cycles and that mean these configurations have an *upper bound delay (UBD)*= 32 cycles for the four-core and UBD= 73 cycles for the eight-core processor (see figure 2.6). The parameter $C_{lock}$ is the overhead for acquiring a ticket lock. The WCET is derived with *OTAWA* (see section 2.4.3).

### 5.2.3   Performance and Impact of Buffer Overhead

The performance and the reduction of the CPU utilization achieved by TIC are investigated by scheduling the TDG for the two processor setups in table 5.1. The speed-up compares the *schedule length (makespan)* of the TDG in figure 5.7 before its transformation with TIC against the transformed TDG that allow free scheduling of tasks. Hence, the speed-up reflects the reduction of the CPU utilization achieved by TIC.

For these experiments, different values for the worst-case overhead for a single buffer operation ($o_B$) are assumed. A setup with two cores is not evaluated here, because the configuration could not take advantage of the multicore processor. The first core is exclusively reserved for the execution of the crank-angle task and all other tasks execute serial on the other core.

*Worst-case performance* — Realistic values for $o_B$ depend on the target platform and the number of comparisons per read or write operation. The assumption here is that the number of comparisons for a read- or write-operation is logarithmic in the number of receiver tasks. As a result, four comparisons are conducted in the worst-case for the case study (the maximum number of receiver tasks is 10). Thus, realistic values for $o_B$ can be approximated based on the UBD and they are 150 and 300 for four cores and eight cores, respectively.

*Best-case performance* — In an idealistic scenario all buffer accesses are precomputed and for example stored in a table to access an overwriteable datum without searching for it. Hence, the overhead for a single buffer access is zero. One would always strive to achieve this in the implementation for mass production to achieve maximal performance.

### 5.2.3.1 Expectations

The impact of the buffer on the performance depends on the frequency of accesses to the buffer from the tasks. The tasks in the use case exchange *several thousand* data with each other. Using TIC means the buffer manages all data and every access is accompanied with overhead. Thus, the expectation is that already a small value for $o_B$ results in a significant reduction of the performance.

### 5.2.3.2 Results

Figure 5.8 shows the best-case and the worst-case performance on four and eight cores, respectively. $Proc_8$ provides the highest speed-up of both configurations with 4.5 in the best-case, which equals an efficiency of 56%. On the processor $Proc_4$, the execution finishes 2.7 times faster in the best-case, which means an efficiency of 67.5% and this is significantly better than for the processor $Proc_8$.

The speed-ups under worst-case assumptions decrease down to a 1.95 times and 2.31 times faster execution on $Proc_4$ and $Proc_8$, respectively. This equals a reduction of 27.7% and 48.6%, respectively. Thus, the buffer overhead has a significant impact on the performance and this behaviour meets the expectations.

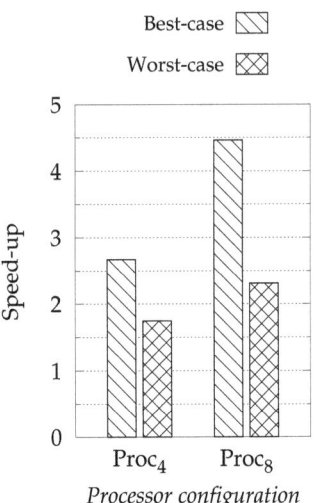

Figure 5.8: Comparison of best-case and worst-case speed-up with TIC on four and eight cores.

**Summary**—The highest speed-up in the ideal case is achieved on the $Proc_8$ (4.5 times faster), but the highest efficiency is achieved on $Proc_4$ (67.5%). Even under more realistic assumption provides $Proc_4$ a comparably good performance and efficiency. For this reason, the processor $Proc_4$ is the preferable target platform for the use case application, when TIC is used for the parallelization.

## 5.2.4  Comparison with Runnable-level Parallelization

This section compares and discusses the approaches for runnable-level parallelization in this thesis (RunPar and Supertask) with the approach for task-level parallelization (TIC). This must allow for better classification of the approaches and show when the approaches are ideally applied. Therefore, the tasks of the use (see section 2.1.3) are parallelized with the following strategies:

1) *Separate* runnable-level parallelization, i.e. RunPar (section 4.1.3) is separately to each task and tasks are executed in a sequential order. These results are labelled as *Separate*.

2) *Supertask* runnable-level parallelization, i.e. tasks are combined in a Supertask first (table 4.4 in section 4.2.3) and RunPar is applied afterwards. These results are labelled as *Supertask*.

3) TIC task-level parallelization, the TDG is transformed with TIC and RunPar is applied to distribute the tasks. The worst-case performance for the buffer overhead is approximated based on the UBD and they are 50 and 100 cycles for two cores and four cores (see the previous section), respectively. These results are labelled as *TIC (WC)*. The best-case results are labelled as *TIC (BC)*, in which zero overhead is considered.

This comparison focuses on the periodic tasks and therefore the two-core processor setup ($Proc_2$ in table 5.1) is considered for TIC. In contrast, considering the eight-core processor setup ($Proc_8$) does not make sense as the results in section 4.3 showed. Thus, this comparison uses $Proc_2$ and $Proc_4$. The evaluation of the coordination of RunPar and TIC is subject to experiments in section 6.2.5.

### 5.2.4.1  Expectations

Task- and runnable-level parallelism provide good performance in potentially different scenarios. The former one for a sufficiently large number of tasks and cores; the latter one for a single task, but it is limited by data dependencies. The expectation is that RunPar and Supertasks provide better performance for small task sets and TIC provides a better performance for large task sets.

### 5.2.4.2  Results

Figure 5.9 shows the results for the speed-up on the two core processor. The x-axis denotes the parallelized task set as defined in table 4.4 of section 4.2.3. The lines are added to ease readability; they do not represent intermediate points. The size of the task set increases from the left to the right.

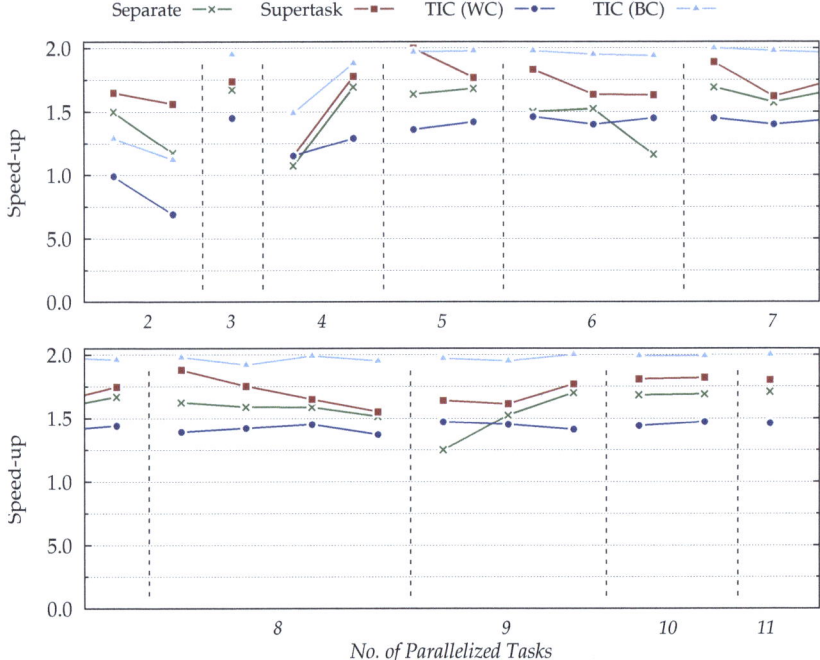

Figure 5.9: Comparison of the speed-up on two cores between the task- and runnable-level parallelization.

The results show a better scalability for Supertasks over Separate task parallelization in any case. The improvement ranges between 5% and 35%. This results in a better performance of runnable-level parallelization compared to TIC (WC). However, TIC provides a better performance when five or more tasks are scheduled in an ideal system setup (TIC (BC)), but this comes at the cost of an increased latency. Thus, runnable-level parallelization provides competitive performance on two cores, without adding latency in the chain of control.

Figure 5.10 shows the results for the speed-up on the four-core processor for the same task set as in figure 5.9. Similar to the two-core processor case, Supertasks obtain a better scalability than separate task parallelization in all cases. Also, on a four-core processor, Supertasks provide better or equal results as TIC (WC) for task sets with a size up to 6 tasks (task sets 1 to 10). However, task-level parallelism outperforms Supertasks for large task sets with 7 or more tasks (task sets 11 to 23).

Nevertheless, task set 22 (ten tasks) finishes 2.52 times and 2.65 times faster with TIC (WC) and Supertasks, respectively. In contrast, TIC (BC) outperforms both with a 3.95 times faster execution than execution is a serial way. The shrinking benefit of Supertasks in comparison to TIC for a large task set results from TIC ignoring inter-task data dependencies, while Supertasks respect all dependencies. Thus, TIC exploits a four-core processor better.

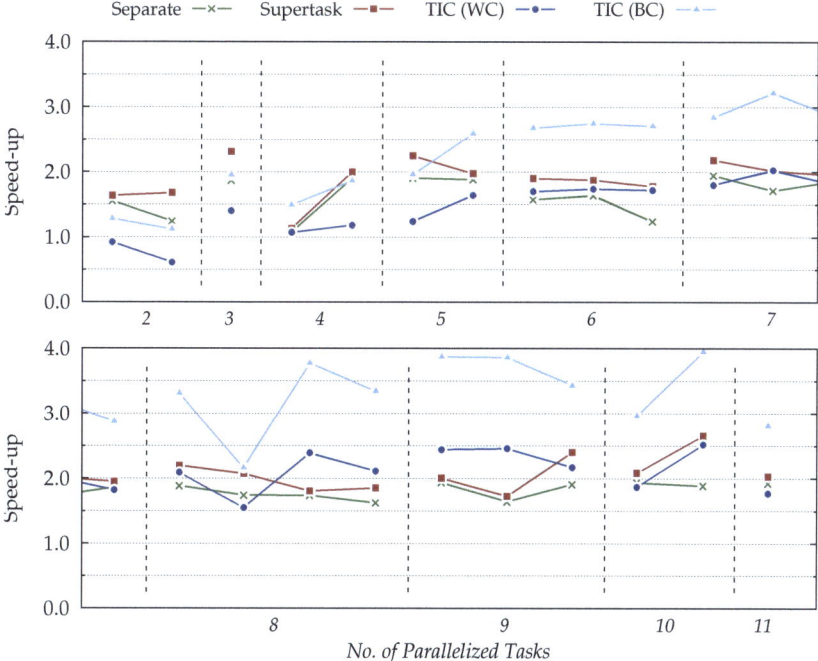

Figure 5.10: Comparison of the speed-up on four cores between the task- and runnable-level parallelization.

These results indicate that none of the approaches is the ultimate choice. The processor utilization changes over time due to simultaneous activation of tasks, in multiperiodic systems like automotive software. Thus, the parallelization method should change as the utilization changes. Runnable-level parallelism is ideal for a few activated tasks and task-level parallelism is ideal when large task sets are activated. Thus, runnable- and task-level parallelism are rather complementary. Combining these two levels of granularity also reduces the end-to-end latency increment of TIC. Moreover, the overall performance is increased. This makes it possible to either execute more complex algorithms or execute the same application on multiple cores with a reduced clock rate (such that deadlines are still kept) to save energy. The latter point is further investigated in chapter 6.

## 5.2.5   Discussion of Research Questions

Due to the evaluation of TIC, it is possible to answer the related research questions from the qualitative discussion.

⋄ *How does the buffer overhead affect the degree of parallelism, when automotive control software uses TIC?*

The buffer overhead has a significant impact on the achievable performance. The potential benefits from buffer optimization increase with the number of cores, because the pessimism increases. A worst-case buffer performance decreased the achievable speed-up by 27% and 48% on four and eight cores, respectively. Thus, it worth spending effort on optimizing of the buffer, because this increases the achievable degree of parallelism in the automotive control application strongly.

⋄ *How performs task-level parallelization with TIC on two and four cores in comparison to runnable-level parallelization with RunPar or Supertasks?*

On the two-core processor, runnable-level parallelization with RunPar and Supertasks provides better performance compared to TIC (WC). Supertasks provide competitive performance on two cores, without adding latency in the chain of control as TIC does. Contrarily, TIC provides similar performance for almost all task set sizes. Also, on four-core processor, Supertasks provide better or equal results as TIC for task sets with a size up to seven. However, for larger task sets TIC utilizes cores better, whereas Supertask performance decreases. The shrinking benefit of Supertasks in comparison to TIC, as the number of runnables increases, results from the fact that TIC ignores inter-task data dependencies, while Supertasks respect all dependencies. Thus, TIC exploits a four-core processor better.

⋄ *When are task-level and runnable-level parallelization ideally applied to automotive control software to maximize the degree of parallelism?*

The results indicate that none of the approaches is the ultimate choice. Runnable-level parallelism is ideal for a few activated tasks and task-level parallelism is ideal when large tasks are activated.

The processor utilization changes over time due to simultaneous activation of tasks, in multiperiodic systems like automotive software. Thus, runnable- and task-level parallelism should be used as complementary methods and used according to the utilization. Combining these two levels of granularity reduces the end-to-end latency increment of TIC and it also increases the overall performance. This makes it possible to either execute more complex algorithms or execute the same application on multiple cores with a reduced clock rate (such that deadlines are still kept) to save energy.

## 5.3   Summary of Task-level Parallelization

This chapter introduced a method for task-level parallelization of automotive control software. The original application's configuration for the single-core used for transforming the communication between tasks. The communication mechanism TIC ensures an identical data-flow for all target ECU platforms. Keeping the original runnable-to-task mapping guarantees predictability and reproducibility, because this maintains a correct data-flow within a task.

TIC is compliant to AUTOSAR and allows current legacy applications to execute tasks in a parallel way without any modification at source code level and it is independent from the workload of the application. Producer and consumer task are decoupled, which makes it possible to treat them as independent during scheduling. However, TIC enlarges the end-to-end path delay.

TIC is evaluated with a diesel EMS as example. When the load is at its maximum, tasks finish 2.7 and 4.5 times faster with TIC on a processor with four and eight cores, respectively. An inefficient buffer management reduces these results significantly and optimizations are recommended.

Additionally, the approach for task-level parallelization is compared against the runnable-level parallelization methods presented in the previous chapter to allow for better classification of the approaches and show when they are ideally applied. Supertasks provide better or equal performance on two cores and better performance for a task set size up to 6 on four cores, respectively. The task-level and runnable-level parallelization methods proposed in this thesis are therefore found to be complementary strategies.

On the one hand, combining them can improve the overall performance of the system on processors with larger core numbers. On the one hand, it can reduce the impact end-to-end latency of TIC. Consequently, the next chapter focuses on the limited use of TIC and the RunPar.

# 6 | Coordination of Concepts

"Evolution is cleverer than you are."

Orgel's Second Rule, Leslie Eleazer Orgel

This chapter proposes a method for combining the approaches for runnable-level (chapter 4) and task-level parallelization (chapter 5) in this thesis into an efficient parallel schedule for a complete hyperperiod. Thereby, latency constraints are respected, the processor's clock rate is reduced to a minimum, and idle intervals are utilized. The method maintains the sensor/actuator data-flow and the critical *first-in-last-out (FILO)* latency, for which the original application's configuration is successfully validated and tested. Parts of this chapter are published as a method named PARCUS in [Keh+17].

The performance evaluation of runnable-level parallelization with RunPar (in section 4.2) and its comparison with task-level parallelization with *timed implicit communication (TIC)* (in section 5.2) showed benefits in different scenarios. Runnable-level parallelism is ideal for a few activated tasks running on a few cores. Contrarily, task-level parallelism is ideal when a large amount of tasks is activated on numerous cores. As a drawback, the FILO latency is increased with TIC. Hence, combining both means to apply the methods in such a manner that individual shortcomings are considered and the drawbacks of the one are compensated by advantages in the other.

Defining a schedule for a hyperperiod means coping with a large solution space. The analysis of mapping and scheduling approaches in section 3.2 showed scheduling meta-heuristics are most suitable for such scheduling problems. However, none of the exiting approaches can be applied straightforward. Evolutionary algorithms for solving the *resource-constrained project scheduling problem (RCPSP)* are among the best performing meta-heuristics with respect to schedule length. However, they are not applicable to real-time scheduling in a straightforward manner, because they do not consider latency constraints periodic task release. *AUTomotive Open System ARchitecture (AUTOSAR)*-specific approaches focus on efficient resource usage in the first. They consider latency constraints, but not to a sufficient degree. Hence, a new parallelization approach is needed for guaranteeing a predictable data-flow, achieving efficient resource usage, and reducing the overall migration cost.

The first part of this chapter describes a method for defining a hyperperiod schedule with the same FILO latency as the reference platform, in which reducing the clock rate to a minimum utilizes idle intervals. This is achieved by scaling all task periods with a constant factor. An evolutionary algorithm is used to generate a set of possible solutions and a metric is established that quantifies the quality of a hyperperiod schedule to allow for choosing the one with the highest gain from parallelization.

The second part evaluates the coordination approach. Subject to evaluation are the ideal configuration of the evolutionary algorithm, the trade-off between clock rate and FILO latency, and the overall performance gain from combining runnable- and task-level parallelism.

# 6.1 Coordination of Runnable- and Task-level Parallelization

Combining the approaches in this thesis requires understanding of their advantages and shortcomings. This was done in the respective chapters 4 and 5. Common for both approaches is a predictable data-flow, which is achieved by either respecting precedence constraints or by logically communicating at the task period boundaries. RunPar utilizes two cores well, but only few tasks take benefit from larger core numbers due to a large amount of data dependencies. This is typical for automotive software, see section 2.1.3 and [Bro06]. TIC provides the best performance when numerous tasks is activated on numerous cores. However, TIC increases the FILO latency and thus applying TIC requires careful choice.

The next section introduces the notations needed for this chapter. Section 6.1.2 describes the impact of TIC on the FILO latency and the impact of the parallelization on idle times in more details. Section 6.1.3 outlines the individual steps of the coordination approach in this chapter. Section 6.1.4 establishes the *parallel schedule quality (PSQ)* metric for quantifying the quality of a parallel schedule. Section 6.1.5 describes an evolutionary algorithm that uses this metric for generating a hyperperiod schedule.

## 6.1.1 Notations

This chapter differs from the previous ones, because the clock rate of the processor is considered. The *worst-case execution time (WCET)* of a runnable is initially expressed in processor cycles and not in time units as it is commonly the case. The actual WCET depends on the clock rate of the processor. Therefore, the frequency-scaled WCET is defined as follows.

**Definition 6.1 (Frequency-scaled WCET):** *Let $G_i$ be the runnable dependence graph (RDG) for a task $\tau_i$ in the AUTOSAR application $\mathcal{A}$. $\gamma_r$ characterises the WCET of runnable $r \in V_i$ in processor cycles. The WCET of the $\tau_i \in \mathcal{A}$, in processor cycles, is denoted as $\Gamma_i$, i.e. the sum of runnable WCETs of $\tau_i$:*

$$\Gamma_i = \sum_{r \in V_i} \gamma_r \tag{6.1}$$

The runnable WCET $c_i$ and the task WCET $C_i$ expressed in time units scale with the processor's clock rate $f$ that executes the application, i.e.

$$c_i = \frac{\gamma_i}{f} \quad and \quad C_i = \frac{\Gamma_i}{f}. \tag{6.2}$$

The clock rate has therefore a direct impact on the schedulability of an application, because a higher clock rate shortens the WCET in time units. The relation between the processor frequency and the feasibility of a schedule is described by constraint 6.1.

**Constraint 6.1 (Schedule feasibility with frequency-scaled WCET):** *Let $\mathcal{A}$ be an AUT-OSAR application according to definition 4.2 with frequency-scaled WCET. Let the tuple $\mathcal{S} = (st_1^0, st_1^1, \ldots, st_i^n)$ be a schedule that assigns start times to the task instances of $\mathcal{A}$. The finish time of a task is*

$$ft_i^p = st_i^p + C_i = st_i^p + \frac{\gamma_i}{f}. \tag{6.3}$$

*Hence, the schedule is feasible under the clock rate $f$, iff*

$$\begin{aligned} o_i^p &\le st_i^p < ft_i^p \le d_i^p \\ o_i^p &\le st_i^p < st_i^p + \frac{\gamma_i}{f} \le d_i^p \end{aligned} \tag{6.4}$$

Nevertheless, minimizing the clock rate is important to construct an energy-efficient embedded system. Idle intervals obtained from parallelization can either be used for additional computations or they can be used for reducing the clock rate. The focus in this chapter is on the latter option, because this leads to a reduction of the processor's energy consumption and this is of high importance for the automotive industry. The reduction of the clock rate reduces the power consumption of the *electronic control unit (ECU)* and allows for a lower supply voltage [Seo+08]. Thus, the target in this chapter is to define a feasible parallel schedule $\mathcal{S}^p$ for the application $\mathcal{A}$ in a way that the clock rate $f$ is minimized. This minimal value is denoted as $f_{min}^p$ for the remainder of this chapter.

## 6.1.2 Problem Description

The original runnable-to-task mapping defines, in combination with the task scheduling, a valid application configuration, for which the application is tested and validated. This configuration defines:

1) A specific data-flow (definition 5.1) that is the order in which runnables process data between the sensor and the actuator.

2) An acceptable upper bound on the response time on a stimulus, which is equal to the end-to-end latency between a sensor and an actuator (section 2.3.2).

The methods for runnable- and task-level parallelization in this thesis are designed to maintain the original application's data-flow. This applies also to combinations of the methods. Hence, the data-flow is no subject to concerns here.

However, minimizing the end-to-end latency [Nat+07] is a typical optimization objective to guarantee the reaction requirements of the embedded system. For example, the maximum time between the push on a gas pedal and the resulting final injection. The primary focus here is on the FILO (explained in section 2.3.2), because this value is considered in situations where it is important to capture the system's reaction delay after a value change.

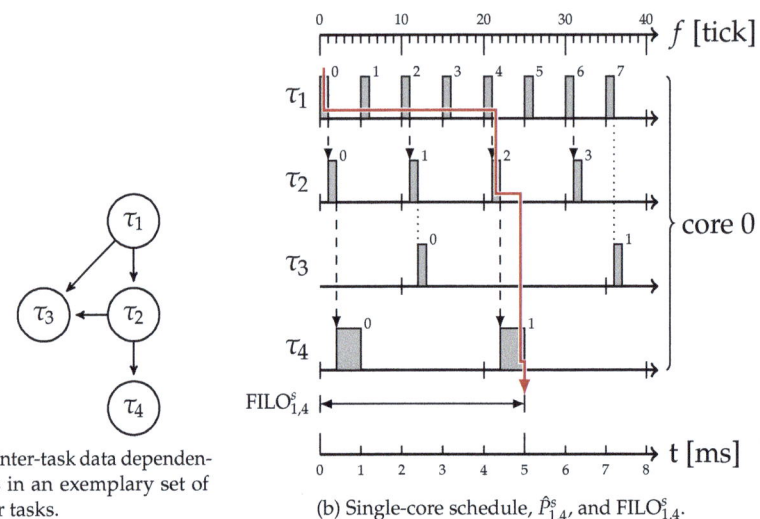

(a) Inter-task data dependencies in an exemplary set of four tasks.

(b) Single-core schedule, $\hat{P}^s_{1,4}$, and $\text{FILO}^s_{1,4}$.

Figure 6.1: Example for an optimized single-core schedule (b) with four tasks (a).

The schedule in figure 6.1 illustrates the baseline situation before the parallelization. The *task dependence graph (TDG)* in figure 6.1a shows an application with four tasks. $\tau_1$, $\tau_2$, $\tau_3$, and $\tau_4$ are released with periods 1, 2, 5, and 4 ms, respectively. The task priorities follow a *rate monotonic (RM)* [LSD89] assignment scheme as typical assumption, i.e. $\pi_1 > \pi_2 > \pi_4 > \pi_3$.

The red arrow in figure 6.1b describes the data-flow through task instances from an initial sensor input between clock tick 0 and 1, entering $\tau_1^0$ (first instance of task 1). In the consequence, the input value is processed in $\tau_1$ and written into a register buffer that is later read by $\tau_2^2$ etc. The critical FILO latency traverses $\tau_1$, $\tau_2$, and $\tau_4$. Apart from this, the task $\tau_3$ represents other computations of the controller that must be considered during scheduling, but they have no immediate impact on the computation within the critical FILO path.

The clock rate is set to 5 kHz (5 ticks per millisecond) in this example to satisfy all deadline constraints. This number and task WCETs are chosen for illustration purposes. For calculating the FILO latency, a situation is considered, in which a value change took place *just after* the sensor read-instruction in $\tau_1$. That means the polling task has just missed the value change and it takes an additional period to recognize the change. In this way the FILO path is constructed. The path, according to equation (5.4), in this example equals:

$$\hat{P}^s_{1,4} = \tau_1^0 \, \tau_1^1 \, \tau_1^2 \, \tau_1^3 \, \tau_1^4 \, \tau_2^2 \, \tau_4^1 \tag{6.5}$$

The resulting FILO latency in the single-core ECU is 5 ms. This value represents the reference value, which must be guaranteed after the parallelization.

Task-level parallelization with TIC keeps the original task configuration, which guarantees a correct data-flow within a task and thus the same traversal time per task instance. However, TIC introduces an additional delay in the communication between tasks and thus increases the FILO latency. Figure 6.2 illustrates the effect of TIC for the example in figure 6.1b. The inter-task communication on the FILO path uses TIC and the clock rate is set to the same value in the single-core ECU.

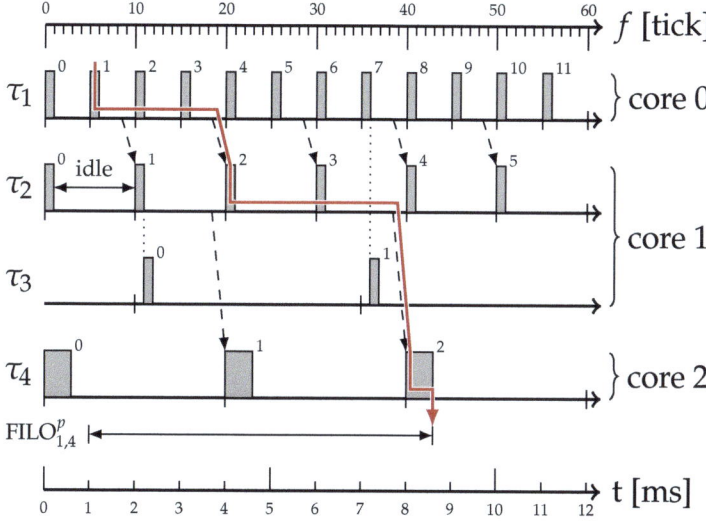

Figure 6.2: $\hat{P}^p_{1,4}$ and $\mathrm{FILO}^p_{1,4}$ with TIC for the example in figure 5.2.

TIC buffers data until publication at the end of the producer task's period. Hence, data are not immediately transmitted and processed by subsequent execution of the receiver task ($\tau_2$). Thus, the resulting FILO path is enlarged:

$$\hat{P}^p_{1,4} = \tau^1_1 \, \tau^2_1 \, \tau^3_1 \, \tau^2_2 \, \tau^3_2 \, \tau^2_4 \tag{6.6}$$

Generally, the FILO latency for a path is at least the sum of task periods composing it plus the WCET of the last task in the data-flow path. However, it is important to remark that the actual value can be smaller or bigger, depending on the finish time of the last task in the data-flow path. Executing $\tau^2_4$ later would be correct, as long as the task finishes before its deadline. *Hence, the task scheduling and each task's WCET are of great importance for computing the latency.* Thus, the latency after the parallelization with TIC equals:

$$\text{FILO}^p_{1,4} = \text{ft}^2_4 - \text{st}^1_1 = T_1 + T_2 + T_3 + (o^p_i - f^2_4) = 7.6 \tag{6.7}$$

Another effect from parallelization is a potentially larger idle interval after a task has finished execution, see $\tau^0_2$ in figure 6.2 for example. These additional idle intervals allow for the aspired reduction of the clock rate.

### 6.1.3 Approach

The challenge in coordinating runnable- and task-level parallelization is to optimize contradictory targets. Parallelization introduces additional idle times that can be used for reducing the clock rate, but TIC and a lower clock rate increase the critical FILO latency. A straightforward way of bounding the latency is limiting the usage of TIC by selecting an appropriate subset of inter-task communication that tolerates a delay.

Figure 6.3 shows a parallel schedule on a multicore ECU for the example from figure 6.2. In this figure, TIC is applied to $\tau_2 \rightsquigarrow \tau_4$ and thus the tasks $\tau_2$ and $\tau_4$ can execute in a parallel way. The effect of limiting the usage of TIC is twofold. First, the reduced FILO latency goes hand in hand with a lower level of parallelism. The communication between $\tau_1$ and $\tau_2$ remains unchanged imposing a precedence constraint $\tau_1 \to \tau_2$. This serialises the execution of both tasks, although they are executed on different cores. However, the resulting idle intervals can be utilized by applying RunPar.

Second, the FILO latency between $\tau_1$ and $\tau_4$ ($\text{FILO}^p_{1,4}$) is reduced by 1 ms ($\Delta$), which is the duration of one period of $\tau_1$. Still, the value is larger than the reference value and it is unknown whether this would lead to correct functional behaviour or not. Applying RunPar to $\tau_1$ and $\tau_2$ reduces the task WCETs and it utilizes the idle intervals, but it does not reduce the latency. Likewise, a higher clock rate cannot compensate

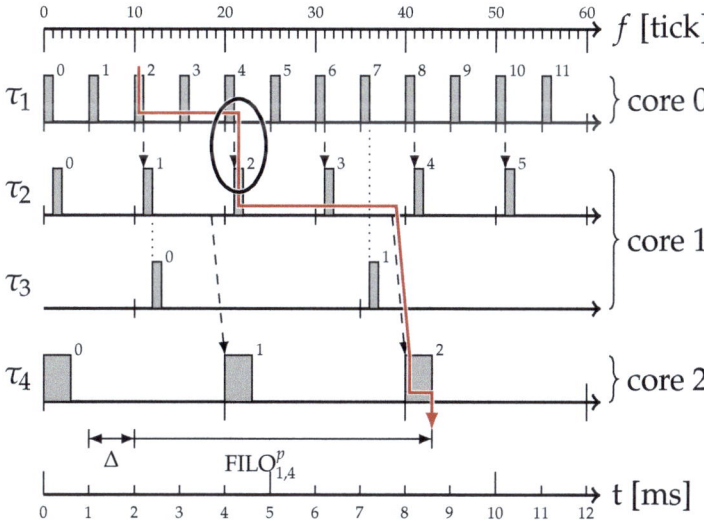

Figure 6.3: FILO latency in a multicore schedule with explicit communication ($\tau_1 \rightarrow \tau_2$) and TIC ($\tau_2 \rightsquigarrow \tau_4$).

the increased latency completely, because TIC buffers data until the end of the task period. This means limiting the usage of TIC is a necessary step, but it is insufficient to reduce the latency down to the reference value.

Instead, all task periods are shortened by the same constant factor to reduce the latency until it is equal to the reference value. Concretely, the coordination of runnable- and task-level parallelization operates in the following steps.

1) *Extraction of latency constraints* — A control application can have one or more critical FILO paths that must satisfy strict timing constraints. The system under control imposes the critical path. The path and its latency are either specified as requirement for the controller or determined by analysing the legacy application and measuring or simulating the single-core scheduling with the methods described in section 2.3.2.

2) *Parallel schedule generation* — A set of hyperperiod schedules is computed at once. Here, an evolutionary algorithm meta-heuristic for solving the RCPSP (described in section 3.2.2.1) is adapted for scheduling automotive control software to deal with the enormous size of the solution space. Computations in this step are repeated in an iterative process based on the results from the previous iteration. The result in each iteration is a set of hyperperiod schedules, in which the FILO latency and the clock rate are minimized.

3) *Schedule adjustment and selection* — An additional metric is established for quantifying the robustness and the efficiency of a parallel schedule. The parallel schedule quality (PSQ) quantifies how good the positive effect of clock rate reduction compensates the negative impact on the FILO latency. Hence, the idea is to prefer schedules that compensate the negative impact on the FILO latency with the positive effect of a clock rate reduction better. Thus, the hyperperiod schedules are rated ordered by their PSQ and the schedule whose configuration achieves the highest quality is selected for implementation.

The extraction of latency constraints is not discussed here. The assumption is that the original platform's clock rate, the critical FILO path, and its latency are known.

The next section introduces notations and the problem formulation for this chapter. Afterwards, section 6.1.4 describes how the clock rate and the FILO latency are derived from a given schedule to compute its PSQ. Generating hyperperiod schedules is explained afterwards in section 6.1.5, because the method is based on the meta-heuristic that makes use of the PSQ metric.

## 6.1.4   Parallel Schedule Quality (PSQ)

Selecting a parallel schedule, for an AUTOSAR application $\mathcal{A}$ according to definition 4.2 with frequency-scaled WCET according to definition 6.1, from a set of possible solutions requires a measure that quantifies when one solution is superior to another. For this, the parallel schedule quality (PSQ) is introduced in this section, which quantifies the quality of a parallel schedule $\mathcal{S}^p$ in comparison to the sequential execution of the same application with schedule $\mathcal{S}^s$. The frequency $f^s_{\min}$ for the serial schedule $\mathcal{S}^s$ is assumed to be given by the original application's configuration.

The first relevant quality criterion for a parallel schedule is the required clock rate, because the parallelization makes it possible to reduce the clock rate. The second criterion is the FILO latency, because TIC and a lower clock rate increase the latency. Therefore, $f^p_{\min}$ and the FILO latency are derived for a given parallel schedule $\mathcal{S}^p$ and considered as criteria to decide if a schedule is superior to another or not. This is realized in two steps for a given parallel schedule $\mathcal{S}^p$:

1) *Task-fitting:* the lowest possible *clock rate is derived*, for filling idle intervals in the schedule.

2) *Latency-fitting:* the task periods and the clock rate are adjusted in a way that the FILO latency of $\mathcal{S}^p$ is equal to the validated reference of the single-core ECU.

### 6.1.4.1  Task-Fitting: Adjustment for Energy-saving

During task-fitting, an intermediate result $f'^p_{min}$ for the frequency is derived, which is thus marked with $\prime$ (prime). For this, the clock rate needed to finish the task instance $\tau^p_i$ before its deadline $d^p_i$ ($\underline{f}^n_i$) is derived. The _ (underline) is used to distinguish the frequency for each task instance from the frequency of the complete application. The final frequency for the parallel schedule is computed after the computation of the latency impact in the next step.

The clock rate $f'^p_{min}$ is computed in three steps as follows.

1) $\mathcal{S}^p$ is initially derived for $f'^p_{min} = 1$. That means the WCET of a task in time units is equal to the WCET in processor cycles:

$$C_i = \gamma_i. \tag{6.8}$$

2) $\underline{f}^n_i$ for $\tau^p_i$ is derived as follows:

$$
\begin{aligned}
\text{ft}^p_i &\leq d^p_i \\
\text{st}^p_i + C_i &\leq d^p_i \\
\text{st}^p_i + \frac{\gamma_i}{\underline{f}^n_i} &\leq d^p_i \\
\underline{f}^n_i &\geq \frac{\gamma_i}{d^p_i - \text{st}^p_i}
\end{aligned}
\tag{6.9}
$$

3) Consequently, the minimal clock rate needed to guarantee all deadlines is

$$f'^p_{min} = \max(\underline{f}^n_i) \tag{6.10}$$

Knowing $f'^p_{min}$ makes it possible to exactly calculate the latency of the FILO path $\hat{P}_{i,j}$, because this specifies the concrete finish time of a task instance (constraint 6.1). This is done analogous to section 2.3.2, whereas the transformation with TIC is respected. That means produced data elements are not available for the receiver task before the end of the producer period, if TIC is used.

The *frequency impact* reflects the improvement by a reduction of the clock rate by parallel execution and defined as follows.

**Definition 6.2 (Frequency Impact):** *Let $f^s_{min}$ and $f'^p_{min}$ represent the minimal clock rate of the sequential schedule $\mathcal{S}^s$ and the parallel schedule $\mathcal{S}^p$ for the AUTOSAR application $\mathcal{A}$, respectively. The frequency impact between the schedules $\mathcal{S}^s$ and $\mathcal{S}^p$ is*

$$\mathcal{F}^{s,p} = \frac{f^s_{min}}{f'^p_{min}} \tag{6.11}$$

The clock rate for the parallel schedule is potentially smaller than the one for the sequential schedule, because parallelization allows more tasks or runnables to execute in a parallel way. Thus, this fraction indirectly reflects the degree of parallelism, similar to the well-known speed-up [Rod85].

For illustration, figure 6.4 shows the schedule for figure 6.2 after task fitting, with a reduced clock rate $f'^p_{min} = 1$ kHz (previously 5 kHz). Here, TIC makes it possible to execute $\tau_1$, $\tau_2$, and $\tau_4$ in a parallel way. The clock rate is reduced until all task deadlines are just met. Here, $\tau_1^n$ and $\tau_3^n$ limit the reduction. Both task instances cannot take more computation time, because other task instances execute on the same core. The frequency impact for this example is

$$\mathcal{F}^{s,p} = \frac{f^s_{min}}{f'^p_{min}} = \frac{5 \text{ kHz}}{1 \text{ kHz}} = 5. \tag{6.12}$$

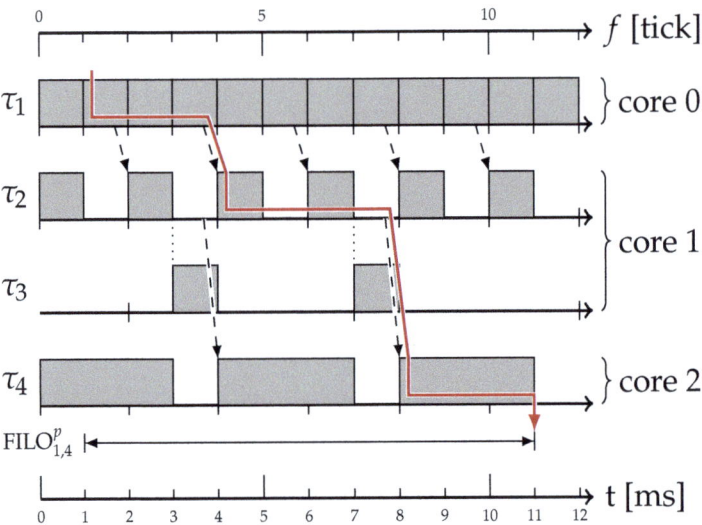

Figure 6.4: Multicore schedule from figure 6.2 with a reduced clock rate ($f'^p_{min} = 1$kHz).

### 6.1.4.2  Latency-Fitting: Adjustment for Robustness

However, the lower clock rate also increases the finish time of $\tau_4^2$ and this enlarges FILO$^p_{1,4}$ from 7.6 ms to 10.0 ms. This negative impact on the critical FILO path, when TIC is used, is reflected by the *latency impact* and defined as follows.

**Definition 6.3 (Latency Impact):** *For the AUTOSAR application $\mathcal{A}$, let $\mathrm{FILO}_{i,j}^s$ represent the latency of the sequential schedule $\mathcal{S}^s$ and let $\mathrm{FILO}_{i,j}^p$ represent the latency of the parallel schedule $\mathcal{S}^p$ after task-fitting. The latency impact is*

$$\mathcal{L}^{s,p} = \frac{\mathrm{FILO}_{i,j}^s}{\mathrm{FILO}_{i,j}^p}. \tag{6.13}$$

The latency impact for the example in figure 6.4 is

$$\mathcal{L}^{s,p} = \frac{\mathrm{FILO}_{i,j}^s}{\mathrm{FILO}_{i,j}^p} = \frac{5 \text{ ms}}{10 \text{ ms}} = \frac{1}{2}. \tag{6.14}$$

For comparison, the frequency impact and latency impact for the schedule in figure 6.3 are $\mathcal{F}^{s,p} = 1$ and $\mathcal{L}^{s,p} = 0.65$, respectively. Both schedules (in figures 6.3 and 6.4) have a negative impact on the FILO latency, which makes a decision for one of the schedules hard. The target platform is potentially not as robust as the original platform and thus both schedules seem to be unsatisfying solutions.

Scaling the original task periods with the factor $\mathcal{L}^{s,p}$ and the previously computed clock rate $f_{\min}^p$ with the factor $1/\mathcal{L}^{s,p}$ guarantees the same FILO latency as in the reference platform.

**Definition 6.4 (Adjustment for Robustness):** *Let $\mathcal{L}^{s,p}$ be the latency impact for a parallel schedule $\mathcal{S}^p$ for the AUTOSAR application $\mathcal{A}$. Let $f_{\min}^p$ be the clockrate for $\mathcal{S}^p$ after task-fitting. The application is adjusted as follows:*

$$f_{\min}^p = f_{\min}'^p \cdot \frac{1}{\mathcal{L}^{s,p}}$$
$$and$$
$$\forall \tau_i(\pi_i, T_i, G_i = (V_i, E_i), C_i, O_i, D_i) \in \mathcal{A} : (\pi_i, T_i \cdot \mathcal{L}^{s,p}, G_i, C_i, O_i, D_i) \tag{6.15}$$

This transformation is valid, because all tasks are scaled with the same constant factor. Scaling the clock rate is necessary to finish all tasks before their deadlines. The resulting parallel schedule with adjusted task periods and frequency is shown in figure 6.5.

### 6.1.4.3 Schedule Quality Quantification

Finally, the parallel schedule quality quantifies whether such a scaling results in an overall benefit for the parallelization. It is defined as follows.

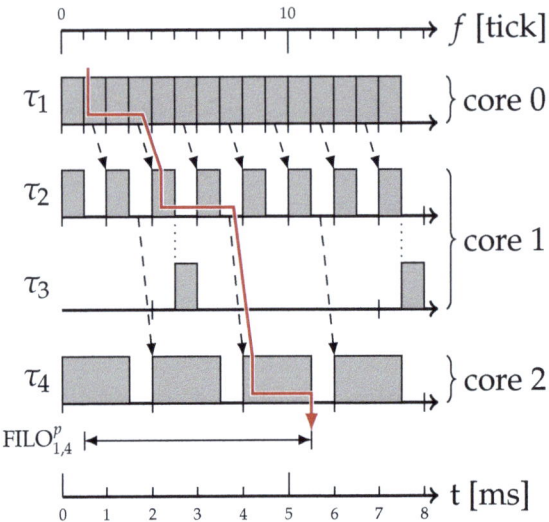

Figure 6.5: Multicore schedule from figure 6.4 with adjusted $f^{p}_{min}$ and task periods according to definition 6.4.

**Definition 6.5 (Parallel Schedule Quality):** *Let $\mathcal{F}^{s,p}$ be the frequency impact and let $\mathcal{L}^{s,p}$ be the latency impact of the parallel schedule $\mathcal{S}^{p}$ over the sequential schedule $\mathcal{S}^{s}$ for the application $\mathcal{A}$. The parallel schedule quality (PSQ) is defined as*

$$PSQ_{s,p} = \mathcal{F}^{s,p} \cdot \mathcal{L}^{s,p} = \frac{f^{s}_{min}}{f'^{p}_{min}} \cdot \frac{FILO^{s}_{i,j}}{FILO'^{p}_{i,j}}. \tag{6.16}$$

Increasing the number of TIC communications in the parallel application changes the fractions $\mathcal{F}^{s,p}$ and $\mathcal{L}^{s,p}$ in opposite directions. The fraction $\mathcal{F}^{s,p}$ (in equation (6.12)) increases, because more tasks can execute in a parallel way and this can result in a reduction of $f^{p}_{min}$. Contrarily, the fraction $\mathcal{L}^{s,p}$ (in equation (6.14)) decreases, because the latency $FILO^{p}_{i,j}$ increases. This criterion means to counterbalance the negative impact of the increased latency with the benefits of parallel execution. This is done by applying TIC to communication that affects the latency fewest and provides the best performance gain. Values larger than 1 represent schedules that benefit from the parallelization.

Applying the metric to the previously mentioned schedules in figures 6.3 and 6.4 gives a PSQ of 0.65 and 2.5, respectively. Hence, the schedule with the reduced clock rate is the superior schedule in this comparison.

## 6.1.5 Schedule Generation

This section describes how the scheduling meta-heuristic proposed by Hartmann [Har02] (described in section 3.2.2.1) is adapted for scheduling automotive control software for a complete hyperperiod. The proposed method is an evolutionary algorithm whose basic scheme is described in section 3.2.1.5.

The input information and the transformation of a computed schedule into a real-time schedule are described next. Extensions of individuals and evolutionary operators are described afterwards.

### 6.1.5.1 Problem Representation and Schedule Transformation

The meta-heuristic

$$\mathbf{M}(\mathcal{J} = \{1,\ldots,J\}, K^\rho, R^\rho_k, \text{Pred} = \{\text{pred}_1,\ldots,\text{pred}_J\}, r_{J,k}, C_J) \qquad (6.17)$$

generates a schedule $\mathcal{S}$ with a minimized *schedule length (makespan)* for a job list $\mathcal{J}$, precedence relations Pred, on the limited renewable resources $K^\rho$ with per-period availability $R^\rho_k$, job resource request $r_{J,k}$, and job processing time $C_J$. Please note, the schedule can be serial or parallel.

The job list $\mathcal{J}$ is composed of all task instances that appear in one hyperperiod of the AUTOSAR application $\mathcal{A}$. The predecessors of $\text{Pred}_J$ of the job $J$ represent the periodic extended precedence constraints between the task instances. The target is an ECU with one processor with multiple cores, i.e.

$$K^\rho = \{1\} \text{ and } R^1_1 = \texttt{procnum}(). \qquad (6.18)$$

The request of job $J$ for processor capacity is equal to the WCET of the corresponding task in processor cycles, i.e.

$$C_i = \Gamma_i \text{ for } J = \tau^n_i. \qquad (6.19)$$

Based on this information, the precedence-based earliest and latest finish time are computed by forward and backwards pass, respectively.

The output of $\mathbf{M}$ is the schedule $\mathcal{S}$, which is not a real-time schedule, because each task instance is scheduled as soon as all their predecessors have finished their execution regardless of the release time of the task. Thus, it is necessary to respect the ticks of a real-time clock to prevent tasks from starting their execution before their periodic release and to let each task instance finish before its relative deadline. The heuristic should thereby remain unchained to maintain its functionality.

Therefore, the proposal is to insert dummy tasks ($\tau_\oplus$) that represent the ticks of a real-time clock. Precedence constraints with these dummies are used to define an execution window, in which a task can be scheduled that is defined by the start and end of its period. The real-time attributes of a dummy task $\tau_\oplus$ are:

$$T_\oplus = 1 \text{ ms}, \quad C_\oplus = \Gamma_\oplus = 0, \quad \text{and} \quad O_\oplus = 1 \tag{6.20}$$

Dummy tasks require no computation time, but they introduce inter-task data dependencies in the TDG to prevent scheduling tasks before their current period has finished. A dummy precedes a task, if both task instances have the same release time:

$$o_\oplus^n = o_i^{n'} \quad \Rightarrow \quad \tau_\oplus^n \rightarrow \tau_i^{n'} \tag{6.21}$$

A task precedes a dummy, if the relative deadline of the task instance is equal to the release time of a dummy task instance:

$$d_i^n = o_\oplus^{n'} \quad \Rightarrow \quad \tau_i^n \rightarrow \tau_\oplus^{n'} \tag{6.22}$$

The original job list $\mathcal{J}$ is extended by dummy jobs and the relations with the dummies extends the precedence constraints Pred. The resulting job list $\mathcal{J}'$ is scheduled with **M** and the dummies in the resulting schedule $\mathcal{S}$ are used to transform the schedule in a real-time schedule $\mathcal{S}'$:

$$\mathcal{S} = \{st_1^0, st_1^1, \ldots, st_i^n\} \quad \Rightarrow \quad \mathcal{S}' = \{st_1'^0, st_1'^1, \ldots, st_i'^n\} \tag{6.23}$$

by adjusting the start time of tasks. This is done in the following two steps:

1) The length of one millisecond $\omega$ (in cycles) is determined by finding the maximum number of cycles between two consecutive dummy tasks:

$$\omega = \max(\tau_\oplus^{n+1} - \tau_\oplus^n) \tag{6.24}$$

2) The start times of all tasks are adjusted based on $\omega$:

$$\begin{aligned} \text{offset} &= st_i^n - o_i^n \\ o_i'^n &= o_i^n \cdot \omega \\ st_i'^n &= o_i'^n + \text{offset} \end{aligned} \tag{6.25}$$

The result is a schedule $\mathcal{S}'$ that defines start times of tasks on a real-time axis, in which a task instance $\tau_i^n$ is not scheduled before its release time $o_i^n$ and it finishes before its relative deadline $d_i^n$.

**Example**—Figure 6.6 shows an exemplary task graph that is scheduled with the **M** and afterwards transformed with the rules defined in the equations (6.24) and (6.25).

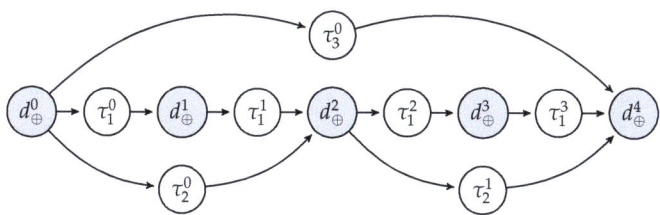

Figure 6.6: Task graph for a period of four milliseconds with three tasks from section 2.1.3.

Here, the assumption is that inter-task communication already uses TIC and the tasks can be scheduled freely within their period. The duration of the tasks is assumed to be $\Gamma_1 = 1, \Gamma_2 = 2, \Gamma_3 = 4$ cycles, respectively.

The input parameters for **M** are:

$$\mathcal{J} = \{1(\tau_\oplus^0), 2(\tau_1^0), \ldots, 11(\tau_1^3), 12(\tau_\oplus^4)\}$$
$$\text{Pred} = \{\{\varnothing\}, \{1\}, \ldots\} \tag{6.26}$$
$$K^p = \{1\}, \quad R_1^p = 2 \quad r_{1,1} = 1, \ldots \quad C_0 = 0, C_1 = \Gamma_1 = 1 \ldots$$

Figure 6.7 shows the results of the scheduling. The tasks are scheduled to the earliest feasible time. The dummy tasks $\tau_\oplus^0$ to $\tau_\oplus^4$ are indicated by arrows as they require zero computation time, but they are used as markers for the start of a new millisecond.

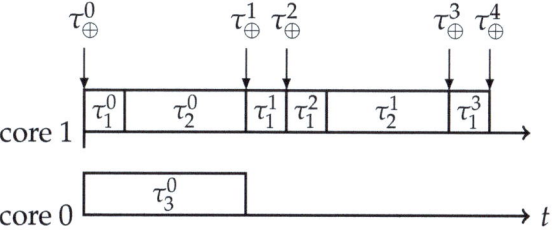

Figure 6.7: The schedule $\mathcal{S}$ for the parameter set equation (6.26).

The transformation first derives the length of one millisecond for the given schedule. The longest duration between two dummy tasks in this example is $\omega = \tau_\oplus^1 - \tau_\oplus^0 = 4$. Subsequently, the start times for each task are derived according to equation (6.25) and the resulting schedule is shown in figure 6.8.

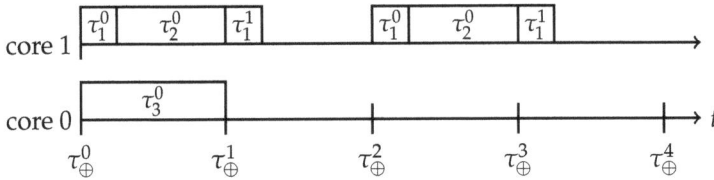

Figure 6.8: The transformed schedule $\mathcal{S}'$ from figure 6.7.

### 6.1.5.2 Meta-heuristic Extensions

The problem representation and schedule transformation in the previous section is enough to use the meta-heuristic **M** for scheduling automotive software on multicore ECUs, if the software is not parallelized. A fitness function guides the search for the best solution with the target to maximize this value. **M** considers the makespan as fitness function.

Using **M** for coordinating runnable- and task-level parallelism requires further extensions of the evolutionary algorithm. The encoding of a schedule solution (genome of an individual) must represent communication that is replaced by TIC and tasks that are parallelized with RunPar. The fitness function must be replaced by the quality metric PSQ introduced in section 6.1.4. These extensions are described in more detail in the following paragraphs.

**Representation of Individuals**—An individual in **M** encodes a schedule solution with one activity list and a *schedule generation scheme (SGS)*. The extension for TIC and RunPar also requires adaptation of the evolutionary operations (crossover and mutation). For TIC a *communication list* $\mu = ((\tau_i, \tau_j), \ldots)$ is added. The tuple $(\tau_i, \tau_j)$ represents a periodic extended precedence constraint between $\tau_i$ and $\tau_j$. For RunPar a *task list* $\delta = \{\tau_1, \cdots, \tau_J\}$ is added that contains all tasks of the application $\mathcal{A}$. It must be possible to test different combinations of both. Therefore, the parameter $w$ represents number of inter-task data dependencies in $\mu$ that are transformed according to equation (5.9) (on page 108). The parameter $u$ represents the tasks in $\delta$ that are parallelized with RunPar. As a result, the representation of each individual is changed as follows:

$$I = (\lambda, SGS) \quad \Rightarrow \quad I' = (\lambda, SGS, \mu, w, \delta, u) \tag{6.27}$$

As a consequence, a task is performed in one out of two modes: *serial* or *parallel*. Executing a task in the serial mode means one core is allocated for the execution ($r_{i,1} = 1$). Contrarily, executing a task in the parallel mode results in the allocation of all cores ($r_{i,1} = R_i^1$), but with a shorter WCET ($C_i = C_i^{\Phi_i}$ as defined by RunPar). $\mu$ and $\delta$ are instantiated with a random order during initialization of the population.

Some inter-task communication can be sensitive to delay, i.e. the communication between tasks on the FILO path. Such *critical* communication is added to the end of the communication list in random order. This guarantees replacement by TIC for less critical communication first. $w$ and $u$ remain static to find an optimal solution for the given parameter set.

**Crossover and Mutation of Individuals**—The crossover of two individuals takes place analogous to [Har02] and this operation must be extended for the two new lists in the individual. The communication lists and the task list of father

$$I^F = (\lambda^F, SGS^F, \mu^F, w^F, \delta^F, u^F) \tag{6.28}$$

and mother

$$I^M = (\lambda^M, SGS^M, \mu^M, w^M, \delta^M, u^M) \tag{6.29}$$

are also merged with a two-point crossover.

For this crossover, four random integers are drawn:

$$1 \le q_1 < q_2 \le |\mu| \quad \text{and} \quad 1 \le q_3 < q_4 \le |\delta| \tag{6.30}$$

Let $x_i^F$ and $x_i^D$ be the i-th position in the communication list of father and mother, respectively. The daughter's communication list takes the positions $i = 1, \ldots, q_1$ from the mother, i.e. $x_i^D = x_i^M$. The positions $i = q_1 + 1, \ldots, q_2$ are taken from the father, $x_i^D = x_i^F$ (already selected pairs are not considered again, i.e. $x_i^F \notin \{x_1^M, \ldots, c_{q_1}^M\}$). The remaining positions are taken from the mother again. The communication list of the son is generated analogously. That means the first and the third part of the list are taken from the father and the second part is taken from the mother.

The task lists are merged in the same way. Let $y_i^F$ and $y_i^D$ be the i-th position in the task list of father and mother, respectively. The daughter's task list takes the positions $i = 1, \ldots, q_3$ from the mother, i.e. $y_i^D = y_i^M$. The positions $i = q_3 + 1, \ldots, q_4$ are taken from the father, $y_i^D = y_i^F$ (already selected tasks are ignored). The remaining positions are taken from the mother again.

Afterwards, both lists are traversed from left to right and an element is shifted to the right with a probability $p_{mutation} = 0.05$. This value is recommended by [Har02].

**Selection of Individuals**—Each iteration follows the basic scheme for evolutionary algorithms as defined by [Hol75; Gol89] (see section 3.2.2.1). The last step in each iteration is the selection of the fittest individuals for reuse in the next iteration. The quality metric PSQ is used as fitness function for an individual whose value must be maximized (see definition 6.5 on page 136). Therefore, frequency impact, latency impact and PSQ are calculated for each schedule in the population ($POP$). Eventually, the individuals (schedules) are ranked by their fitness (PSQ) The schedules with the highest fitness value are selected for survival of the iteration.

A mechanism known as *clone detection* is used to avoid redundant calculations. Each individual has a unique encoding that identifies it. A database stores the description of each individual and the resulting PSQ. Thus, the fitness of a repeatedly occurring individuals is directly taken from the database without further computation.

## 6.2  Performance Evaluation

The evaluation of the coordination of runnable- and task-level parallelization is conducted in several steps. First, a qualitative analysis is conducted, in which the objectives from section 3.1 are discussed and research questions are derived. Second, the questions are investigated in experiments. Here, an initial set of experiments is conducted to derive an optimal configuration for the meta-heuristic **M**. The experiments in section 6.2.4 investigate the impact of selectively applying TIC on critical FILO paths of a real control application. Section 6.2.5 investigates how selectively applying RunPar in combination with TIC can improve the overall system performance.

### 6.2.1  Qualitative Analysis and Resulting Research Questions

This section discusses the coordination of runnable- and task-level parallelization in the context of the functional and non-functional objectives defined in section 3.1. Research questions for the quantitative evaluation are derived whenever necessary.

#### 6.2.1.1  Functional Objectives

*Subtask decomposition* — The coordinating approach is designed to consider data dependencies on two levels of granularity. On runnable-level, a RDG (definition 4.1) defines precedence constraints between runnables. Section 4.1.2 described how the graph is derived from an existing application. On task-level, periodic extended precedence constraints (definition 2.5) define inter-task data dependencies as repetitive pattern. From this, a job list of task instances with precedence constraints for one hyperperiod is derived. In the job list, tasks that are parallelized on runnable-level are considered with a shorter WCET and with a higher resource consumption (all available cores).

The FILO paths and their latency are mandatory input parameters for the coordination. These paths are derived for each computed solution and considered during the selection process. Particularly sensitive paths are annotated.

*Mapping and scheduling* — The job list is used to compute a schedule for a complete hyperperiod, whereas two levels of granularity and the processor specific WCET are considered. A task executes either on one core (task WCET plus overhead for TIC) or on all cores following a RunPar schedule (task WCET of the static partitioning). That means runnable- and task-level parallelism are combined in a divide and conquer manner, whereas different combinations are explored. Robust paths are preferred for usage with TIC. The clock rate is adjusted to guarantee the schedule's feasibility.

### 6.2.1.2 Non-functional Objectives

*Predictable interprocessor communication* — The evolutionary algorithm constructs a static schedule, in which *logical execution times (LETs)* for the execution of a single runnable or a complete task are specified. On runnable-level, the definition of these LETs is based on the precedence constraints defined in the RDG. Hence, the computed schedule is predictable by construction. On task-level, the LETs are defined based on the precedence constraints in the job list. Tasks that execute in a parallel way are either independent from each other or they use TIC. TIC guarantees a predictable data-flow regardless of the actual execution of a task. This means the interprocessor communication is predictable.

*Robustness* — The FILO latency of a critical sensor/actuator chain is considered as part of the schedule generation process. The use of TIC is limited to keep the latency within acceptable bounds, but the task periods and the clock rate are adjusted by a constant factor, in such a manner that the latency of the parallel schedule is equal to the value of the reference platform. Therefore, the latency is derived from the parallel schedule considering the smallest possible clock rate. Then, a constant adjustment factor is computed to scale the task periods and the clock rate. This factor also serves as a quality criterion in selecting a schedule that minimizes latency and clock rate.

*Data consistency* — The static schedule respects data dependencies and thus prevents access to shared memory locations. Moreover, the access to shared memory locations always takes places in the same order. Computations based on communication with TIC are performed on a copy of a datum and this allows simultaneous access to the same variable without corruption. Encapsulating shared functions in client/server-calls prevents lost updates. Thus, data consistency is ensured by construction and lost updates are impossible.

*Efficiency* — Reducing the clock rate utilizes idle intervals obtained from parallelization and it reduces the energy consumption. TIC enables more scheduling possibilities, because fewer inter-task data dependencies need to be respected. This allows for better load balancing and larger idle intervals. The experiments in section 5.2 already analysed the improvements with TIC for the time slot when the utilization is maximal. This situation appears once in a hyperperiod and the impact on the complete hyperperiod is not studied so far. Thus, the following research question arises:

◇ *To what extent reduces selectively using TIC and RunPar in a hyperperiod the required clock rate $f_{min}$?*

Nevertheless, a reduction of the clock rate is bound to the impact on the critical FILO latency. This is reflected by the quality metric PSQ. TIC provides a benefit only, if the positive effect of a clock rate reduction compensates the negative impact on the FILO latency. Consequently, the following research question arises:

◇ *What is the trade-off between the selective use of TIC and benefit from the parallelization?*

The qualitative discussion of TIC in section 5.2.1 already concluded that the method cannot be applied to all inter-task data dependencies. Otherwise, critical FILO paths experience an unacceptable high latency. However, applying RunPar can still improve the performance in such cases. This results in the research question:

◇ *How does the combination of RunPar and TIC influence the quality of the parallelization in comparison to the individual mechanisms?*

*Scalability* — The scheduling for a hyperperiod is an NP-complete problem [GJ90] and thus finding an optimal solution in reasonable time is hard. Therefore, a meta-heuristic is used to compute a large set of possible solutions and select the best one. However, no guarantee can be given whether found solution is optimal. An evolutionary algorithm maintains a population and adapts the genome of individuals in an evolution-like process. A critical parameter for finding good solutions is the population size and the necessary number of iterations. Hence, a fundamental question about this approach equals:

◇ *Which population size and how many iterations are necessary to find a good solution with the proposed evolutionary algorithm?*

The two new lists in the genome, the communication list $\mu$ and the task list $\delta$, increase the computational time for the crossover operation minimal. The number of tasks and the number of connections in between is typically much smaller than the length of the activity list. Moreover, the communication list specifies constraints that can be ignored by the scheduling heuristic, which is in favour of the computation time. That means the additional overhead is assumed to be small.

To proof the scalability of the approach, a real automotive control application is used for the evaluation. The following research question must be answered by the experiments:

⋄ *How much computation time is required to generate a hyperperiod schedule for a real application?*

*Low cost* — Limiting the FILO latency to an acceptable bound reduces cost of human labour for the migration, because the effort for re-validation is drastically reduced.

*Compliance, portability, and minimal standard modification* — The evolutionary algorithm generates a static schedule for a complete hyperperiod. The concrete implementation is left to the integrator and this allows for optimizations. However, the implementation must guarantee that tasks do not start before their defined start time to maintain predictability. For instance, this can be done with schedule tables.

*Summary of non-functional objectives* — The approach in this chapter generates robust and feasible schedules, in which runnable- and task-level parallelization are combined. The expected cost is low and the generated schedules are compliant to AUTOSAR. The integrator, however, has to take care about the implementation of the schedule. Nevertheless, the scalability and the efficiency need to be investigated in experiment. Therefore, the evaluation in the next four sections investigates the aforementioned research questions.

Section 6.2.3 investigates the ideal configuration of the evolutionary algorithm when a real application is used. Therefore, the value of the fittest schedule (expressed by the PSQ metric) in the population of one iteration is used as metric. Printing the value over time shows when the approach converges and one can derive an ideal population size and a minimal number of iterations.

Section 6.2.4 investigates the trade-off between the selective use of TIC and the clock rate and the FILO latency. Therefore, overall benefit of the parallelization is quantified with the PSQ metric. The same metrics are used for investigating the combination of TIC and RunPar in section 6.2.5.

The experiments with the evolutionary algorithm are conducted on a compute cluster that is equipped with five 64Bit Intel Xeon E5-2650 CPUs (each with eight cores) running at 2.3GHz providing 40 cores in total and 252 GB RAM of which less than 20GB are needed by the simulator.

## 6.2.2   Experiment Configurations

The experiments in this section investigate the impact of TIC on the critical FILO latency and the coordination of TIC and RunPar. Therefore, two task dependence graphs (TDGs) are used: a *randomly generated* TDG and a *real case study* TDG. This must ensure the general validity of the results in practice. The randomly generated TDG is denoted as $G_p$ and a TDG of the case study is denoted as $G_c$. Both are explained in the following in greater detail.

### 6.2.2.1   Random Task Dependence Graph

A random TDG is generated with the Erdős-Rényi model, which is described in section 2.4.4. The properties of the generated TDGs are derived from the use case that is used for the previous experiments, described in section 2.1.3. Table 6.1 lists the properties of $G_p$. The amount of tasks is reduced to eight, because the number of experiments with these graphs is high, 32 per data point, and this still allows for conducting experiments in reasonable time.

| Parameter | Value |
|---|---|
| Tasks | $8\ (\tau_2, \tau_3, \tau_4, \tau_5, \tau_6, \tau_7, \tau_8, \tau_9)$ |
| Hyperperiod | 320 ms |
| Jobs | 875 |
| $G_p$ | A random graph in the set $G_{8,32}$ |
| WCET | $C_i$ chosen from $\{C_2, C_3, C_4, C_5, C_6, C_7, C_8, C_9\}$ |

Table 6.1: Properties of $G_p$.

The eight tasks with the lowest periods in the use case have 32 inter-task data dependencies. Thus, the TDG is selected randomly from the graph set $G_{8,32}$, which means each graph for a single experiment is composed of eight tasks and exactly 32 inter-task data dependencies. Each inter-task data dependency between two tasks can appear with uniform probability. The WCET of a task is randomly chosen from the WCETs in the use case, whereas each $C_i$ is assigned to one task only.

### 6.2.2.2   Case Study Task Dependence Graph

Additionally, the same experiments are conducted with the same use case as in the previous chapters (section 2.1.3) to investigate how valid the results of a randomly generated TDGs are for real applications. However, the tasks $\tau_1$ and $\tau_{12}$ are not considered here. The former one is the crank-angle task, which already communicates asynchronously with periodic tasks and its impact can be considered by assuming a periodic task with maximal period that adds a constant worst-case load. The latter one has a comparably high period (1024 ms) and it only communicates with two other tasks. Thus, this task is not responsible for critical operation of the controller. Ignoring this task significantly reduces the computation time of the experiments, but their expressiveness remains. Table 6.2 summarizes the parameters of the TDG based on the case study.

| Parameter | Value |
|---|---|
| Tasks | 10 ($\tau_2$, $\tau_3$, $\tau_4$, $\tau_5$, $\tau_6$, $\tau_7$, $\tau_8$, $\tau_9$, $\tau_{10}$, $\tau_{11}$) |
| Hyperperiod | 1920 ms |
| Jobs | 5285 |
| $G_c$ | 22798 resulting from 51 inter-task data dependencies |
| WCET | $C_i$ as derived by OTAWA (section 2.4) |

Table 6.2: Properties of $G_c$.

## 6.2.3 Ideal Configuration

Table 6.3 list the configuration for two experiments, which are conducted to find an ideal configuration for the evolutionary algorithm for further experiments. Therefore, the *population size (POP)* and the number of iterations are derived.

### 6.2.3.1 Experiment Configuration

The first set of experiments (A) is conducted with random TDGs as defined in table 6.1 and the second set of experiments (B) is conducted with the use case TDG as defined in table 6.2.

| Setup | $A_1$ | $A_2$ | $A_3$ | $A_4$ | $B_1$ | $B_2$ | $B_3$ | $B_4$ |
|---|---|---|---|---|---|---|---|---|
| POP | 30 | 50 | 100 | 150 | 30 | 50 | 100 | 150 |
| Runs | 32 | | | | 12 | | | |
| Iterations | 7 | | | | | | | |
| w | 32 (all connections use TIC) | | | | 21 (partly use of TIC) | | | |
| u | 0 (no RunPar tasks) | | | | | | | |
| TDG | $G_p \in G_{8,32}$ | | | | $G_c$ | | | |

Table 6.3: Configuration for experiment A with $G_p$ and for experiment B with $G_c$ for deriving an ideal configuration.

Four different configurations are tested per experiment, in which $POP$ is varied. The article of [Har98] found that a $POP$ of 40 and 25 iterations are ideal for solving the RCPSP for 30 jobs with 81.5% optimal. However, the number of jobs is larger for automotive control software due to the long hyperperiod and $POP$ is therefore set to 30, 50, 100, and 150 individuals, respectively. An advantage for the calculation is the frequent serialization from dummy jobs (section 5.1.3), because this limits the schedulable range for a task. Hence, the number of iterations is limited to seven, and one initializing iteration in the beginning of the run.

The parameters in for an individual (equation (6.27) on page 140) are set to $w = 32$ and $u = 0$ in experiment $A$ and they are set to $w = 21$ and $u = 0$ in experiment $B$, respectively. That means none of the tasks uses RunPar, all inter-task data dependencies are ignored in experiment $A$, and a fraction of inter-task data dependencies is ignored in experiment $B$. In the latter on, 21 out of the 51 inter-task communication selectively uses TIC. The motivation for this configuration is, the evolutionary algorithm is forced to test many different combinations, over several iterations, until the optimization criterion PSQ converges towards a maximal value.

### 6.2.3.2 Expectations

The size of the population can have a significant impact on the computation time and the convergence of an evolutionary algorithm. However, the frequent serialisation, caused by a precedence relation with dummy activities, shrinks the solution space. The expectation for both experiments is a good solution is found in reasonable computation time. Nevertheless, the computation time in experiment $B$ is expected to be larger, because the hyperperiod of the schedule is larger.

### 6.2.3.3 Results of Experiment A

Figure 6.9 shows the computation time per iteration for the four setups in table 6.3 for $G_p$ with 95%-confidence intervals computed over 32 runs. The labels $POP$ 30, $POP$ 50, $POP$ 100, and $POP$ 150 denote the setups $A_1$, $A_2$, $A_3$, and $A_4$, respectively. The lines are added to ease readability; they do not represent intermediate points.

The duration of the first iteration is smaller than subsequent iterations. The reason for this is the first iteration in each run only computes the initial population of size $|POP|$, whereas subsequent iterations compute twice as much. They also generate the offspring by the crossover and mutation, which is the reason for increasing the computation time between the first three iterations. The results show: a larger population significantly increases the computation time.

Figure 6.10 shows the required clock rate $f_{min}$ for the best schedule in each iteration for experiment A, before adjusting task periods and frequency (definition 6.4 on page 135).

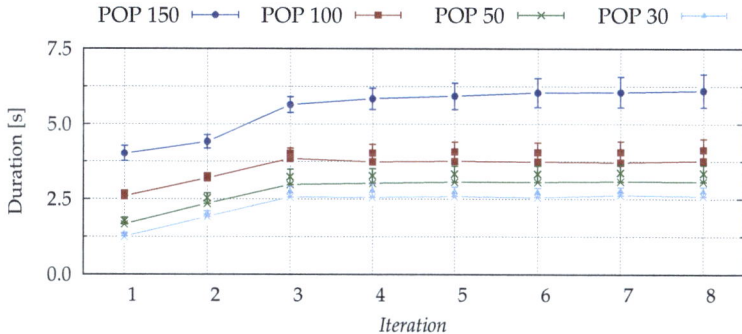

Figure 6.9: Computation time per iteration of the evolutionary algorithm for scheduling $G_p$ in experiment A.

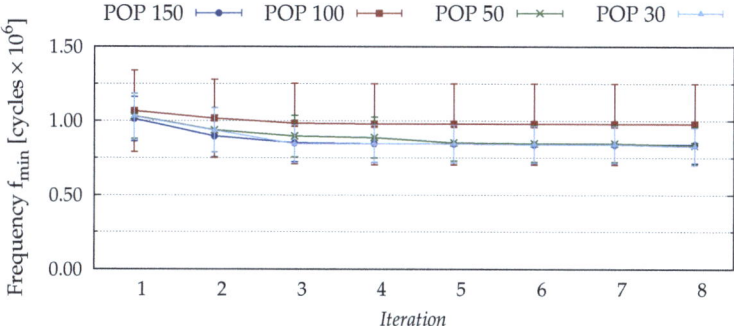

Figure 6.10: Convergence of the required clock rate $f_{min}$ in experiment A. Smaller values are better.

The number of TIC connections increases from left to right. 95%-confidence intervals were computed over 32 runs. The lines are added to ease readability; they do not represent

The confidence intervals in this figure overlap. However, of particular interest in this figure is the lower end of the confidence interval, because it marks better results. A larger population ($POP$ 100) has a wider confidence interval than a small population ($POP$ 30). That means the solutions span a wider range and an optimal solution is found in fewer iterations. Nevertheless, the lower end of the confidence interval is equal in all experiments after iteration five. A population with 150 individuals, however, does not shorten the convergence time further.

#### 6.2.3.4  Results of Experiment B

Figure 6.11 shows the computation time per iteration for $G_c$ with 95%-confidence intervals computed over 12 runs. The labels *POP 30*, *POP 50*, *POP 100*, and *POP 150* denote the setups $B_1$, $B_2$, $B_3$, and $B_4$, respectively. Like in experiment A, the duration of the first iteration is smaller than subsequent iterations. Although, the effect is less significant than in experiment A; and the computation time for $B_1$ and $B_2$ are equivalent.

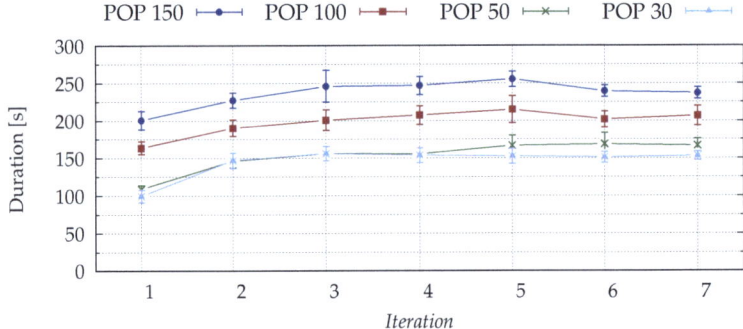

Figure 6.11: Computation time per iteration of the evolutionary algorithm for scheduling $G_c$ in experiment B.

Figure 6.12a shows the required clock rate $f_{min}$ for the best schedule per iteration for experiment B, before adjusting task periods and frequency (definition 6.4 on page 135). 95%-confidence intervals were computed over 12 runs.

In contrast to experiment A, the values overlap each other and they do not change over the iterations. That means the best schedule solution with respect to a minimal clock rate is already found in the first iteration. However, $f_{min}$ is insufficient for making conclusions about the convergence for the use case.

For this reason, the quality of the schedule (PSQ) is shown additionally in figure 6.12b. The figure shows the value of the best schedule per iteration with 95%-confidence intervals computed over 12 runs. The size of the population does not make a difference in the achieved fitness. However, the value increases after three iterations, which means a schedule with a lower latency and the same clock rate is found.

The overlapping results in this experiment results from repeating the experiment with the same use case and configuration. The variation in the initial population was small and thus all repetitions computed similar results.

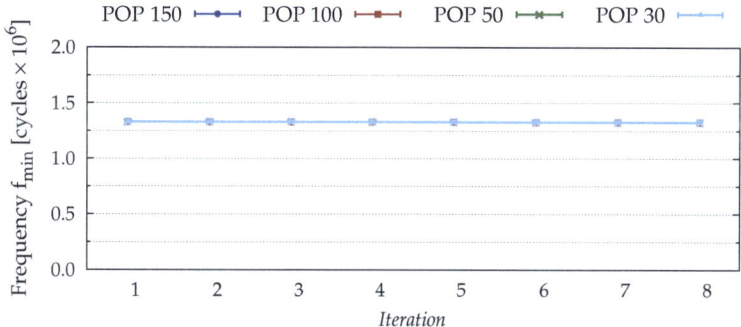

(a) The required clock rate $f_{min}$ per iteration. Smaller values are better.

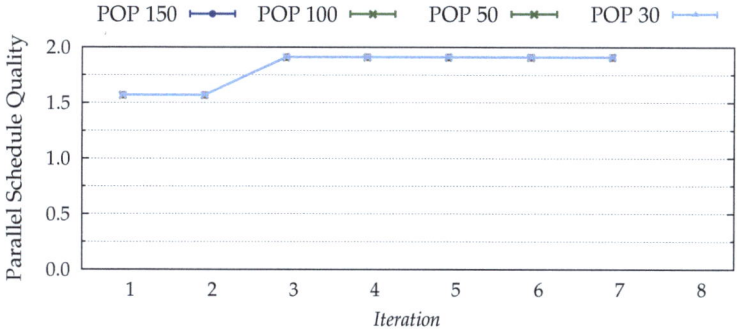

(b) Maximal achieved fitness per iteration. Higher values are better.

Figure 6.12: Convergence of the evolutionary algorithm for scheduling $G_c$ in experiment B.

### 6.2.3.5 Summary

The population size does not significantly affect the quality of the result, but a good solution is found with fewer iterations when the population is large. Both experiments converged in few iterations (three and five). Therefore, all further experiments are conducted with a *population size of 100* individuals and *six iterations*.

## 6.2.4 Trade-off Between Clock Rate and FILO Latency

This section investigates the impact of TIC on the end-to-end latency of automotive control software. Therefore, two experiments are conducted that investigate the changes in the critical and in the longest end-to-end chain, respectively.

### 6.2.4.1 Experiment Configuration

Again, the first set of experiments (*A*) is conducted with random TDGs as defined in table 6.1 and the second set of experiments (*B*) is conducted with the use case TDG as defined in table 6.2.

The second column in table 6.4 lists the configuration for experiment *A*. This first set of experiments concerns the impact of TIC on the clock rate $f_{min}$ and only on the critical FILO latency. Therefore, one pair of tasks is randomly selected and their communication is considered as critical FILO chain, which means the critical path is considered for computing the schedule quality PSQ (definition 6.5 on page 136).

The parameter $w$ is varied in steps of two from 0 to 32 (all inter-task communication uses TIC) to get an overview and still keep the simulation time on a reasonable level. RunPar is not used in the experiments as the impact of TIC is investigated here and this means the parameter $u = 0$. A four-core processor ($Proc_4$ in table 5.1 of section 5.2.2) is considered as target platform.

The third column in table 6.4 lists the configuration for experiment *B*. The focus of this second set of experiments is on investigating the impact of TIC on the critical FILO latency and on the longest possible end-to-end chain at the same time. The use case is larger and, thus, the parameter $w$ is varied in steps of three from 0 to 51 (all inter-task communication uses TIC). Again, RunPar is not used and the same four-core processor is considered as target platform.

| Parameter | Experiment A | Experiment B |
|:---:|:---:|:---:|
| Task graph | $G_p$ from table 6.1 | $G_c$ from table 6.2 |
| Processor | $Proc_4$ from table 5.1 | |
| Runs | 32 | 1 |
| Population size | 100 | |
| Iterations | 6 | |
| $u$ | 0 (no RunPar tasks) | |
| $w$ | 0, 1, 3, 5, 7, 9, 11, 13, 15, 17, 19, 21, 23, 25, 27, 29, 31, 32 | 0, 3, 6, 9, 12, 15, 18, 21, 24, 27, 30, 33, 36, 39, 42, 45, 48, 51 |

Table 6.4: Configuration for experiment *A* with $G_p$ and for experiment *B* for investigating the impact of TIC on the FILO latency.

The critical computation in a diesel *engine management system (EMS)* is the *gas pedal/injection* FILO chain. Analysis of the use case showed that these chain begins in the use case in $\tau_6$ (gas pedal sensor acquire) and ends in $\tau_8$ (injection quantity and timing calculation). The tasks are executed one after another in the original application's configuration and the resulting data-flow (definition 5.1) equals:

$$P_{6,8}^s = \tau_6^{n_0} \tau_8^{n_1}.$$ (6.31)

The associated FILO latency is denoted as $\text{FILO}_{6,8}^s$. The necessary analysis to identify these chains in the use case has been conducted in the Master's thesis of Hassan [Has15].

The longest inter-task communication data-flow chain in a hyperperiod (considering several sensor/actuator chains in one long chain) is composed of 8 tasks:

$$P_{2,11}^s = \tau_2^{n_0} \tau_3^{n_1} \tau_4^{n_2} \tau_5^{n_3} \tau_6^{n_4} \tau_8^{n_5} \tau_9^{n_6} \tau_{11}^{n_7}.$$ (6.32)

The associated FILO latency is thus denoted as $\text{FILO}_{2,11}^s$.

### 6.2.4.2 Expectations

The expectation for experiment $A$ is that $f_{\min}^p$ is lower than $f_{\min}^s$ and it decreases when inter-task communication uses TIC. Some tasks have only few data dependencies with other tasks, for example $\tau_{12}$ has only two inter-task data dependencies. Thus, a reduction can be expected even without using TIC, because tasks can already execute in a parallel way. However, increasing the amount of TIC connections should further reduce $f_{\min}^p$.

The FILO latency is expected to increase, because the chain is considered by the optimization criterion of the evolutionary algorithm that selects the best combination between latency increment and frequency reduction.

Likewise, for experiment $B$ a reduction of $f_{\min}^p$ in comparison to $f_{\min}^s$ is expected when the number of TIC connections increases. Contrarily, $\text{FILO}_{2,11}^p$ is expected to be higher than $f_{\min}^s$ already for small values of $w$. Thereby, the evolutionary algorithm potentially prefers a replacing of inter-task data dependencies between tasks with low period, because the impact on the optimization criterion PSQ is smaller. The reason is, TIC adds latency in the length of one producer task period to $\text{FILO}_{2,11}^p$. Hence, inter-task communication with tasks of low period are preferable candidates for the use with TIC.

Considering critical communication at least causes an impact on the critical chain not until almost all inter-task data communication uses TIC. That means the expectation is that $f_{\min}^p$ decreases with every increment of $w$, whereas $\text{FILO}_{2,11}^p$ increases slowly with every increment of $w$. A high number of data dependencies must be replaced to reach the minimal possible clock rate.

### 6.2.4.3   Results of Experiment A

Figure 6.13 shows the minimum frequency $f^p_{min}$ that is required to fulfil all task dead-lines for experiment A, before adjusting task periods and frequency (definition 6.4 on page 135). The number of TIC connections increases from left to right. 95%-confidence intervals were computed over 32 runs. The lines are added to ease readability; they do not represent intermediate points. The dashed line represents the baseline frequency that is $f^p_{min}$ for the sequential execution of the tasks *on one core*. This value is derived from a separate set of simulations with the same configuration, but with a non-preemptive scheduling on one core only.

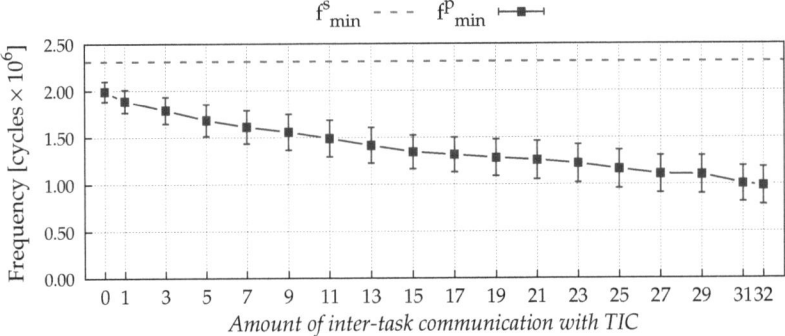

Figure 6.13: The impact of TIC on the clock rate $f^p_{min}$ for $G_{8,32}$ on four cores.

The figure shows a reduction for $f^p_{min}$ already for $w = 0$ by 13.5%. That means some tasks can execute in a parallel way without TIC, because they are not constrained by inter-task data dependencies. Increasing the amount of TIC further reduces the clock rate down to 43% of the reference value.

Figure 6.14 shows the impact of TIC on the critical FILO latency relative to the baseline value. Like the baseline frequency, this value is derived from a separate set of simulations with the same configuration of one core. As expected, introducing TIC increases the latency in the FILO chain already for $w \geq 3$. The evolutionary algorithm prefers combinations, in which a latency increment can be compensated by a reduction of the clock rate. The latency increases until $w = 5$ and keeps steady until $w = 29$. The last two data points represent schedules that replace also the critical chain, leading to a higher latency increment.

The evolutionary algorithm prefers an increment of the latency due to the higher PSQ of such individuals. The values of the fitness function for the best schedule are shown in figure 6.15. The PSQ increases with every increment of $w$. The two highest values are achieved when all inter-task communication uses TIC, although the latency increases by 21%. The reduction of $f^p_{min}$ by 43% outweighs this.

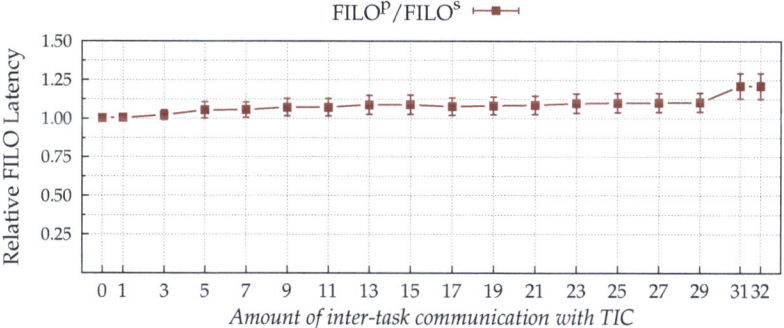

Figure 6.14: Impact of TIC on the critical FILO latency in $G_{8,32}$ on a processor with four cores.

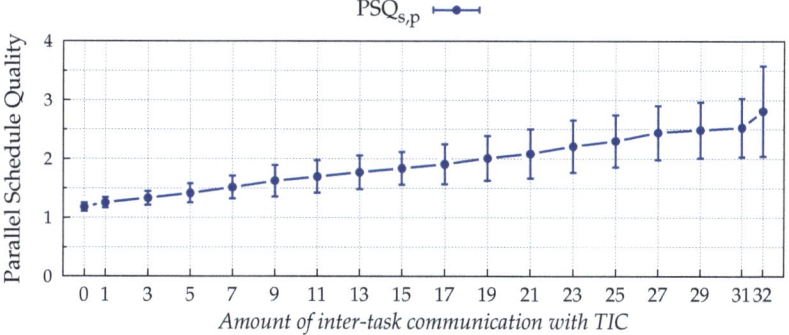

Figure 6.15: The fitness function parallel schedule quality (PSQ) on four cores.

#### 6.2.4.4 Results of Experiment B

Figure 6.16 shows the minimum frequency $f^p_{min}$ that is required to fulfil all task deadlines for experiment B, before adjusting task periods and frequency (definition 6.4 on page 135). The number of TIC connections increases from left to right. 95%-confidence intervals were computed over 12 runs. The dashed line represents the baseline frequency that is $f^p_{min}$ for the sequential execution of the tasks ($w = 0$). The figure shows that introducing TIC reduces $f^p_{min}$ already for small values of $w$.

However, further increasing the number of TIC connections does not immediately lead to further reduction of $f^p_{min}$. The improvements are stepwise in contrast to the expectations. Concretely, the first step ranges from 3 to 6, the next from 9 to 24, and the last from 30 to 51. These steps result from the high number of inter-task data

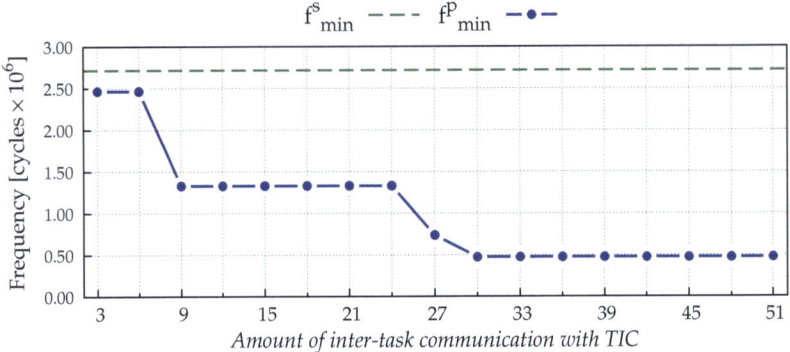

Figure 6.16: The impact of TIC on the clock rate $f_{min}^{p}$.

dependencies per task. All data dependencies of a task must be replaced with TIC before it can execute totally free within its period and a benefit is taken from this. As a result, the lowest clock rate requires a replacement of more than half (30) of the connections with TIC and this leads to a reduction of 82%.

Figure 6.17 shows the impact of TIC on the latency FILO paths $FILO_{2,11}$ and $FILO_{6,8}$. The dashed lines represent the latency in the single-core configuration and they are used for comparison purposes here. As expected, introducing TIC increases the latency in both FILO chains. The latency in the longer chain $FILO_{2,11}$ increases slowly and shows also stepwise changes. Concretely, the first step ranges from 3 to 6, the next from 9 to 21, and the latency totally exacerbates from 39 on.

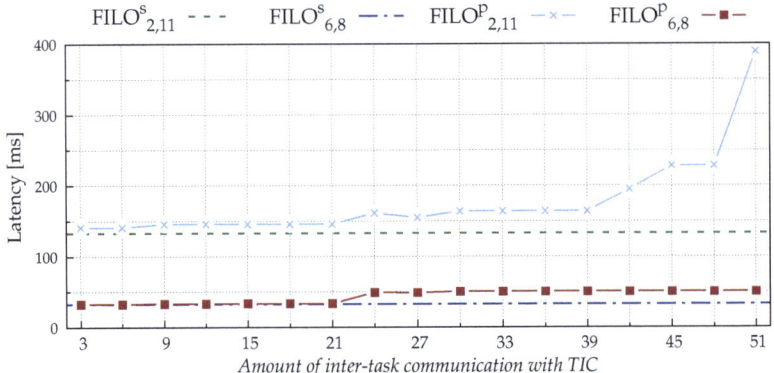

Figure 6.17: Impact of TIC on $FILO_{2,11}^{s}$ and $FILO_{6,8}^{s}$ in experiment B.

However, the impact on the shorter, but more critical, chain $\hat{P}^p_{6,8}$ is less severe, because the optimization criterion prefers combinations with less impact on the latency. Here, the latency does not suffer any variation until $w = 21$, where the frequency reduction is 51% (figure 6.16). Interestingly, the frequency impact with larger values of $w$ outweighs the disadvantages of the increased delay. A superior schedule is found, but the critical latency is increased.

Figure 6.18 shows the $PSQ_{s,p}$ resulting from combining the plots figures 6.16 and 6.17. The stepwise reduction of the clock rate leads to stepwise changes in the $PSQ_{s,p}$. The frequency impact (definition 6.2 on page 133) outweighs the latency impact (definition 6.3 on page 134), although the latency increases slowly. The $PSQ_{s,p}$ reaches its maximal value in the interval $w = (30, 39)$. Interestingly, the overall performance decreases for larger values, because the frequency impact cannot compensate the latency impact any more.

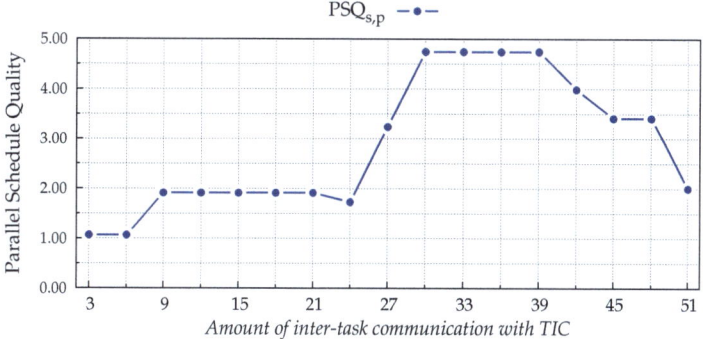

Figure 6.18: The fitness function PSQ on four cores.

### 6.2.4.5 Summary

Both experiments confirmed that a gain in the frequency impact (definition 6.2) can outweigh the disadvantage of the latency impact (definition 6.3), when TIC is used for inter-task communication. Considering one long end-to-end FILO chain and one critical FILO chain prevents an immediate impact on the latter one.

The experiments with the case study from section 2.1.3 showed a stepwise reduction of the minimal clock rate. The reason is a high number of inter-task data dependencies with the same task, which all have to be replaced before the clock rate reduces further. This should be considered when the mechanism is applied.

The highest overall gain from task-level parallelization is achieved, if more than half of the inter-task communication used TIC. Below this, most of the tasks are still executed in a sequential order. This keeps the FILO latency low, but the quality of the schedule is low. RunPar can reduce the WCET in such cases and utilize idle interval, whereas the latency remains almost equal. This imposes the question:

⋄ *Is it possible to further reduce the clock rate for $G_c$ running on* Proc$_4$ *in the range* $w \in (3, 21)$ *with RunPar?*

This question is investigated in the next section.

## 6.2.5  Coordination of TIC and RunPar

In this section, TIC and RunPar are used as complementary mechanisms. Moreover, they are compared against each other in one hyperperiod.

The previous section showed that applying TIC to less than half (21) of the inter-task communication of the use case results in a low latency increment. Furthermore, re-placing communication can reduce the clock rate, but this also increases the latency. Fortunately, RunPar finds ideal usage here. RunPar distributes runnables to the available cores and data dependencies are respected. Thus, the task WCET is shortened, idle intervals are utilized, and the clock rate is reduced without further increasing the latency.

### 6.2.5.1  Experiment Configuration

Again, two experiments are conducted, where the first set of experiments ($A$) uses the random TDGs, as defined in table 6.1, and the second set of experiments ($B$) uses the case study TDG, as defined in table 6.2.

The second column of table 6.5 lists the configuration for experiment $A$. The configuration is almost identical to experiment A in the previous section, except for the amount of RunPar tasks that is set to eight ($u = 8$). This allows for a direct comparison against a setup with $u = 0$, which was computed in the previous experiment. Likewise, a four-core processor is considered as target platform, one pair of tasks is randomly selected as critical FILO chain, and the parameter $w$ is varied in steps of two from 0 to 32.

The third column of table 6.5 lists the configuration for experiment $B$. Experiment B from the previous section is repeated, but the amount of RunPar tasks is varied: $u = 0, 3, 6$, and 10. This allows for investigating the improvement by complementary use of runnable- (RunPar) and task-level (TIC) parallelization.

The evolutionary algorithm computes for every pair of $w$ and $u$ the schedule with the highest PSQ. The interest in these experiments is on the impact of TIC, i.e. parameter

| Parameter | Experiment A | Experiment B |
|---|---|---|
| Task graph | $G_p$ from table 6.1 | $G_c$ from table 6.2 |
| Processor | Proc$_4$ from table 5.1 | |
| Runs | 32 | 1 |
| Population size | 100 | |
| Iterations | 6 | |
| $u$ | 0 (no RunPar tasks), 8 (8 RunPar tasks) | 0, 3, 6, 10 |
| $w$ | 0, 1, 3, 5, 7, 9, 11, 13, 15, 17, 19, 21, 23, 25, 27, 29, 31, 32 | 0, 3, 6, 9, 12, 15, 18, 21 |

Table 6.5: Configuration for experiment $A$ with $G_p$ and for experiment $B$ for comparing and coordinating TIC and RunPar.

$w$. There is a series of measurements for every $u$. The schedules for experiment A are denoted as $\mathcal{S}^{p,0}$ and $\mathcal{S}^{p,8}$. The schedules for experiment B are denoted as $\mathcal{S}^{p,0}$, $\mathcal{S}^{p,3}$, $\mathcal{S}^{p,6}$, and $\mathcal{S}^{p,10}$.

### 6.2.5.2 Expectations

The comparison in section 5.2.4 showed an advantage for RunPar when only few (less than eight) tasks are active. The task set in experiment $A$ contains eight tasks and, thus, the performance of both is expected to be equivalent when all inter-task communication uses TIC. For smaller amounts of TIC, RunPar is expected to require a lower clock rate.

The TDG for experiment $B$ contains a larger task set. Hence, TIC is expected to require a lower clock rate when all inter-task communication uses TIC. In contrast, RunPar is expected to require a lower clock rate in the range $w = 0$ to $w = 21$. Moreover, the combination of both approaches is expected to perform better than the individual approaches.

### 6.2.5.3 Results of Experiment A

Figure 6.19 compares $f_{\min}$ between TIC and RunPar for $G_p$ in experiment A, before adjusting task periods and frequency (definition 6.4 on page 135). 95%-confidence intervals were computed over 12 runs. The lines are added to ease readability; they do not represent intermediate points. The curves for $\mathcal{S}^{p,0}$ and $\mathcal{S}^{p,8}$ are named as $f_{\min}^{p,0}$ (only TIC) and $f_{\min}^{p,8}$ (only RunPar tasks), respectively. The line $f_{\min}^{s}$ denotes the baseline value from the original application.

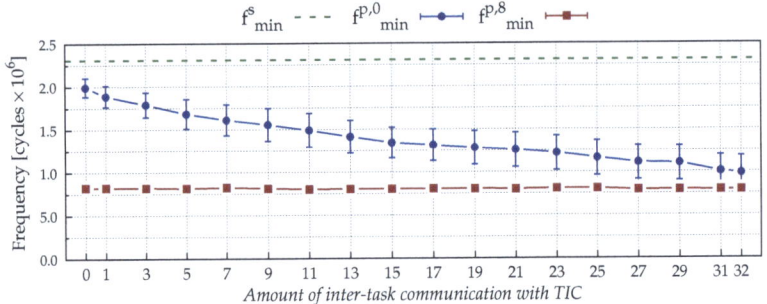

Figure 6.19: Comparison of $f_{\min}$ with RunPar and TIC for $G_p$.

The results show that solely relying on RunPar ($f_{\min}^{p,8}$) results in a lower clock rate than only using TIC ($f_{\min}^{p,0}$). Both achieve a comparable low clock rate when all inter-task communication uses TIC, i.e. at $w = 32$. However, RunPar provides the same performance without increasing the critical FILO latency. These results match with the expectations and they support the findings in section 5.2.4.

### 6.2.5.4  Results of Experiment B

Figure 6.20 shows the minimal required clock rate $f_{\min}$ when TIC and RunPar are combined in experiment B. Again, the values are derived before adjusting task periods and frequency (definition 6.4 on page 135). 95%-confidence intervals were computed over 12 runs. The curves for the clock frequency are names as follows:

▷ $\mathcal{S}^{p,0}$ without RunPar tasks: $f_{\min}^{p,0}$

▷ $\mathcal{S}^{p,3}$ with 3 RunPar tasks: $f_{\min}^{p,3}$

▷ $\mathcal{S}^{p,6}$ with 6 RunPar tasks: $f_{\min}^{p,6}$

▷ $\mathcal{S}^{p,10}$ with 8 RunPar tasks: $f_{\min}^{p,10}$

Unfortunately, not all measurement points could be derived due to implementation issues.

The plot is separated in two regions. The first region, from $w = 3$ to $w = 21$, represents the range in which TIC can be applied safely, which means the critical FILO latency is increased to an acceptable amount. The second region, from $w = 21$ to $w = 51$, represents the range in which TIC increases the critical FILO latency more severe, which requires a larger compensation by a clock rate reduction.

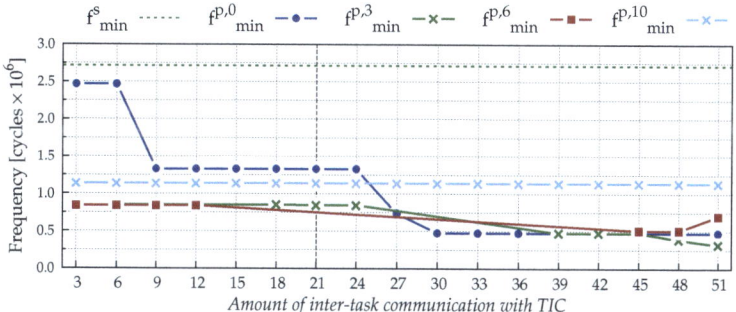

Figure 6.20: Comparison of $f_{min}$ with different fractions of RunPar tasks and TIC for $G_c$.

Solely relying on RunPar ($f_{min}^{p,10}$) results in a lower required clock rate than only using TIC ($f_{min}^{p,0}$) within the first region (from $w = 3$ to $w = 21$). In contrast, $f_{min}^{p,0}$ requires a much lower clock rate in the second region (from $w = 21$ to $w = 51$). The reason for this is the larger task set profits from the reduction of inter-task data dependencies more than a small task set, like in experiment A. This also matches with the findings in section 5.2.4.

Combination both approaches further reduces the clock rate below the value of the individual approaches in the first region. The performance is equivalent to $f_{min}^{p,0}$ in the second region. Consequently, the quality of the parallel schedule is increased in this region.

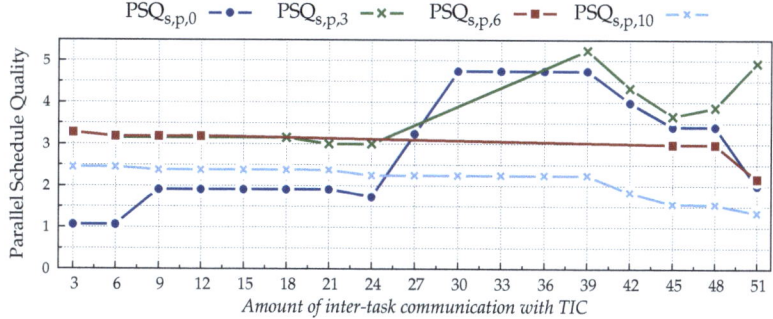

Figure 6.21: Parallel schedule quality for different combinations of runnable- and task-level parallelism.

Figure 6.21 shows the PSQ for the combinations of runnable- and task-level parallelism. The PSQ curves for the parallel schedules are named as follows:

▷ $\mathcal{S}^{p,0}$ without RunPar tasks: $PSQ_{s,p,0}$

▷ $\mathcal{S}^{p,3}$ with 3 RunPar tasks: $PSQ_{s,p,3}$

▷ $\mathcal{S}^{p,6}$ with 6 RunPar tasks: $PSQ_{s,p,6}$

▷ $\mathcal{S}^{p,10}$ with 8 RunPar tasks: $PSQ_{s,p,10}$

In the region of interest ($w \leq 24$), the quality of the combines parallel schedules $PSQ_{s,p,3}$ and $PSQ_{s,p,6}$ is significantly higher than the quality of the individual approaches $PSQ_{s,p,0}$ and $PSQ_{s,p,10}$, respectively. In addition, $PSQ_{s,p,3}$ outperforms $PSQ_{s,p,0}$ also for larger values of $w$.

These results indicate that a the overall best schedule quality is achieved, if a large amount of inter-task communication uses TIC (39 out of 51) and if a large part of the task is parallelized with RunPar (6 out of 10). Hence, combining both methods outperforms the individual approach.

### 6.2.5.5  Summary

The results in this section confirmed a better performance for runnable- over task-level parallelization for small task sets and a better performance for the task- over runnable-level parallelization for large task sets. TIC can be applied safely up to a certain degree and the combination with RunPar further improves the system performance, without further increasing the critical end-to-end latency. In addition to section 5.2.4, the results in this section support the combination of runnable- and task-level parallelism to maintain the application's response time and exploit the performance of the multicore.

## 6.2.6   Discussion of Research Questions

Due to the evaluation of the evolutionary algorithm for coordinating runnable- and task-level parallelization, it is possible to answer the related research questions from the qualitative discussion in section 6.2.1.

◇ *Which population size and how many iterations are necessary to find a good solution with the proposed evolutionary algorithm?*

Contrary to the expectation, the population size does not significantly affect the quality of the result. However, a good solution is found with fewer iterations when the population is large due to frequent serialization by dummy jobs that limit the scheduling possibilities. Thus, few iterations (five) and a small population (30) were sufficient to find a good solution. Nevertheless, simulations were conducted with more iterations and larger populations.

◇ *How much computation time is required to generate a hyperperiod schedule for a real application?*

The computation time for a short schedule (875 jobs in 320 ms) with 150 individuals took only few seconds on average per iteration. A large schedule (5285 jobs in 1920 ms) with 150 individuals took 225 seconds on average per iteration. In all experiments, the duration of the first iteration is smaller than subsequent ones. The reason for this is the computation of the initial population with half size. A larger population size significantly increases the computation time.

◇ *To what extent reduces selectively using TIC and RunPar in a hyperperiod the required clock rate $f_{min}$?*

Both methods reduce the required clock rate. In a small task set, both showed an equivalent reduction by 43%. The benefit of RunPar here is an unchanged FILO latency. For larger task sets, RunPar also produces schedules with a smaller required clock rate as long as a critical FILO latency given as strict constraint. Still, a reduction by 51% is possible with this configuration.

◇ *What is the trade-off between the selective use of TIC and benefit from the parallelization?*

The experiments showed that a gain in the frequency impact (definition 6.2 on page 133) can outweigh the disadvantage of the latency impact (definition 6.3 on page 134), when TIC is used for inter-task communication. Considering one long end-to-end FILO chain and one critical FILO chain prevents an immediate impact on the latter one.

The experiments with the case study from section 2.1.3 showed a stepwise reduction of the minimal clock rate. The reason is a high node degree of a task in the TDG, which all have to be replaced before a clock rate reduces further. Moreover, TIC could be applied safely to a subset of the of inter-task data dependencies. Nevertheless, TIC can outweigh the negative impact beyond this point and, thus, provide the overall better performance in this case (a reduction by 58%).

◇ *How does the combination of RunPar and TIC influence the quality of the parallelization in comparison to the individual mechanisms?*

The combination of RunPar and TIC improves the performance over the individual approaches. In addition to section 5.2.4, the results in this section support the combination of runnable- and task-level parallelism to maintain the application's response time and exploit the performance of the multicore. The results in this section confirmed a better performance for runnable- over task-level parallelization for small task sets and a better performance for the task- over runnable-level parallelization for large task sets.

## 6.3 Summary of Coordination of Concepts

Based on the investigations in the previous chapters, this chapter introduced a mechanism for combining the approaches for runnable- and task-level parallelization into an efficient parallel schedule for a complete hyperperiod. The parallelization is based on the original application's configuration for the single-core ECU. That means precedence constraints are considered on two levels of granularity and critical sensor/actuator latencies from the reference platform are maintained.

Coordinating runnable- and task-level parallelization means to optimize contradictory targets. However, each approach has individual advantages that can be used to compensate the shortcomings in the other. To achieve this, an evolutionary algorithm for solving the resource-constrained project scheduling problem is adapted to generate a set of possible hyperperiod schedules. The parallel schedule quality (PSQ) is established as a metric for quantifying the quality of a schedule. This allows for selecting the schedule with the highest overall benefit from parallelization.

The computed schedule is predictable, robust, efficient, cost-effective, and can be implemented in AUTOSAR straightforward. The FILO latency is identical to the reference platform. Reducing the processor's clock rate to a minimum utilizes idle intervals. This is achieved by scaling all task periods with a constant factor.

The evolutionary algorithm is investigated in extensive experiments with a real diesel EMS as an example, whereas the data-flow from the gas pedal sensor to the injector is considered as critical sensor/actuator path. The experiments focused on investigating the ideal configuration of the evolutionary algorithm, the trade-off between clock rate and FILO latency, and the overall performance gain from combining runnable- and task-level parallelism.

The results show that small populations (30 individuals) deliver satisfactory results after few iterations (five). RunPar and TIC significantly reduce the clock rate, whereas TIC achieves a much lower value (58% less than RunPar). RunPar's impact on the latency is negligible, whereas TIC has a high impact. Thus, solely using RunPar provides an overall better performance, if less than half of the inter-task communication uses TIC. The trend reverses when more inter-task communication is replaced. The overall best result is found when 39 out of 51 inter-task data dependencies use TIC. However, combining runnable- and task-level parallelism outperforms the individual approaches.

# 7 | Conclusion and Future Work

> "A longer sentence brings no more
> Than one that I had said before."
>
> ―――――――――――――――――――――
> I can talk – Two Door Cinema Club, 2010

This final chapter repeats the initial motivation for this thesis and presents the proposed solutions for the parallelization of automotive control software. The main results of their evaluation and ideas for future research directions are given.

The central requirements for parallelizing automotive control software are *predictability* and *robustness*. That means the execution order of runnables must be deterministic to form a predictable data-flow from sensor to actuator. It is important for a correct control function to guarantee an upper bound on the traversal time for this data-flow.

The cores of a multicore processor perform calculations independent of each other, but they share resources such as bus, memory, or other peripherals. Frequent access from different cores to the shared memory is a particular characteristic of automotive control software. Thus, the challenge in this Ph.D. thesis was to schedule tasks to cores in a way that the data dependencies are respected and the data-flow between sensor and actuator produces a valid result with a low latency. This was initially formulated as a guiding research question:

⋄ *How can parallel execution of communicating runnables be enabled, but sensor/actuator data-flows be guaranteed with a worst-case latency?*

The *AUTomotive Open System ARchitecture (AUTOSAR)* standard itself imposes limitations on the parallelization. The challenge here is to minimize these changes and remain compliant to the standard as far as possible. This brought up a second guiding research question.

⋄ *Which extensions for the AUTOSAR standard are required to guarantee efficient and deterministic parallel execution on a multicore electronic control unit (ECU)?*

Due to the analysis of state-of-the-art approaches and the evaluation of new approaches, it is possible to answer these questions.

# 7.1   Summary

In this thesis, objectives for automotive software parallelization were defined, taking the properties of legacy automotive embedded control software and the AUTOSAR standard's methodology into account. A qualitative comparison and a discussion of existing approaches revealed several deficiencies: they require a re-validation of the functional correctness, their applicability is limited, or they are not compatible with AUTOSAR. Furthermore, the AUTOSAR standard itself does not provide a method for predictable interprocessor communication. Alternative mechanisms ensure determinism. However, they are not real-time capable, have strict time budgets that cannot be exceeded, or the data-flow is changed. Some approaches relax inter-task data dependencies to improve parallel performance by reading less up-to-date input data. However, a predictable and reproducible sensor/actuator data-flow and an upper bound on end-to-end latency are not guaranteed.

Two methods for runnable-level parallelization for automotive control software are introduced: *RunPar* and the concept of a *Supertask*. Both maintain the same application configuration to avoid costly re-validation. Runnables (and not tasks) are considered as the *unit of scheduling (UoS)*. The original application's configuration is used to derive precedence constraints within the task. The concept of Supertasks is introduced to increase the level of parallelism already achieved by RunPar. Therefore, consecutively executed tasks are grouped and executed with a period equal to the least common multiple of tasks composing it. The parallel static schedule is efficiently implemented with the concept of *logical execution times (LETs)*, either directly with AUTOSAR schedule tables or with an efficient synchronization operation. Hence, idle intervals between parallelized tasks are utilized and the validation effort after the migration is drastically reduced.

The performance evaluation was conducted to investigate the efficiency, scalability, and practicability with a complex diesel *engine management system (EMS)*, with several hundred runnables and thousands of data dependencies, as an example. The combined utilization in combination with a worst-fit decreasing heuristic provided the best results. On a four-core processor, Supertasks provide a shorter task *worst-case execution time (WCET)* than the separate parallelization. However, these results show that a high number of data dependencies prevent the efficient parallelization with more than two cores.

Consequently, the results of runnable-level parallelization motivated for investigating the parallel execution of complete tasks by reducing the impact of inter-task communication. Thus, *timed implicit communication (TIC)* was introduced as a method for task-level parallelization of automotive control software, which transforms the communication between tasks based on the original application's configuration for the single-core ECU. TIC is a communication mechanism that ensures an identical data-flow for all target ECU platforms. Keeping the original runnable-to-task mapping guarantees predictability and reproducibility, because this maintains a correct data-flow within a task. TIC is compliant to AUTOSAR and it allows current legacy applications to execute tasks in a parallel way without any modification at source code level. Producer and consumer task are decoupled, which makes it possible to treat them as independent during scheduling. However, the use of TIC enlarges the sensor/actuator end-to-end latency.

A comparison was made with runnable-level parallelization methods (RunPar and Supertask). They showed that Supertasks provide better or equal performance on two cores and better performance for small task sets (up to six) on four cores, respectively. Contrarily, runnable-level parallelization provided better performance for large task sets and core numbers. Thus, the task-level and runnable-level parallelization methods proposed in this thesis are therefore found to be complementary strategies. Consequently, their combination was investigated to improve the overall performance of the system and to reduce the impact end-to-end latency of TIC.

The combination of runnable- and task-level parallelization is conducted with an evolutionary algorithm whose objective is to maximize the *parallel schedule quality* in a hyperperiod. Therefore, the parallelization is based on the original application's configuration for the single-core ECU. The negative impact of TIC on the latency and the positive impact on the processor's clock rate from parallelism are derived to quantify the quality of a schedule. Hence, the best schedule can be selected from a set of possible solutions.

The approach considers precedence constraints on two levels of granularity and maintains the critical sensor/actuator latencies from the reference platform. The individual advantages of each approach are used to compensate the shortcomings in the other. To achieve this, an existing approach for solving the *resource-constrained project scheduling problem* is extended to support real-time scheduling and end-to-end latency constraints.

The computed schedule is predictable, robust, efficient, cost-effective, and can be implemented in AUTOSAR straightforward. The *first-in-last-out (FILO)* latency is identical to the reference platform and reducing the processor's clock rate to a minimum utilizes idle intervals. This is achieved by scaling all task periods with a constant factor.

The evolutionary algorithm was investigated in extensive experiments with randomly generated task graphs and with a real diesel EMS. For the latter one, the data-flow from the gas pedal to the injector was considered as critical sensor/actuator chain.

The proposed algorithm delivered satisfactory results with small populations and after few iterations. RunPar and TIC significantly reduce the clock rate, whereas TIC achieves a much lower value. RunPar's impact on the latency is negligible, whereas TIC has a high impact. Thus, solely using RunPar provides an overall better performance, if less than half of the inter-task communication uses TIC. The trend reverses when more inter-task communication is replaced. However, combining runnable- and task-level parallelism outperforms the individual approaches.

## 7.2 Future Work

Apart from the current integration of the methods on an Infineon AURIX processor, further scientific and technical investigations are ongoing as a future work beyond this thesis.

The way how sporadic tasks are scheduled with RunPar, section 4.1.5.3, imposes the question, whether this could lead to a significant performance degradation. Although, the frequency of sporadic tasks can be high, but the WCET of the sporadic task is comparatively small in the investigated case study. The use of multiple cores can shorten this time, because the runnables within the task are distributed to these cores. However, a static schedule becomes inefficient, when the load from sporadic tasks increases and when they are considered as periodic task with minimal possible period. Thus, an investigation of systems with high system load from sporadic tasks is necessary.

A crucial factor for the use of TIC is an efficient implementation of the wait-free buffer. Additional work is necessary to quickly store a new datum from a producer task with its timestamp and to quickly find an old datum. Therefore, a support by specialized hardware or the use of a data structure (for which the access pattern is optimized) are possible. The hardware-supported approach requires integration of the buffer within the processor architecture such that both operations (read and write as defined in section 5.1.4) complete within few cycles. A list is possibly a suitable data structure for buffering data. Pushing a new datum to the end of the list keeps the order data in the order, in which they are produced. However, it must be decided where the list is located, on the producer or consumer side, and how the search for a datum with a specific timestamp is conducted.

The coordination of RunPar and TIC outweighs the negative impact on one FILO latency chain and one critical path. Control applications can contain more than these two important chains and the critical chain can contain more than two tasks. Therefore, the timing validation has to be extended to support multiple and longer FILO latency chains.

The investigations in this thesis are based on one case study, which can be seen as a representative application for a complex automotive control software, and randomly generated task graphs. However, applying the methods in this thesis to other control software is necessary to show the applicability of the approaches in a more general way. Moreover, a benchmark of alternative approaches is needed to investigate the possible performance improvements in comparison with existing approaches. In addition to common performance metrics, robustness, and predictability have to be considered in the benchmark.

An important premise in this thesis is the compliance of the approaches with AUT-OSAR. The mechanisms must be made available for others by standardising them. Extensions are required for distributing *software-components (SW-Cs)*, start and termination of tasks, and the error handling must span multiple cores. Furthermore, this requires a new set of development tools for integrating the methods in the AUTOSAR methodology.

# A | Migration in an Industrial Environment

This appendix describes the applicability of the approach in an industrial mass production environment. The tools required to implement the parallelization approach are listed and migration process is described step by step to ease its reproduction. Furthermore, the impact on the *AUTomotive Open System ARchitecture (AUTOSAR)* methodology is described.

## A.1 Prerequisites and Required Tools

To apply the parallelization approach described in this thesis, the following prerequisites must be satisfied:

a) Legacy application

    a) The original *operating system (OS)* configuration for the single-core *electronic control unit (ECU)*, which serves as a foundation to derive parallelization constraints. The implementation of the OS is not required for the migration, because it is replaced by an AUTOSAR-compliant OS.

    b) The source code, including all parts of the control function, libraries, and *complex device drivers (CDDs)*.

    c) Trace-files are required for the validation after the migration.

b) Analysis tools for

    a) Control flow and dependency analysis (for example Understand™[Inc16] described in section 2.4 on page 30) tools are needed to identify precedence constraints between runnables and for identifying inter-task data dependencies.

    b) Static and/or measurement-based *worst-case execution time (WCET)* analysis (for example *Open Toolbox for Adaptive WCET Analysis (OTAWA)* [Bal+11] on page 30, RapiTime [Rap08], or the Timing Architects™Tool Suite [Gmb14]) are needed to derive a trustworthy upper bound on the execution time (WCET) of runnables and tasks.

c) Parallelization

    a) RunPar (Python script) to implement chapter 4.

    b) *Timed implicit communication (TIC)* overhead computation (C++ program) that implements chapter 5.

    c) Hyperperiod scheduling (C++ program) that implements chapter 6.

d) Migration to AUTOSAR

    a) ARText is used for textual description of AUTOSAR *software-components (SW-Cs)*. From this, AUTOSAR XML-files can be generated imported into an *run-time environment (RTE)* generator.

The use of these tools and parallelization methods is described in the *Business Process Model and Notation (BPMN)* [OMG11] in the following sections.

## A.2   Stepwise Migration to Multicore

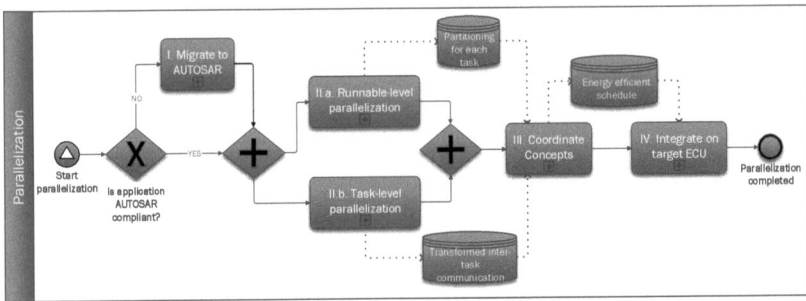

Figure A.1: Overview about the migration approach.

Figure A.1 shows the overall parallelization process, which considers AUTOSAR compliant and proprietary legacy applications. Immediately after the start of the parallelization, it must be decided whether a migration to AUTOSAR is necessary. Non-compliant applications are migrated (I.), with the methods described in section 2.1.2, to an AUTOSAR application as preparation for the parallelization. This migration is necessary, because the AUTOSAR model defines a formal model of the application including components and interfaces in between.

The extraction of runnable-level parallelism (II.a.) and task-level parallelism (II.b.) can be done independent of each other, i.e. in a parallel way. These steps execute the methods described chapter 4 and chapter 5, respectively. The outcome of the former one is a static partitioning for each task and Supertask in the application. The outcome of the latter one is a transformed inter-task communication pattern, i.e. timestamps for reading and writing data shared between tasks.

The results of steps II.a. and II.b. are combined (III.) into one hyperperiod schedule that is energy-efficient. The methods thereby considers the end-to-end latency of critical *first-in-last-out (FILO)* chains. This step executes the methods described in chapter 6. The computed schedule is integrated with an AUTOSAR compliant OS (which is extended for the use with the proposed mechanisms) in the last step (IV.).

## A.2.1 Migration to AUTOSAR

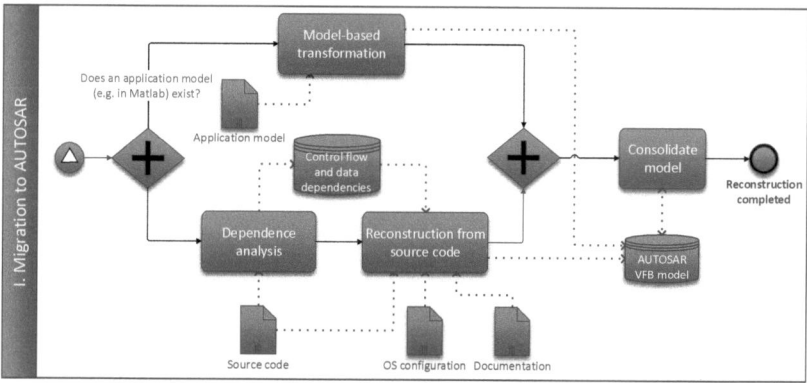

Figure A.2: Migration to AUTOSAR.

Figure A.2 shows the process of migrating legacy software to an AUTOSAR *virtual function bus (VFB)* model. This migration can be based on model-based transformation, if such a model for the application exists, or it can be done by interpretation of the source code. The model-based transformation is straightforward for proprietary environments such as MATLAB/Simulink. The Embedded Coder supports the export of AUTOSAR XML from an existing model.

The migration from plain source code requires a dependency analysis of the complete code first. Subsequently, further information are taken from the original OS config-uration (task bodies, task priorities and periods, etc.) and documentation. All these information are used to interpret the data dependencies of the source code to generate the VFB model of the application. A combination of both methods is possible, whereas a consolidating task combines the results from both in one model.

During this process, each runnables must be encapsulated in one SW-C to allow a free allocation to cores later. The reconstruction from plain source code requires a refactoring of the original code, furthermore. Thereby, read and write accesses to shared variables are replaced by call through the RTE-*application programming interface (API)*.

## A.2.2 Runnable-level Parallelization: RunPar

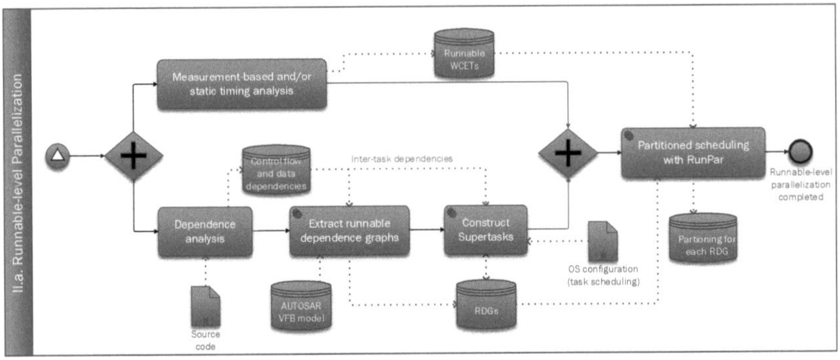

Figure A.3: Extraction of runnable-level parallelism.

Figure A.3 shows the process for extracting runnable-level parallelism with the Run-Par allocation algorithm. On the one hand, the WCET of each runnable must be determined section 2.4.3 with a measurement-based or static timing analysis approach. A combination of both methods is possible to improve the confidence in the estimated values (improved trustworthiness). On the other hand, *runnable dependence graphs (RDGs)* are derived for each task separately in several steps. The first step is a dependency analysis of the task's source code. Control flow and data dependencies, between runnables and between tasks, are extracted and stored in a database. The next step is the extraction of the RDGs for each original task. Therefore, the step uses the results from the dependency analysis and the AUTOSAR VFB model. Afterwards, Supertasks are constructed from the original task scheduling from the existing RDGs and from original task scheduling.

Finally, each runnable in the RDG is enriched with a WCET estimate and scheduled with RunPar. The static partitioning is stored in a database for use in further process steps.

## A.2.3 Task-level Parallelization: Timed Implicit Communication

Figure A.4 shows the process for extracting task-level parallelism with TIC. The first step is a dependency analysis of the task's source code. Data dependencies between tasks are extracted and stored in a database. The next step is the extraction of the inter-task communication as repetitive pattern, according to constraints 2.4 and 2.5. Therefore, the results from the dependency analysis, the original task scheduling, and the AUTOSAR software component and system description of the application are used. Afterwards, the communication pattern is transformed with TIC and stored in

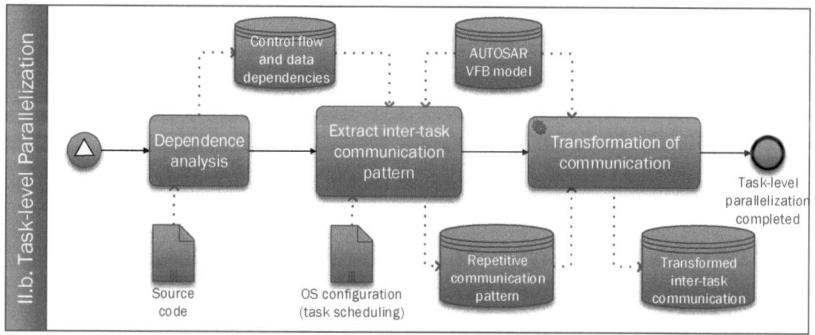

Figure A.4: Extraction of task-level parallelism.

a database for use in later process steps. This pattern represents the predictable and reproducible data-flow between tasks.

## A.2.4 Coordination of Concepts

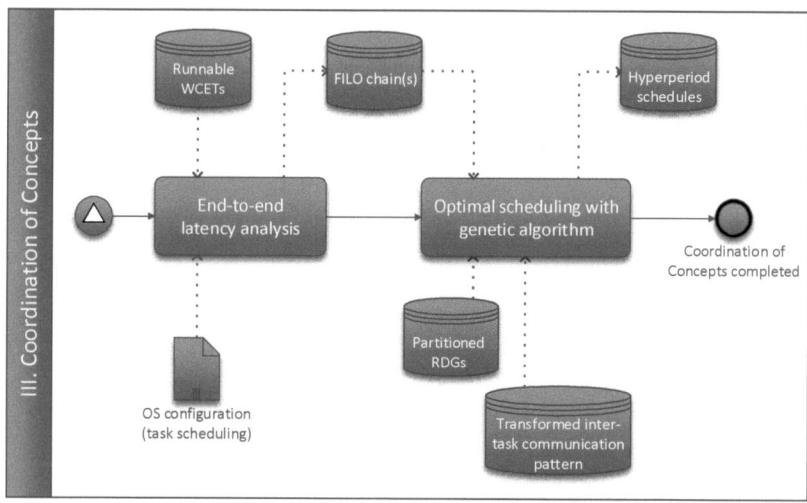

Figure A.5: Coordination of concepts.

Figure A.5 shows the process of coordinating the results from runnable- and task-level parallelization into an efficient hyperperiod schedule. First, critical end-to-end FILO chains are extracted from the original application's configuration. The methods in section 2.3.2 can be used for this. These chains are necessary to ensure the hyperperiod schedule guarantees the same upper bound latency as the original implementation on the single-core ECU.

The schedule is derived with an evolutionary algorithm that searches for an optimal result in a repetitive process. Therefore, an initial set of hyperperiod schedule is randomly defined from the partitioned RDGs (RunPar) and the transformed inter-task communication pattern (TIC). Here, the amount of TIC can be defined as a parameter.

In each iteration, the schedules with the highest *parallel schedule quality (PSQ)* are selected for the next iteration. The process finished, if the maximum number of iteration is reached or if a time limited is reached.

## A.2.5  Integration on the Target

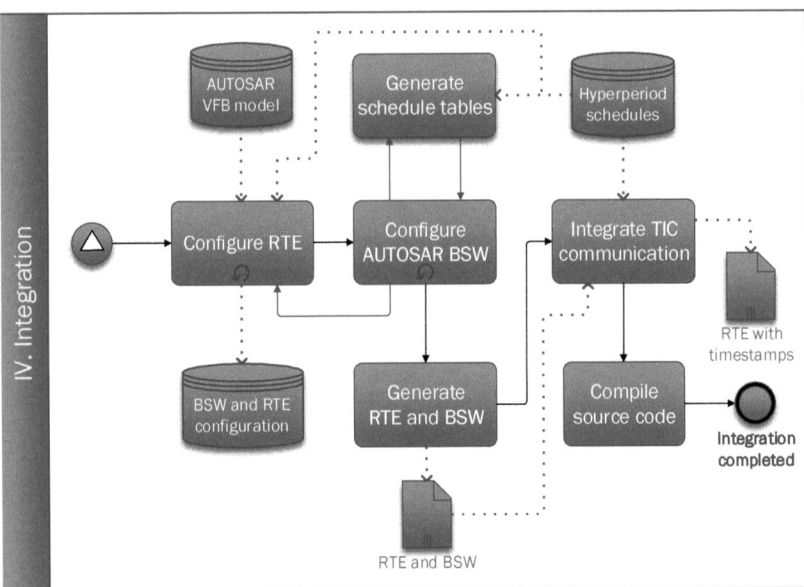

Figure A.6: Integration on the target ECU.

The final step of the parallelization is the integration on the target ECU, as shown in figure A.6. For this, an AUTOSAR *basic software (BSW)* stack is needed that supports multicore processors. The AUTOSAR RTE and BSW are configured in an agile process. Schedule tables are generated from the best hyperperiod schedule computed in step III. Finally, RTE and BSW are generated.

The implementation of the generated RTE is replaced by TIC where the hyperperiod schedule defines. That means the data elements are sent to and read from a non-blocking buffer that attaches timestamps. The executable can be executed on the target after compilation.

*Migration in an Industrial Environment*

## A.3  Proof of Concept

This section describes the integration of RunPar on the Infineon AURIX [Inf] as a proof of concept. The same *engine management system (EMS)* application that is used for the evaluation of the thesis is used for the evaluation in chapters 4 to 6.

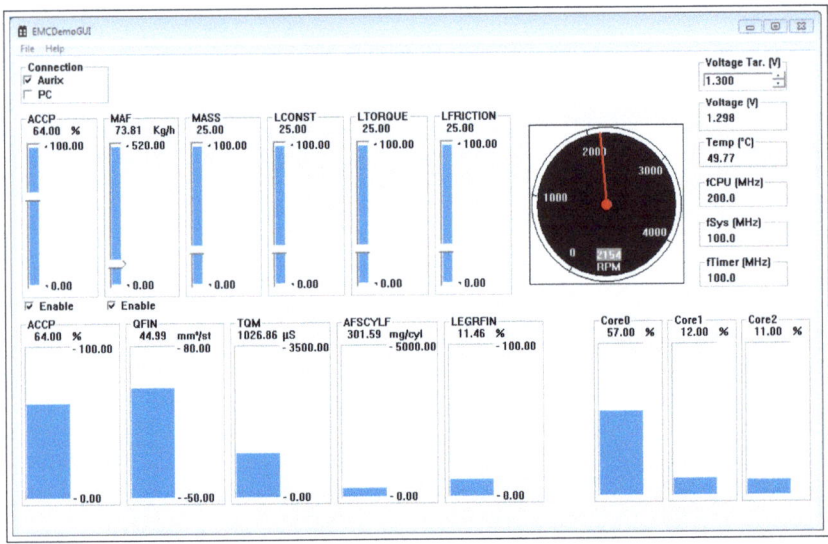

Figure A.7: Screenshot of the GUI.

The EMS runs on the Infineon AURIX TriBoard TC277 using the Elektrobit AutoCore Generic 6.5 [Ele14]. For comparison, an initial implementation one core has been configured. This implementation serves as a reference for a comparison later. The second implementation uses all three cores. Core 0 executes the BSW, the crank-angle task, and an Ethernet task that communicates with a host PC. The host PC emulates a simple engine and visualizes platform's response. Besides displaying the values the GUI (figure A.7) also offers the possibility to interact with the simulation or to provide driver input. That means the GUI allows to change the characteristics of the simulated vehicle-engine system, set certain sensor values, or connect an accelerator pedal.

The cores 1 and 2 provide a higher performance and they are used to execute all parallelized periodic tasks. Thus, each task is distributed over two of the three cores. This allows for evaluating RunPar on a *commercial off-the-shelf* platform and it allows for a comparison with parMERASA processor.

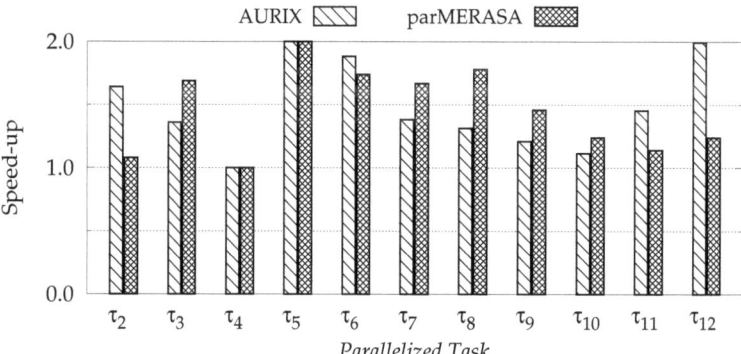

Figure A.8: Comparison of per-task speed-up between AURIX and parMERASA processors.

Figure A.8 compares the measured speed-ups on the AURIX against the parMERASA processor. The achieved values differ, except for $\tau_4$ (contains only one runnable) and $\tau_5$. The difference mainly result from the difference in the processor architectures and from the difference in the BSW. Nevertheless, the average speed-ups (1.46 times faster on the AURIX and 1.49 times faster on the parMERASA processor) are similar.

# References

[ACK87]   Randy Allen, David Callahan, and Ken Kennedy. "Automatic Decomposition of Scientific Programs for Parallel Execution". In: *14th SIGACTSIGPLAN Symposium on Principles of Programming Languages (POPL)*. ACM, 1987, pp. 63–76.

[AIS09]   Ankur Agarwal, Cyril Iskander, and Ravi Shankar. "Survey of Network on Chip (NoC) Architectures & Contributions". In: *Journal of Engineering, Computing and Architecture* 3.1 (2009), pp. 21–27.

[Amz+96]  Cristiana Amza, Alan L Cox, Sandhya Dwarkadas, Pete Keleher, Honghui Lu, Ramakrishnan Rajamony, Weimin Yu, and Willy Zwaenepoel. "Treadmarks: Shared Memory Computing on Networks of Workstations". In: *Computer* 29.2 (1996), pp. 18–28. DOI: 10.1109/2.485843.

[ASU86]   Alfred V Aho, Ravi Sethi, and Jeffrey D Ullman. *Compilers, Principles, Techniques*. Addison Wesley, 1986.

[Aud+91]  Neil C Audsley, Alan Burns, Mike F Richardson, and Andy J Wellings. "Real-time Scheduling: the Deadline-monotonic Approach". In: *IEEE Workshop on Real-Time Operating Systems and Software*. Citeseer. 1991.

[Aug+11]  David I August, J Huang, T B Jablin, Hanjun Kim, T R Mason, P Prabhu, A Raman, and Yun Zhang. "Automatic Extraction of Parallelism from Sequential Code". In: *Fundamentals of Multicore Software Development*. Ed. by Victor Pankratius, Ali-Reza Adl-Tabatabai, and Walter Tichy. Chapman & Hall / CRC Press, 2011. Chap. 9, pp. 201–238.

[Aus+10]  C Aussagues, D Chabrol, V David, D Roux, N Willey, A Tournadre, and M Graniou. "PharOS, a Multicore OS Ready for Safety-related Automotive Systems: Results and Future Prospects". In: *Embedded Real Time Software and Systems (ERTS²)*. 2010.

[AUT14a]  AUTOSAR GbR. *AUTomotive Open System ARchitecture (AUTOSAR)*. Standard. 2014. URL: www.autosar.org.

[AUT14b]  AUTOSAR GbR. *Explanation of Error Handling on Application Level*. Standard. 2014. URL: www.autosar.org.

[Axe+14]  Philip Axer, Rolf Ernst, Heiko Falk, Alain Girault, Daniel Grund, Nan Guan, Bengt Jonsson, Peter Marwedel, Jan Reineke, Christine Rochange, et al. "Building Timing Predictable Embedded Systems". In: *ACM Transactions on Embedded Computing Systems (TECS)* 13.4 (2014), p. 82.

[Bal+11]   Clément Ballabriga, Hugues Cassé, Christine Rochange, and Pascal Sain-
           rat. "OTAWA: An Open Toolbox for Adaptive WCET Analysis". In: *Soft-
           ware Technologies for Embedded and Ubiquitous Systems*. Ed. by Sang Lyul
           Min, Robert Pettit, Peter Puschner, and Theo Ungerer. Vol. 6399. Lecture
           Notes in Computer Science. Springer, 2011, pp. 35–46. DOI: 10.1007/
           978-3-642-16256-5.

[Bar+12]   Sunandan Baruah, Vincenzo Bonifaci, Alberto Marchetti-Spaccamela,
           Leen Stougie, and Andreas Wiese. "A Generalized Parallel Task Model
           for Recurrent Real-time Processes". In: *IEEE Real-Time Systems Symposium
           (RTSS)*. IEEE. 2012, pp. 63–72.

[BCG13]    Tom Bergan, Luis Ceze, and Dan Grossman. "Input-covering Schedules
           for Multithreaded Programs". In: *ACM SIGPLAN Notices*. Vol. 48. 10.
           ACM. 2013, pp. 677–692.

[Bec14]    Jorge Alberto Becerril-Sandoval. *Parallelization Concepts for Automotive
           Software*. Master's Thesis. Cologne University of Applied Sciences, 2014.

[Ber+11]   T Bergan, J Devietti, N Hunt, and L Ceze. "The Deterministic Execution
           Hammer: How Well Does it Actually Pound Nails?" In: *Workshop on
           Determinism and Correctness in Parallel Programming (WoDet)*. 2011.

[Ber+16]   Michel Berkelaar, Jeroen Dirks, Kjell Eikland, Peter Notebaert, and Juer-
           gen Ebert. *Mixed Integer Linear Programming (MILP) solver – lp_solve*.
           2016. URL: http://lpsolve.sourceforge.net/5.5 (visited on
           2016-01-06).

[Ber66]    Arthur J Bernstein. "Analysis of Programs for Parallel Processing". In:
           *IEEE Transactions on Electronic Computers* 5 (1966), pp. 757–763.

[BHS12]    Vladimir Belau, Hermann von Hasseln, and Martin Simons. "Coordi-
           nating AUTOSAR Runnable Entities Using Giotto - First Concepts". In:
           *Workshop on Designing for Embedded Parallel Computing Platforms (DEPCP):
           Architectures, Design Tools, and Applications*. 2012.

[Bin07]    David Binkley. "Source code analysis: A road map". In: *Future of Software
           Engineering*. IEEE Computer Society. 2007, pp. 104–119.

[BKU14]    Christian Bradatsch, Florian Kluge, and Theo Ungerer. "Synchronous
           Execution of a Parallelised Interrupt Handler". In: *Work-in-Progress Session
           20th IEEE Real-Time and Embedded Technology and Applications Symposium
           (RTAS)*. 2014, pp. 9–10.

[Bro06]    Manfred Broy. "Challenges in Automotive Software Engineering". In:
           *28th International Conference on Software Engineering*. ACM. 2006, pp. 33–
           42.

[But11]    Giorgio C Buttazzo. *Hard Real-time Computing Systems: Predictable Schedul-
           ing Algorithms and Applications*. Vol. 24. Springer Science & Business Media,
           2011.

[CAD09]    Damien Chabrol, Christophe Aussaguès, and Vincent David. "A Spatial and Temporal Partitioning Approach for Dependable Automotive Systems". In: *International Conference on Emerging Technologies and Factory Automation (ETFA)*. IEEE. 2009, pp. 1–8.

[Car94]    John B Carter. "Efficient Distributed Shared Memory Based on Multiprotocol Release Consistency". PhD thesis. Rice University, 1994.

[CH00]     Ben-Chung Cheng and Wen-Mei W Hwu. "Modular Interprocedural Pointer Analysis Using Access Paths: Design, Implementation, and Evaluation". In: *ACM SIGPLAN Notices* 35.5 (2000), pp. 57–69.

[Cha+04]   Damien Chabrol, Guy Vidal-Naquet, Vincent David, Christophe Aussagues, and Stéphane Louise. "OASIS: A Chain of Development for Safety-critical Embedded Real-time Systems". In: *2nd European Congress Embedded Real Time Software (ECRTS)*. 2004.

[Cha+13]   Damien Chabrol, Didier Roux, Vincent David, Mathieu Jan, Moha Ait Hmid, Patrice Oudin, and Gilles Zeppa. "Time-and Angle-triggered Real-time Kernel". In: *Design, Automation & Test in Europe Conference & Exhibition (DATE), 2013*. IEEE. 2013, pp. 1060–1062.

[CMM10]    Daniel Cordes, Peter Marwedel, and Arindam Mallik. "Automatic Parallelization of Embedded Software Using Hierarchical Task Graphs and Integer Linear Programming". In: *8th International Conference Hardware/Software Codesign and System Synthesis (CODES+ISSS)*. New York, USA: ACM Press, 2010, pp. 267–276. DOI: 10.1145/1878961.1879009.

[Cor09]    Thomas H Cormen. *Introduction to Algorithms*. MIT press, 2009.

[Cos+07]   Manuel Costa, Miguel Castro, Lidong Zhou, Lintao Zhang, and Marcus Peinado. "Bouncer: Securing Software by Blocking Bad Input". In: *ACM SIGOPS Operating Systems Review*. Vol. 41. 6. ACM. 2007, pp. 117–130.

[CSG99]    David E Culler, Jaswinder Pal Singh, and Anoop Gupta. *Parallel Computer Architecture: A Hardware/software Approach*. Gulf Professional Publishing, 1999.

[Cui+10]   Heming Cui, Jingyue Wu, Chia-Che Tsai, and Junfeng Yang. "Stable Deterministic Multithreading Through Schedule Memoization". In: *9th USENIX Conference on Operating Systems Design and Implementation*. USENIX Association. 2010, pp. 1–13.

[Cui+11]   Heming Cui, Jingyue Wu, John Gallagher, Huayang Guo, and Junfeng Yang. "Efficient Deterministic Multithreading through Schedule Relaxation". In: *23rd ACM Symposium on Operating Systems Principles*. ACM. 2011, pp. 337–351.

[Dav+98]   Vincent David, Jean Delcoigne, Evelyne Leret, Alain Ourghanlian, Phi-
           lippe Hilsenkopf, and Philippe Paris. "Computer Safety, Reliability and
           Security: 17th International Conference, SAFECOMP'98 Heidelberg, Ger-
           many, October 5–7". In: ed. by Wolfgang Ehrenberger. Berlin, Heidelberg:
           Springer Berlin Heidelberg, 1998. Chap. Safety Properties Ensured by
           the OASIS Model for Safety Critical Real-Time Systems, pp. 45–59. DOI:
           10.1007/3-540-49646-7_4.

[Dav81]    James Russell Beckman Davies. *Parallel Loop Constructs for Multiprocessors.*
           Master's Thesis. Department of Computer Science, University of Illinois
           at Urbana-Champaign, 1981.

[DB11]     Robert I Davis and Alan Burns. "A Survey of Hard Real-Time Scheduling
           for Multiprocessor Systems". In: *ACM Computing Surveys (CSUR)* 43.4
           (2011), p. 35.

[DT11]     "Computational Intelligence and Information Technology: 1st Interna-
           tional Conference, CIIT 2011, Pune, India, November 7-8". In: ed. by
           Vinu V. Das and Nessy Thankachan. Berlin, Heidelberg: Springer Berlin
           Heidelberg, 2011. Chap. A Paradigm Shift from Legacy to AUTOSAR
           Architecture in Future Automotives, pp. 548–553. DOI: 10.1007/978-
           3-642-25734-6_94.

[Ele14]    Elektrobit Automotive GmbH. *EB tresos AutoCore - Elektrobit Automo-
           tive.* 2014. URL: http://automotive.elektrobit.com/ecu/eb-
           tresos-autocore (visited on 2014-12-03).

[EMC14]    EMC² Consortium c/o Infineon Technologies AG, Project Coordinator
           Werner Weber. *EMC²: Embedded Multi-Core systems for Mixed Criticality ap-
           plications in dynamic and changeable real-time environments.* ARTEMIS Joint
           Undertaking: Grant agreement no. 621429. 2014. URL: www.artemis-
           emc2.eu.

[Erd59]    A. Erdös P.; Renyi. "On random graphs I". In: *Publicationes Mathematicae* 6
           (1959), pp. 290–297.

[Far+14a]  H.R. Faragardi, B. Lisper, K. Sandstrom, and T. Nolte. "A Communication-
           aware Solution Framework for Mapping AUTOSAR Runnables on Multi-
           core Systems". In: *International Conference on Emerging Technologies and
           Factory Automation (ETFA).* IEEE. 2014, pp. 1–9. DOI: 10.1109/ETFA.
           2014.7005244.

[Far+14b]  H.R. Faragardi, B. Lisper, K. Sandstrom, and T. Nolte. "An Efficient
           Scheduling of AUTOSAR Runnables to Minimize Communication Cost in
           Multi-core Systems". In: *7th International Symposium on Telecommunications
           (IST).* IEEE, 2014, pp. 41–48. DOI: 10.1109/ISTEL.2014.7000667.

[Fei+08]   Nico Feiertag, Kai Richter, Johan Nordlander, and Jan Jonsson. "A Com-
           positional Framework for End-to-End Path Delay Calculation of Automo-
           tive Systems Under Different Path Semantics". In: *Workshop Compositional
           Theory and Technology for Real-Time Embedded Systems (CRTS).* 2008.

[For+10]   Julien Forget, Frédéric Boniol, Emmanuel Grolleau, David Lesens, and Claire Pagetti. "Scheduling Dependent Periodic Tasks Without Synchronization Mechanisms". In: *16th IEEE Real-Time and Embedded Technology and Applications Symposium (RTAS)*. IEEE. 2010, pp. 301–310.

[Fos95]    Ian Foster. *Designing and Building Parallel Programs*. Vol. 95. Addison-Wesley Reading, 1995.

[FOW87]    Jeanne Ferrante, Karl J Ottenstein, and Joe D Warren. "The Program Dependence Graph and Its Use in Optimization". In: *ACM Transactions on Programming Languages and Systems (TOPLAS)* 9.3 (1987), pp. 319–349.

[Fre15]    Freescale Semiconductor Inc. *Qorivva MPC5748G Family*. Fact Sheet Document number: MPC5748GFS REV 1. 2015. URL: http://cache.freescale.com/files/microcontrollers/doc/fact_sheet/MPC5748GFS.pdf.

[Für10]    Simon Fürst. "Challenges in the Design of Automotive Software". In: *Design, Automation & Test in Europe Conference & Exhibition (DATE)*. IEEE, 2010, pp. 256–258. DOI: 10.1109/DATE.2010.5457201.

[GG08]     Rim Guermazi and Laurent George. "Worst Case End-to-end Response Times of Periodic Tasks with an AUTOSAR/Flexray Infrastructure". In: *7th International Workshop on Real-Time Networks (RTN)*. Citeseer. 2008, p. 8.

[GGL12]    Tobias Grosser, Armin Groesslinger, and Christian Lengauer. "Polly: Performing Polyhedral Optimizations On A Low-level Intermediate Representation". In: *Parallel Processing Letters* 22.04 (2012), p. 1250010. DOI: 10.1142/S0129626412500107.

[Gho+04]   Arkadeb Ghosal, Thomas A. Henzinger, Christoph M. Kirsch, and Marco A. A. Sanvido. "Hybrid Systems: Computation and Control: 7th International Workshop, HSCC 2004, Philadelphia, PA, USA, March 25-27, 2004. Proceedings". In: ed. by Rajeev Alur and George J. Pappas. Berlin, Heidelberg: Springer Berlin Heidelberg, 2004. Chap. Event-driven Programming with Logical Execution Times, pp. 357–371. DOI: 10.1007/978-3-540-24743-2_24.

[GJ90]     Michael R. Garey and David S. Johnson. *Computers and Intractability; A Guide to the Theory of NP-Completeness*. 1990.

[Gli+11]   Peter Gliwa, Jens Hanisch, Ursula Kelling, and Christoph Ficek. *From Single-Core to Multi-Core Platforms - Systematic Migration of Hard Real-Time Software in AUTOSAR*. Whitepaper. 2011.

[Gmb14]    Timing-Architects Embedded Systems GmbH. *Model-Based Development Tools for Embedded Multi-Core Systems*. Whitepaper. Timing-Architects Embedded Systems GmbH, 2014. URL: www.timing-architects.com/fileadmin/user_upload/downloads/TA_Brochure.pdf.

[Gol89]     David E. Goldberg. *Genetic Algorithms in Search, Optimization, and Machine Learning*. 2. Addison-Wesley, Reading, MA, 1989.

[GP92]      Milind Girkar and Constantine D Polychronopoulos. "Automatic Extraction of Functional Parallelism from Ordinary Programs". In: *Transactions on Parallel and Distributed Systems* 3.2 (1992), pp. 166–178.

[GP94]      M Girkar and C D Polychronopoulos. "The Hierarchical Task Graph as a Universal Intermediate Representation". In: *International Journal of Parallel Programming* 22.5 (1994), pp. 519–551.

[Gra03]     Ananth Grama. *Introduction to Parallel Computing*. Pearson Education, 2003.

[Har02]     Sönke Hartmann. "A Self-adapting Genetic Algorithm for Project Scheduling Under Resource Constraints". In: *Naval Research Logistics (NRL)* 49.5 (2002), pp. 433–448.

[Har98]     Sönke Hartmann. "A Competitive Genetic Algorithm for Resource-constrained Project Scheduling". In: *Naval Research Logistics (NRL)* 45.7 (1998), pp. 733–750.

[Has15]     Ahmad Hassan. *Verification of End-to-End Delay Constraints in Parallelized Automotive Control Applications*. Master's Thesis. TU Chemnitz, Department of Computer Science, Professorship of Computer Engineering, 2015.

[Hen+05]    Rafik Henia, Arne Hamann, Marek Jersak, Razvan Racu, Kai Richter, and Rolf Ernst. "System Level Performance Analysis–the SymTA/S Approach". In: vol. 152. 2. IET, 2005, pp. 148–166.

[Hen08]     T. A. Henzinger. "Two Challenges in Embedded Systems Design: Predictability and Robustness". In: *Philosophical Transactions of the Royal Society A: Mathematical, Physical and Engineering Sciences* 366.1881 (2008), pp. 3727–3736.

[HHK01]     Thomas A. Henzinger, Benjamin Horowitz, and Christoph Meyer Kirsch. "Embedded Software: 1st International Workshop, EMSOFT 2001 Tahoe City, CA, USA, October 8–10". In: ed. by Thomas A. Henzinger and Christoph M. Kirsch. Springer. Springer Berlin Heidelberg, 2001. Chap. Giotto: A Time-triggered Language for Embedded Programming, pp. 166–184. DOI: 10.1007/3-540-45449-7_12.

[Hin01]     Michael Hind. "Pointer Analysis: Haven't We Solved This Problem Yet?" In: *ACM SIGPLAN-SIGSOFT Workshop on Program Analysis for Software Tools and Engineering*. ACM. 2001, pp. 54–61.

[HK00]      Sönke Hartmann and Rainer Kolisch. "Experimental Evaluation of State-of-the-Art Heuristics for the Resource-constrained Project Scheduling Problem". In: *European Journal of Operational Research* 127.2 (2000), pp. 394–407.

[HL95]     B. Hendrickson and R. Leland. "A Multi-level Algorithm for Partitioning Graphs". In: *Supercomputing, 1995. Proceedings of the IEEE/ACM SC95 Conference*. 1995, pp. 28–28. DOI: 10.1109/SUPERC.1995.242799.

[HM92]     Jeffrey K Hollingsworth and Barton P Miller. "Parallel Program Performance Metrics: a Comprison and Validation". In: *ACM/IEEE Conference on Supercomputing*. IEEE Computer Society Press. 1992, pp. 4–13.

[Hol75]    John Henry Holland. *Adaptation in Natural and Artificial Systems*. The University of Michigan Press, 1975.

[HS07]     Thomas A Henzinger and Joseph Sifakis. "The Discipline of Embedded Systems Design". In: *Computer* 40.10 (2007), pp. 32–40.

[Hur+97]   Ali R Hurson, Joford T Lim, Krishna M Kavi, and Ben Lee. "Parallelization of DOALL and DOACROSS Loops: A Survey". In: *Advances in Computers* 45 (1997), pp. 53–103.

[Inc16]    Scientific Toolworks Inc. *Understand™Static Code Analysis Tool*. 2016. URL: www.scitools.com (visited on 2016-01-06).

[Inf]      Infineon. *AURIX - TC27x B-Step, 32-bit Single-Chip Micro-controller, User's Manual, v14.1*.

[Int15]    International Organization for Standardization (ISO). *ISO 11898: Road vehicles — Controller area network (CAN)*. Standard. 2015. URL: www.autosar.org.

[Ish+05]   Kazuhisa Ishizaka, Takamichi Miyamoto, Jun Shirako, Motoki Obata, Keiji Kimura, and Hironori Kasahara. "Languages and Compilers for High Performance Computing: 17th International Workshop, LCPC 2004, West Lafayette, IN, USA, Revised Selected Papers". In: ed. by Rudolf Eigenmann, Zhiyuan Li, and Samuel P. Midkiff. Berlin, Heidelberg: Springer Berlin Heidelberg, 2005. Chap. Performance of OSCAR Multigrain Parallelizing Compiler on SMP Servers, pp. 319–331. DOI: 10.1007/115323\-78_23.

[Joh+12]   Nick P Johnson, Hanjun Kim, Prakash Prabhu, Ayal Zaks, and David I August. "Speculative Separation for Privatization and Reductions". In: *ACM SIGPLAN Notices*. Vol. 47. 6. ACM. 2012, pp. 359–370.

[Jou+06]   Frédéric Jouault, Freddy Allilaire, Jean Bézivin, Ivan Kurtev, and Patrick Valduriez. "ATL: a QVT-like Transformation Language". In: *Companion to the 21st ACM SIGPLAN symposium on Object-oriented programming systems, languages, and applications*. ACM. 2006, pp. 719–720.

[KA02]     Ken Kennedy and John R. Allen. *Optimizing Compilers for Modern Architectures: A Dependence-based Approach*. San Francisco, CA, USA: Morgan Kaufmann Publishers Inc., 2002.

[Kan+13]   Yohei Kanehagi, Dan Umeda, Akihiro Hayashi, Keiji Kimura, and Hironori Kasahara. "Parallelization of Automotive Engine Control Software on Embedded Multi-core Processor Using OSCAR Compiler". In: *Cool Chips XVI (COOL Chips)*. IEEE. 2013, pp. 1–3.

[Kas+92]   Hironori Kasahara, Hiroki Honda, A Mogi, A Ogura, K Fujiwara, and Seinosuke Narita. "A Multi-grain Parallelizing Compilation Scheme for OSCAR (Optimally SCheduled Advanced multiprocessoR)". In: *Languages and Compilers for Parallel Computing*. Springer, 1992, pp. 283–297.

[Kas+95]   H Kasahara, H Honda, K Aida, M Okamoto, A Yoshida, and W Ogata. "OSCAR Fortran Multigrain Compiler". In: *Parallel Language and Compiler Research in Japan*. Springer, 1995, pp. 271–301.

[KB03]     H. Kopetz and G. Bauer. "The time-triggered architecture". In: *Proceedings of the IEEE* 91.1 (2003-01), pp. 112–126. DOI: 10.1109/JPROC.2002.805821.

[Keh+15]   Sebastian Kehr, Eduardo Quiñones, Bert Böddeker, and Günter Schäfer. "Parallel Execution of AUTOSAR Legacy Applications on Multicore ECUs with Timed Implicit Communication". In: *Proceedings of the 52nd Annual Design Automation Conference*. DAC '15. San Francisco, California: ACM, 2015, 42:1–42:6. DOI: 10.1145/2744769.2744889.

[Keh+16]   Sebastian Kehr, Miloš Panić, Eduardo Quiñones, Bert Boeddeker, Jorge Becerril Sandoval, Jaume Abella, Francisco J. Cazorla, and Guenter Schaefer. "Supertask: Maximizing Runnable-level Parallelism in AUTOSAR Applications". In: *Design, Automation & Test in Europe Conference & Exhibition (DATE)*. IEEE. 2016.

[Keh+17]   Sebastian Kehr, Eduardo Quiñones, Dominik Langen, Bert Böddeker, and Günter Schäfer. "Parcus: Energy-aware and Robust Parallelization of AUTOSAR Legacy Applications". In: *Accepted at 2017 IEEE Real-Time and Embedded Technology and Applications Symposium (RTAS)*. IEEE. 2017-04.

[KH06]     Rainer Kolisch and Sönke Hartmann. "Experimental Investigation of Heuristics for Resource-constrained Project Scheduling: An Update". In: *European Journal of Operational Research* 174.1 (2006), pp. 23–37.

[KK98]     George Karypis and Vipin Kumar. "A Fast and High Quality Multilevel Scheme for Partitioning Irregular Graphs". In: *SIAM Journal on Scientific Computing* 20.1 (1998), pp. 359–392.

[Knü+10]   Christian Knüchel, Michael Rudorfer, Stefan Voget, Stephan Eberle, Romain Sezestre, and Aldric Loyer. "Artop – An Ecosystem Approach for Collaborative AUTOSAR Tool Development". In: *International Congress on Embedded Real Time Software and Systems*. 2010.

[KOI01]    Hironori Kasahara, Motoki Obata, and Kazuhisa Ishizaka. "Automatic Coarse Grain Task Parallel Processing on SMP using OpenMP". In: *Languages and Compilers for Parallel Computing*. Springer, 2001, pp. 189–207.

[Kol96]     Rainer Kolisch. "Serial and Parallel Resource-constrained Project Schedul-
            ing Methods Revisited: Theory and Computation". In: *European Journal of
            Operational Research* 90.2 (1996), pp. 320–333.

[Kop+95]    Hermann Kopetz, Martin Braun, Christian Ebner, Andreas Kruger, Diet-
            mar Millinger, Roman Nossal, and Anton Schedl. "The Design of Large
            Real-time Systems: the Time-triggered Approach". In: *IEEE Real-Time
            Systems Symposium (RTSS)*. IEEE. 1995, pp. 182–187.

[KS12]      Christoph M. Kirsch and Ana Sokolova. "Advances in Real-Time Sys-
            tems". In: ed. by Samarjit Chakraborty and Jörg Eberspächer. Berlin, Hei-
            delberg: Springer Berlin Heidelberg, 2012. Chap. The Logical Execution
            Time Paradigm, pp. 103–120. DOI: 10.1007/978-3-642-24349-3_5.

[Kum+08]    Daehyun Kum, Gwang-Min Park, Seonghun Lee, and Wooyoung Jung.
            "AUTOSAR Migration from Existing Automotive Software". In: *Interna-
            tional Conference on Control, Automation and Systems (ICCAS)*. IEEE. 2008,
            pp. 558–562.

[LA04]      Chris Lattner and Vikram Adve. "LLVM: A compilation framework for
            lifelong program analysis & transformation". In: *International Symposium
            on Code Generation and Optimization (CGO)*. IEEE. 2004, pp. 75–86.

[Lam78]     Leslie Lamport. "Time, Clocks, and the Ordering of Events in a Dis-
            tributed System". In: *Communications of the ACM* 21.7 (1978), pp. 558–565.
            DOI: 10.1145/359545.359563.

[LAN+16]    Los Alamos National Laboratory (LANL) et al. *NetworkX*. 2016. URL:
            https://networkx.github.io/ (visited on 2016-01-17).

[Leh90]     John P Lehoczky. "Fixed Priority Scheduling of Periodic Task Sets with Ar-
            bitrary Deadlines." In: *IEEE Real-Time Systems Symposium (RTSS)*. Vol. 90.
            1990, pp. 201–209.

[Lem+11]    Matthieu Lemerre, Emmanuel Ohayon, Damien Chabrol, Mathieu Jan,
            and M-B Jacques. "Method and Tools for Mixed-criticality Real-time
            Applications Within PharOS". In: *IEEE International Symposium on Object/-
            Component/Service-Oriented Real-Time Distributed Computing Workshops
            (ISORCW)*. IEEE. 2011, pp. 41–48.

[LK13]      Dominique LaSalle and George Karypis. "Multi-threaded graph parti-
            tioning". In: *27th IEEE International Symposium on Parallel & Distributed
            Processing (IPDPS)*. IEEE. 2013, pp. 225–236.

[LL73]      C. L. Liu and James W. Layland. "Scheduling Algorithms for Multipro-
            gramming in a Hard-Real-Time Environment". In: *J. ACM* 20.1 (1973-01),
            pp. 46–61. DOI: 10.1145/321738.321743. URL: http://doi.acm.
            org/10.1145/321738.321743.

[LM95]      Yau-Tsun Steven Li and Sharad Malik. "Performance Analysis of Em-
            bedded Software Using Implicit Path Enumeration". In: *ACM SIGPLAN
            Notices*. Vol. 30. 11. ACM. 1995, pp. 88–98.

[LO12]      Matthieu Lemerre and Emmanuel Ohayon. "A Model of Parallel Deter-
            ministic Real-Time Computation". In: *IEEE Real-Time Systems Symposium
            (RTSS)*. IEEE. 2012, pp. 273–282.

[Lou+02]    Stéphane Louise, Vincent David, Jean Delcoigne, and Christophe Aus-
            sagues. "OASIS Project: Deterministic Real-time for Safety Critical Em-
            bedded Systems". In: *10th Workshop on ACM SIGOPS European Workshop*.
            EW 10. Saint-Emilion, France: ACM, 2002, pp. 223–226. DOI: 10.1145/
            1133373.1133419.

[LS99]      Thomas Lundqvist and Per Stenström. "Timing Anomalies in Dynami-
            cally Scheduled Microprocessors". In: *IEEE Real-Time Systems Symposium
            (RTSS)*. IEEE. 1999, pp. 12–21.

[LSD89]     J Lehoczky, Lui Sha, and Y Ding. "The Rate Monotonic Scheduling Al-
            gorithm: Exact Characterization and Average Case Behavior". In: *IEEE
            Real-Time Systems Symposium (RTSS)*. 1989, pp. 166–171. DOI: 10.1109/
            REAL.1989.63567.

[Lu+14]     Kai Lu, Xu Zhou, Tom Bergan, and Xiaoping Wang. "Efficient Deter-
            ministic Multithreading Without Global Barriers". In: *ACM SIGPLAN
            Symposium on Principles and Practice of Parallel Programming*. ACM. 2014,
            pp. 287–300.

[Lu+15]     Kai Lu, Xu Zhou, Xiao-Ping Wang, Tom Bergan, and Chen Chen. "An
            Efficient and Flexible Deterministic Framework for Multithreaded Pro-
            grams". In: *Journal of Computer Science and Technology* 30.1 (2015), pp. 42–
            56.

[LZG15]     Martin Lowinski, Dirk Ziegenbein, and Sabine Glesner. "Partitioning
            Embedded Real-time Control Software Based on Communication Depen-
            dencies". In: *International Workshop on Modelling in Automotive Software
            Engineering (MASE)* (2015).

[MB09]      Gary Morgan and Andrew Borg. *Multi-core Automotive ECUs: Software and
            Hardware Implications*. Whitepaper. ETAS Group, 2009.

[MHL]       Dror E. Maydan, John L. Hennessy, and Monica S. Lam. "Effectiveness of
            Data Dependence Analysis". In: *International Journal of Parallel Program-
            ming* 23.1 (), pp. 63–81. DOI: 10.1007/BF02577784.

[Mon+10]    Aurélien Monot, Nicolas Navet, Bernard Bavoux, Françoise Simonot-Lion,
            et al. "Multicore Scheduling in Automotive ECUs". In: *Embedded Real Time
            Software and Systems (ERTS²)*. 2010.

[Mon+12]    Aurélien Monot, Nicolas Navet, Bernard Bavoux, and Françoise Simonot-
            Lion. "Multisource Software on Multicore Automotive ECUs Combining
            Runnable Sequencing With Task Scheduling". In: *IEEE Transactions on
            Industrial Electronics* 59.10 (2012), pp. 3934–3942.

[Mös10]     J Mössinger. "Software in Automotive Systems". In: *IEEE Software* 27.2
            (2010), pp. 92–94. DOI: 10.1109/MS.2010.55.

[Mot+08]  Motor Industry Software Reliability Association et al. *MISRA-C: 2004: Guidelines for the Use of the C Language in Critical Systems*. 2008.

[Muc97]  Steven S. Muchnick. *Advanced Compiler Design Implementation*. Morgan Kaufmann, 1997.

[Nat+07]  Marco Di Natale, Wei Zheng, Claudio Pinello, Paolo Giusto, and Alberto Sangiovanni Vincentelli. "Optimizing End-to-end Latencies by Adaptation of the Activation Events in Distributed Automotive Systems". In: *IEEE Real-Time and Embedded Technology and Applications Symposium (RTAS)*. IEEE. 2007, pp. 293–302.

[NBN09a]  F Nemati, M Behnam, and T Nolte. "Efficiently Migrating Real-time Systems to Multi-cores". In: *International Conference on Emerging Technologies and Factory Automation (ETFA)*. IEEE. 2009, pp. 1–8.

[NBN09b]  Farhang Nemati, Moris Behnam, and Thomas Nolte. "Multiprocessor Synchronization and Hierarchical Scheduling". In: *International Conference on Parallel Processing Workshops ICPPW*. IEEE. 2009, pp. 58–64.

[NNB10]  Farhang Nemati, Thomas Nolte, and Moris Behnam. *Blocking-Aware Partitioning for Multiprocessors*. Tech. rep. Mälardalen University, School of Innovation, Design and Engineering, 2010, p. 10.

[OAA09]  Marek Olszewski, Jason Ansel, and Saman Amarasinghe. "Kendo: Efficient Deterministic Multithreading in Software". In: *ACM SIGPLAN Notices* 44.3 (2009), pp. 97–108.

[OMG11]  OMG. *Business Process Model and Notation (BPMN), Version 2.0*. Object Management Group, 2011. URL: http://www.omg.org/spec/BPMN/2.0.

[ORS13]  Haluk Ozaktas, Christine Rochange, and Pascal Sainrat. "Automatic WCET Analysis of Real-Time Parallel Applications". In: *13th International Workshop on Worst-Case Execution Time Analysis*. Ed. by Claire Maiza. Vol. 30. OpenAccess Series in Informatics (OASIcs). Dagstuhl, Germany: Schloss Dagstuhl–Leibniz-Zentrum fuer Informatik, 2013, pp. 11–20. DOI: http://dx.doi.org/10.4230/OASIcs.WCET.2013.11.

[ORS14]  Haluk Ozaktas, Christine Rochange, and Pascal Sainrat. "Minimizing the Cost of Synchronisations in the WCET of Real-time Parallel Programs". In: *17th International Workshop on Software and Compilers for Embedded Systems*. ACM. 2014, pp. 98–107.

[OSE05]  OSEK/VDX Group. *Offene Systeme und deren Schnittstellen fuer die Elektronik im Kraftfahrzeug (OSEK) Operating System Specification*. Standard. 2005. URL: www.osek-vdx.org.

[Ott+05]  Guilherme Ottoni, Ram Rangan, Adam Stoler, and David I August. "Automatic Thread Extraction with Decoupled Software Pipelining". In: *IEEE/ACM International Symposium on Microarchitecture*. IEEE Computer Society. 2005, pp. 105–118.

[Pag+11]   Claire Pagetti, Julien Forget, Frédéric Boniol, Mikel Cordovilla, and David Lensens. "Multi-task Implementation of Multi-periodic Synchronous Programs". In: *Discrete Event Dynamic Systems* 21.3 (2011), pp. 307–338. DOI: 10.1007/s10626-011-0107-x. URL: http://dx.doi.org/10.1007/s10626-011-0107-x.

[Pan+14]   Miloš Panić, Sebastian Kehr, Eduardo Quiñones, Bert Böddecker, Jaume Abella, and Francisco J Cazorla. "RunPar: An Allocation Algorithm for Automotive Applications Exploiting Runnable Parallelism in Multicores". In: *Proceedings of the 2014 International Conference Hardware/Software Codesign and System Synthesis*. CODES '14. New Delhi, India: ACM, 2014, 29:1–29:10. DOI: 10.1145/2656075.2656096.

[Pao+09]   Marco Paolieri, Eduardo Quiñones, Francisco J Cazorla, Guillem Bernat, and Mateo Valero. "Hardware Support for WCET Analysis of Hard Real-time Multicore Systems". In: *ACM SIGARCH Computer Architecture News*. Vol. 37. 3. ACM. 2009, pp. 57–68.

[par11]    parMERASA Consortium c/o University Augsburg, Project Coordinator Theo Ungerer. *parMERASA: Multi-Core Execution of Parallelized Hard Real-Time Applications Supporting Analysability*. FP-7 funded Research Project: Project Ref. 287519. 2011. URL: www.parmerasa.eu.

[Per+07]   Simon Perathoner, Ernesto Wandeler, Lothar Thiele, Arne Hamann, Simon Schliecker, Rafik Henia, Razvan Racu, Rolf Ernst, and Michael González Harbour. "Influence of Different System Abstractions on the Performance Analysis of Distributed Real-time Systems". In: *7th ACM & IEEE international conference on Embedded software*. ACM. 2007, pp. 193–202.

[PK03]     Kleanthis Psarris and Konstantinos Kyriakopoulos. "The Impact of Data Dependence Analysis on Compilation and Program Parallelization". In: *17th International Conference on Supercomputing*. ACM. 2003, pp. 205–214.

[PKH07]    David J Pearce, Paul HJ Kelly, and Chris Hankin. "Efficient Field-sensitive Pointer Analysis of C". In: *ACM Transactions on Programming Languages and Systems* 30.1 (2007), p. 4.

[PKS14]    Stefan Poledna, Hermann Kopetz, and Wilfried Steiner. "Deterministic System Design with Time-triggered Technology". In: *Microelectronic Systems Symposium (MESS)*. IEEE. 2014, pp. 1–4.

[PQC12]    M Paolieri, E Quinones, and FJ Cazorla. "Timing Effects of the Memory System in Real-time Multicore Integrated Architectures: Problems and Solutions". In: *Transactions on Embedded Computing Systems* (2012).

[PW86]     David A Padua and Michael J Wolfe. "Advanced Compiler Optimizations for Supercomputers". In: *Communications of the ACM* 29.12 (1986), pp. 1184–1201.

[Raj+10]   AC Rajeev, Swarup Mohalik, Manoj G Dixit, Devesh B Chokshi, and S Ramesh. "Schedulability and End-to-end Latency in Distributed ECU Networks: Formal Modeling and Precise Estimation". In: *10th ACM SIGBED International Conference on Embedded Software (EMSOFT)*. ACM. 2010, pp. 129–138.

[Raj91]    Ragunathan Rajkumar. "Synchronization in Multiple Processor Systems". In: *Synchronization in Real-Time Systems*. Springer, 1991, pp. 61–118.

[Ram+08]   Easwaran Raman, Guilherme Ottoni, Arun Raman, Matthew J Bridges, and David I August. "Parallel-stage Decoupled Software Pipelining". In: *6th IEEE/ACM International Symposium on Code Generation and Optimization*. ACM. 2008, pp. 114–123.

[Ram+10]   Arun Raman, Hanjun Kim, Thomas R Mason, Thomas B Jablin, and David I August. "Speculative Parallelization Using Software Multi-threaded Transactions". In: *ACM SIGARCH Computer Architecture News*. Vol. 38. 1. ACM. 2010, pp. 65–76.

[Rap08]    Rapita Systems Ltd. *RapiTime White Paper – Worst-Case Execution Time Analysis*. Whitepaper. 2008. URL: www . edn . com / Pdf / ViewPdf ? contentItemId=4137753.

[Rei+06]   Jan Reineke, Björn Wachter, Stefan Thesing, Reinhard Wilhelm, Ilia Polian, Jochen Eisinger, and Bernd Becker. "A Definition and Classification of Timing Anomalies". In: *6th International Workshop on Worst-Case Execution Time Analysis (WCET'06)*. Ed. by Frank Mueller. Vol. 4. OpenAccess Series in Informatics (OASIcs). Dagstuhl, Germany: Schloss Dagstuhl–Leibniz-Zentrum fuer Informatik, 2006.

[Roc+12]   Antoni Roca, Carles Hernandez, José Flich, Federico Silla, and José Duato. "Enabling High-Performance Crossbars Through a Floorplan-Aware Design". In: *41st International Conference on Parallel Processing (ICPP)*. IEEE. 2012, pp. 269–278.

[Rod85]    David P. Rodgers. "Improvements in Multiprocessor System Design". In: *SIGARCH Comput. Archit. News* 13.3 (1985-06), pp. 225–231. DOI: 10 . 1145/327070.327215.

[SA14]     Cedomir Segulja and Tarek S Abdelrahman. "What Is the Cost of Weak Determinism?" In: *23rd International Conference on Parallel Architectures and Compilation*. ACM. 2014, pp. 99–112.

[Sel+12]   Gehan MK Selim, Shige Wang, James R Cordy, and Juergen Dingel. "Model Transformations for Migrating Legacy Models: an Industrial Case Study". In: *Modelling Foundations and Applications*. Springer, 2012, pp. 90–101.

[Seo+08]   Euiseong Seo, Jinkyu Jeong, Seonyeong Park, and Joonwon Lee. "Energy Efficient Scheduling of Real-time Tasks on Multicore Processors". In: *IEEE Transactions on Parallel and Distributed Systems* 19.11 (2008), pp. 1540–1552.

[Sin07a]     Oliver Sinnen. *Task Scheduling for Parallel Systems*. Newark: Wiley, 2007.

[Sin07b]     Oliver Sinnen. "Task Scheduling for Parallel Systems". In: Newark: Wiley, 2007. Chap. 5. Fundamental Heuristics, pp. 108–144.

[SKS10a]     K. Scheidemann, M. Knapp, and C. Stellwag. *Load Balancing in AUTOSAR-Multicore-Systemen (Teil 1)*. 2010. URL: http://www.elektroniknet.de/automotive/tools/artikel/26546/ (visited on 2015-10-06).

[SKS10b]     K. Scheidemann, M. Knapp, and C. Stellwag. *Load Balancing in AUTOSAR-Multicore-Systemen (Teil 2)*. 2010. URL: http://www.elektroniknet.de/automotive/tools/artikel/26538/ (visited on 2015-10-06).

[The15a]     The MathWorks Inc. *Embedded Coder*. 2015. URL: http://de.mathworks.com/products/embedded-coder (visited on 2015-10-01).

[The15b]     The MathWorks Inc. *Generate Code That Is Compliant with the AUTOSAR Standard*. 2015. URL: http://de.mathworks.com/help/ecoder/examples/autosar-code-generation.html (visited on 2015-10-01).

[THW94]      KW Tindell, Hans Hansson, and Andy J Wellings. "Analysing Real-time Communications: Controller Area Network (CAN)". In: *Real-Time Systems Symposium, 1994., Proceedings*. IEEE. 1994, pp. 259–263.

[Ung+13]     T Ungerer, C Bradatsch, M Gerdes, F Kluge, R Jahr, J Mische, J Fernandes, P G Zaykov, Z Petrov, B Boddeker, S Kehr, H Regler, A Hugl, C Rochange, H Ozaktas, H Casse, A Bonenfant, P Sainrat, I Broster, N Lay, D George, E Quiñones, M Panic, J Abella, F Cazorla, S Uhrig, M Rohde, and A Pyka. "parMERASA – Multi-core Execution of Parallelised Hard Real-Time Applications Supporting Analysability". In: *Euromicro Conference on Digital System Design (DSD)*. 2013, pp. 363–370. DOI: 10.1109/DSD.2013.46.

[Ung+16]     Theo Ungerer, Christian Bradatsch, Martin Frieb, Florian Kluge, Jörg Mische, Alexander Stegmeier, Ralf Jahr, Mike Gerdes, Pavel Zaykov, Lucie Matusova, Zai Jian Jia Li, Zlatko Petrov, Bert Böddeker, Sebastian Kehr, Hans Regler, Andreas Hugl, Christine Rochange, Haluk Ozaktas, Hugues Cassé, Armelle Bonenfant, Pascal Sainrat, Nick Lay, David George, Ian Broster, Eduardo Quiñones, Milos Panic, Jaume Abella, Carles Hernandez, Francisco Cazorla, Sascha Uhrig, Mathias Rohde, and Arthur Pyka. "Parallelizing Industrial Hard Real-Time Applications for the parMERASA Multicore". In: *ACM Trans. Embed. Comput. Syst.* 15.3 (2016-05), 53:1–53:27. DOI: 10.1145/2910589. URL: http://doi.acm.org/10.1145/2910589.

[Vac+07]     Neil Vachharajani, Ram Rangan, Easwaran Raman, Matthew J Bridges, Guilherme Ottoni, and David I August. "Speculative Decoupled Software Pipelining". In: *16th International Conference on Parallel Architecture and Compilation Techniques*. IEEE Computer Society. 2007, pp. 49–59.

[Wil+08]    R Wilhelm, J Engblom, A Ermedahl, N Holsti, S Thesing, D Whalley, G Bernat, C Ferdinand, R Heckmann, T Mitra, et al. "The Worst-case Execution-time Problem – Overview of Methods and Survey of Tools". In: *ACM Transactions on Embedded Computing Systems (TECS)* 7.3 (2008), p. 36.

[Wol96]    Michael Wolfe. "Parallelizing Compilers". In: *ACM Computing Surveys (CSUR)* 28.1 (1996), pp. 261–262.

[Woz+13]    Ernest Wozniak, Asma Mehiaoui, Chokri Mraidha, Sara Tucci-Piergiovanni, and Sebastien Gerard. "An Optimization Approach for the Synthesis of AUTOSAR Architectures". In: *International Conference on Emerging Technologies and Factory Automation (ETFA)*. IEEE. 2013, pp. 1–10.

# Terms and Abbreviations

*POP* . . . . . . population size

**API** . . . . . . . application programming interface

**AR-OS** . . . . . AUTOSAR operating system

**ASIL** . . . . . . Automotive Safety Integrity Level

**ATL** . . . . . . . ATLAS Transformation Language

**AUTOSAR** . . AUTomotive Open System ARchitecture

**BPMN** . . . . . Business Process Model and Notation

**BSW** . . . . . . basic software

**CAN** . . . . . . controller area network

**CDD** . . . . . . complex device driver

**CDG** . . . . . . control dependence graph

**CFG** . . . . . . control flow graph

**COTS** . . . . . commercial off-the-shelf

**CPS** . . . . . . . cyber-physical system

**DAG** . . . . . . directed acyclic graph

**DDG** . . . . . . data dependence graph

**DLC** . . . . . . deterministic logical clock

**DLT** . . . . . . . deterministic logical time

**DM** . . . . . . . deadline monotonic

**DMT** . . . . . . deterministic multithreading

**E/E** . . . . . . . electrical/electronic

**ECU** . . . . . . electronic control unit

**EDF** . . . . . . . earliest deadline first

**EEC** . . . . . . . earliest executable condition

**EMS** . . . . . . engine management system

**FDIR** . . . . . . fault detection, isolation, and recovery

**FF** . . . . . . . . first-fit

**FIFO** . . . . . . first-in-first-out

**FILO** . . . . . . first-in-last-out

**FP** . . . . . . . . fixed priority

**GCS** . . . . . . global critical section

**GM** . . . . . . . General Motors

**HPC** . . . . . . high performance computing

**HTG** . . . . . . hierarchical task graph

**ILP** . . . . . . . integer linear programming

**IOC** . . . . . . . inter-OS-application communicator

**IRV** . . . . . . . inter-runnable-variable

**ISA** . . . . . . . instruction set architecture

**LET** . . . . . . . logical execution time

**LIFO** . . . . . . last-in-first-out

**LILO** . . . . . . last-in-last-out

**makespan** . . . schedule length

**MFG** . . . . . . macro-flow graph

**MMU** . . . . . memory management unit

**MPCP** . . . . . Multiprocessor Priority Ceiling Protocol

**MPU** . . . . . . memory protection unit

**MT** . . . . . . . macro task

**NoC** . . . . . . network-on-chip

**OS** . . . . . . . operating system

**OSCAR** . . . . optimally scheduled advanced multiprocessor

**OSEK** . . . . . Offene Systeme und deren Schnittstellen für die Elektronik in Kraftfahrzeugen

**OTAWA** . . . . Open Toolbox for Adaptive WCET Analysis

**PDG** . . . . . . program dependence graph

**PIM** . . . . . . per-instance memory

**PSQ** . . . . . . parallel schedule quality

**RAW** . . . . . . read-after-write

**RCPSP** . . . . . resource-constrained project scheduling problem

**RDG** . . . . . . runnable dependence graph

**RM** . . . . . . . rate monotonic

**RTE** . . . . . . . run-time environment

**SGS** . . . . . . . schedule generation scheme

**SW-C** . . . . . . software-component

**SymTA/S** . . . symbolic timing analysis for systems

**TCA** . . . . . . time-constrained automata

**TDG** . . . . . . task dependence graph

**TIC** . . . . . . . timed implicit communication

**TP** . . . . . . . . timed path

**TTA** . . . . . . . time-triggered architecture

**UBD** . . . . . . upper bound delay

**UoS** . . . . . . . unit of scheduling

**VFB** . . . . . . . virtual function bus

**WAR** . . . . . . write-after-read

**WAW** . . . . . . write-after-write

**WCET** . . . . . worst-case execution time

**WF** . . . . . . . worst-fit